BODY ART

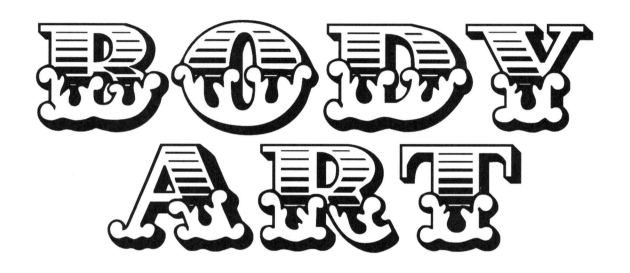

A TATTOO DESIGN COLORING BOOK

BODY ART

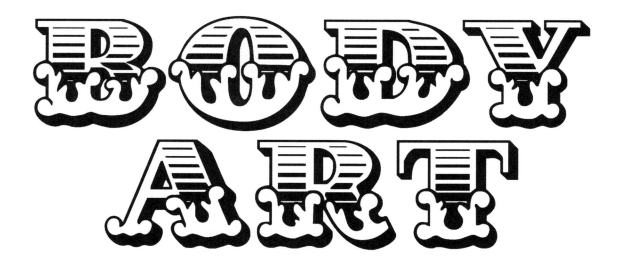

A TATTOO DESIGN COLORING BOOK

ERIK SIUDA

Racehorse Publishing

Copyright © 2017 by Erik Siuda

All rights reserved. No part of this book may be reproduced in any manner without the express written consent of the publisher, except in the case of brief excerpts in critical reviews or articles. All inquiries should be addressed to Racehorse Publishing, 307 West 36th Street, 11th Floor, New York, NY 10018.

Racehorse Publishing books may be purchased in bulk at special discounts for sales promotion, corporate gifts, fund-raising, or educational purposes. Special editions can also be created to specifications. For details, contact the Special Sales Department, Skyhorse Publishing, 307 West 36th Street, 11th Floor, New York, NY 10018 or info@skyhorsepublishing.com.

Racehorse Publishing™ is a pending trademark of Skyhorse Publishing, Inc.®, a Delaware corporation.

Visit our website at www.skyhorsepublishing.com.

10 9 8 7 6 5 4 3 2 1

Cover and interior artwork by Erik Siuda

Print ISBN: 978-1-944686-87-1

Printed in the United States of America

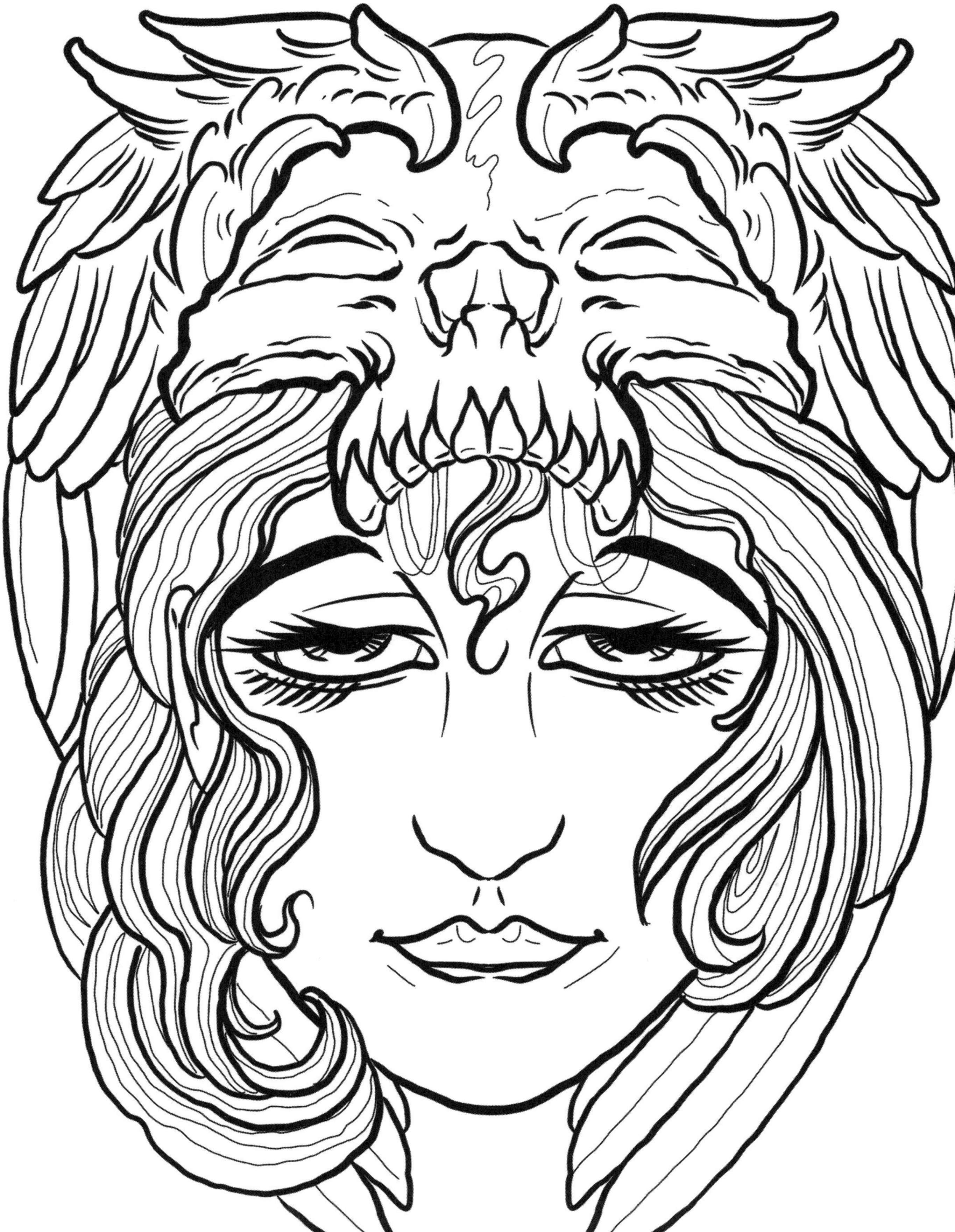

← 1

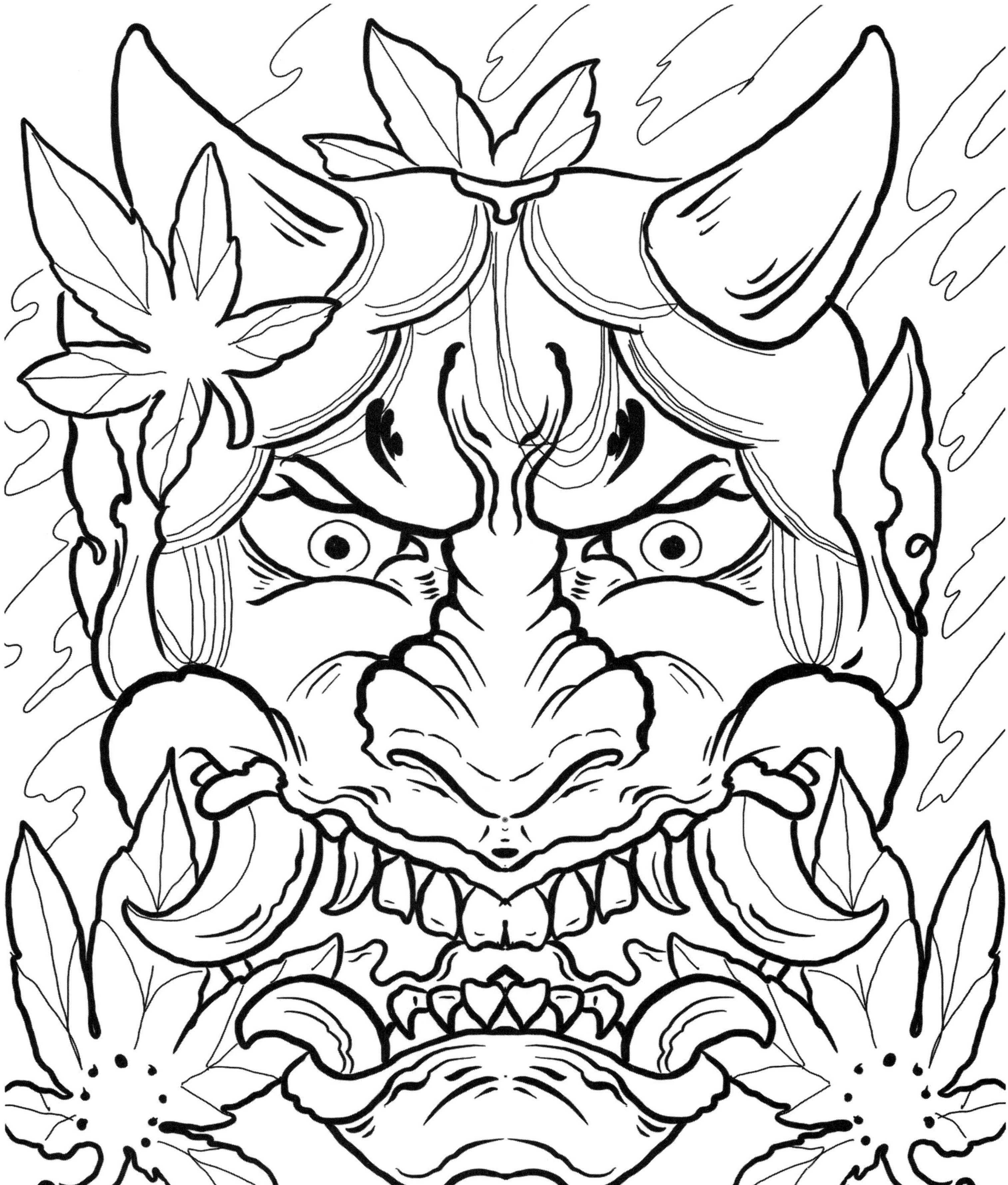

← 2

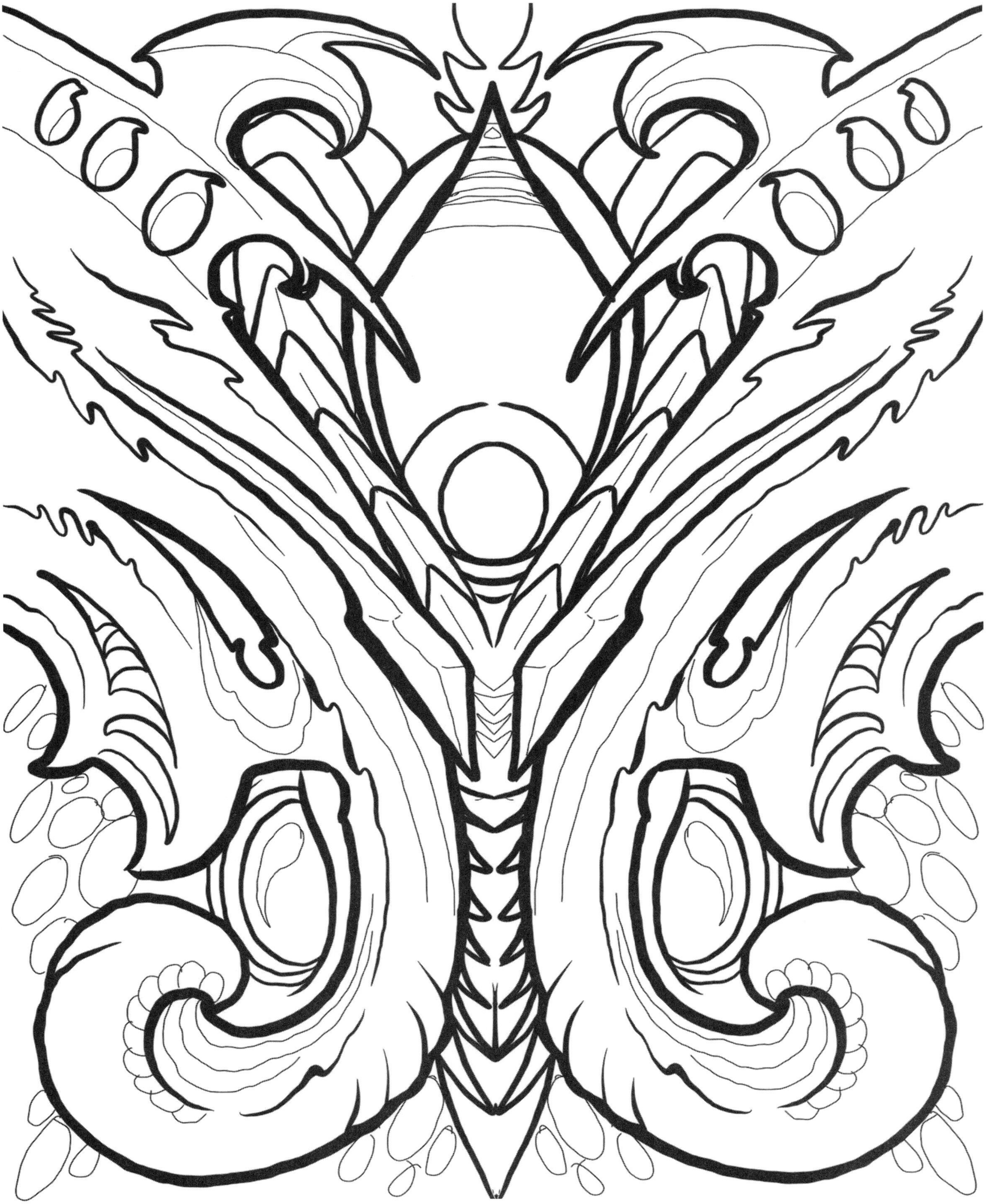

← 3

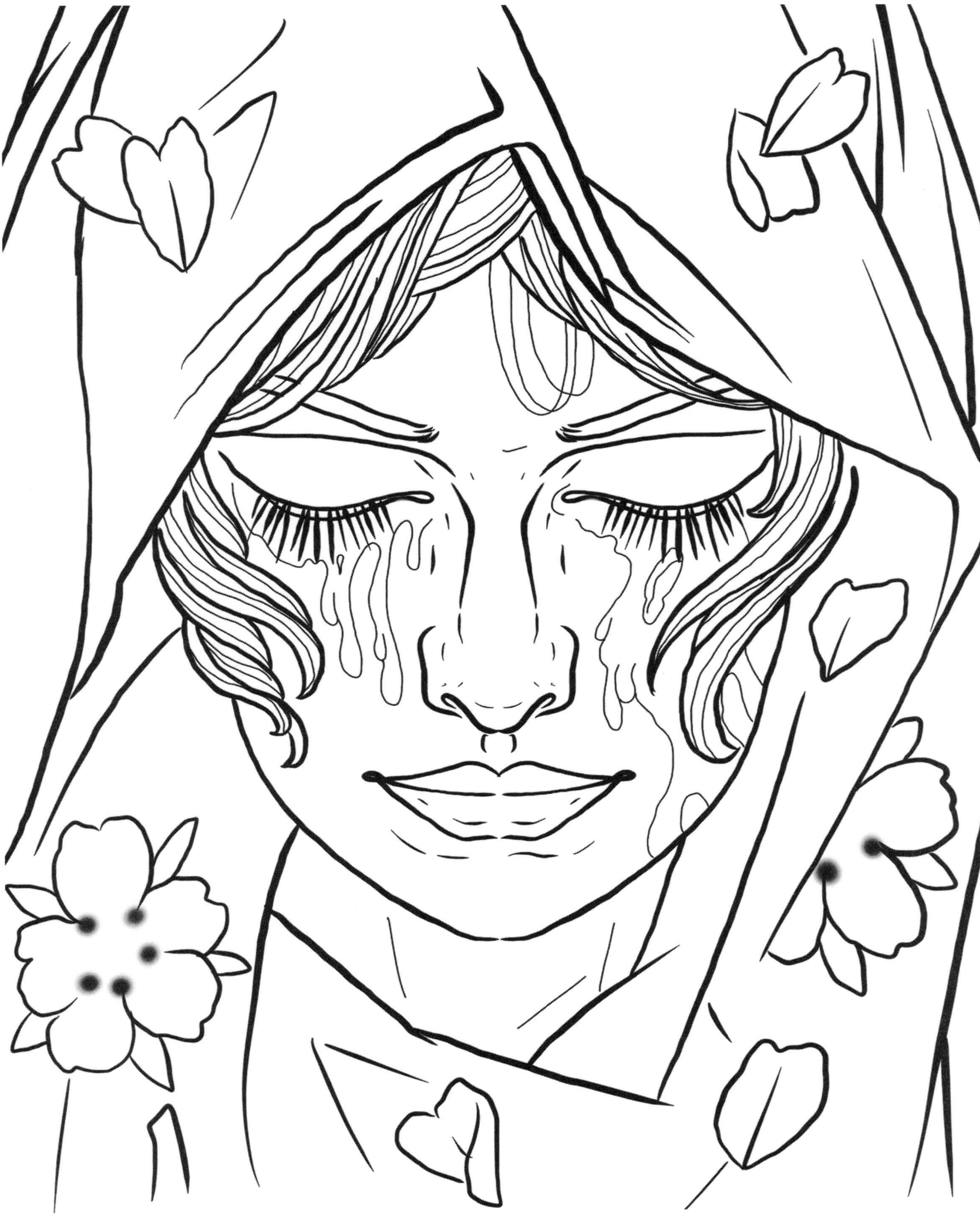

← 4

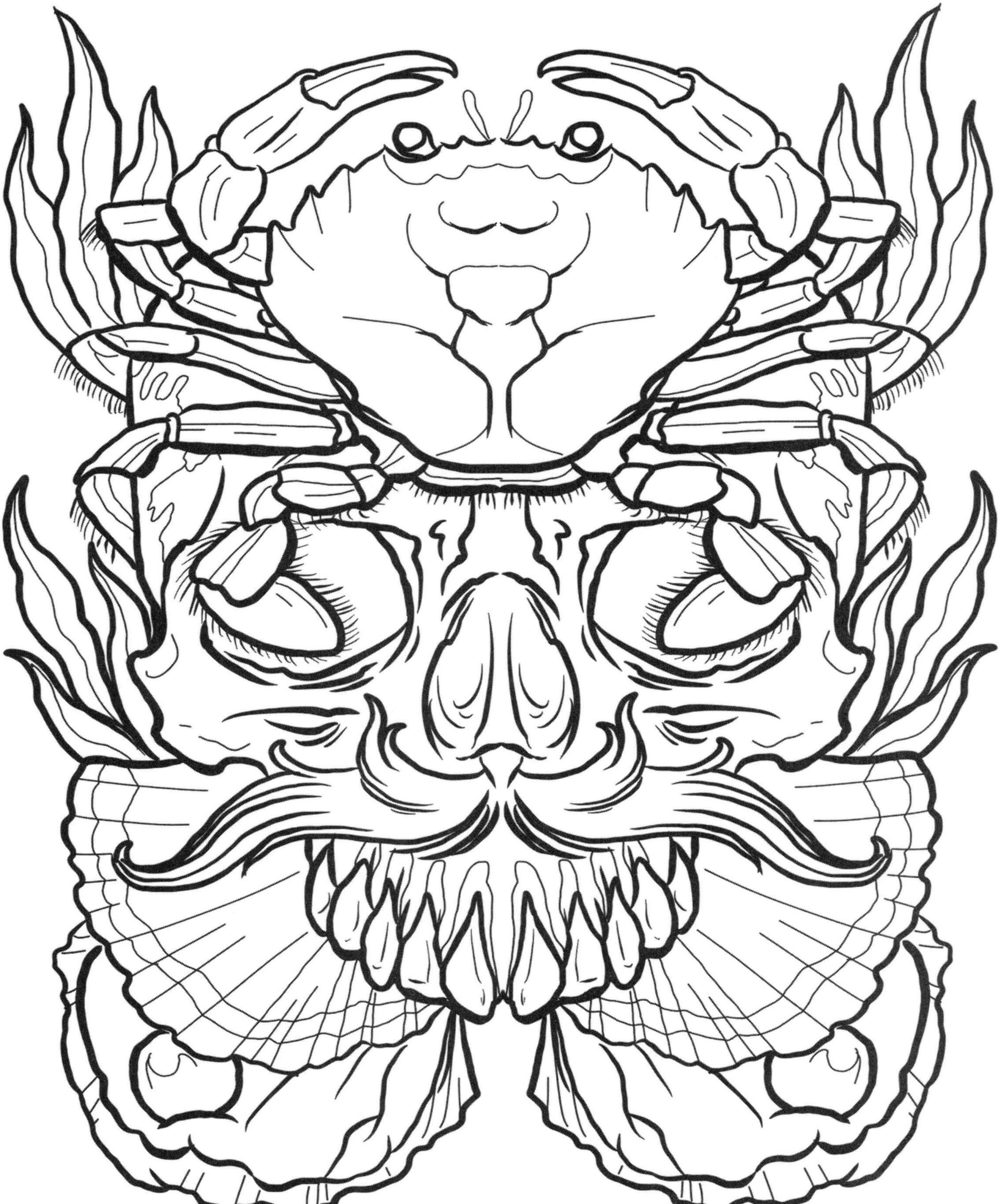

← 5

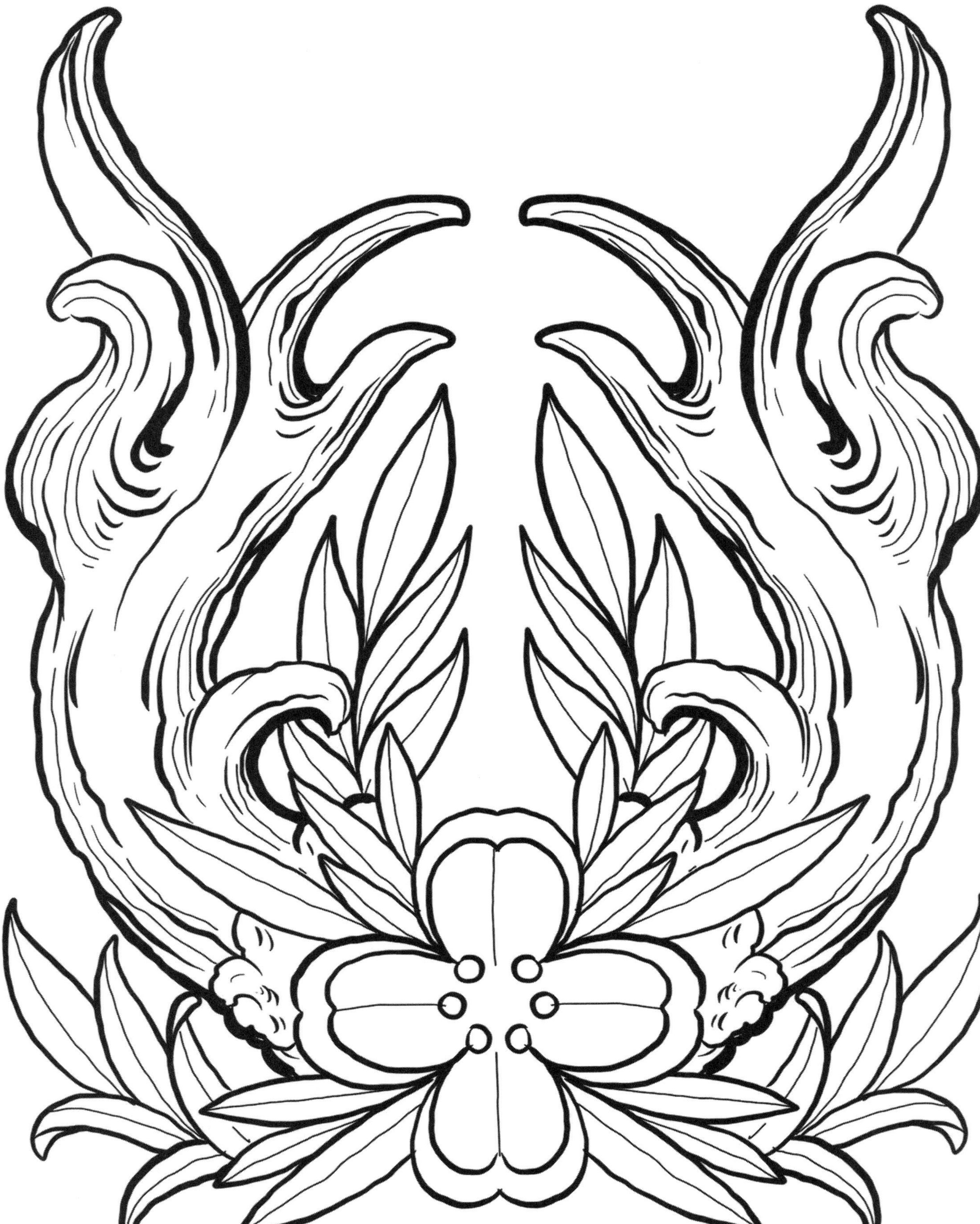

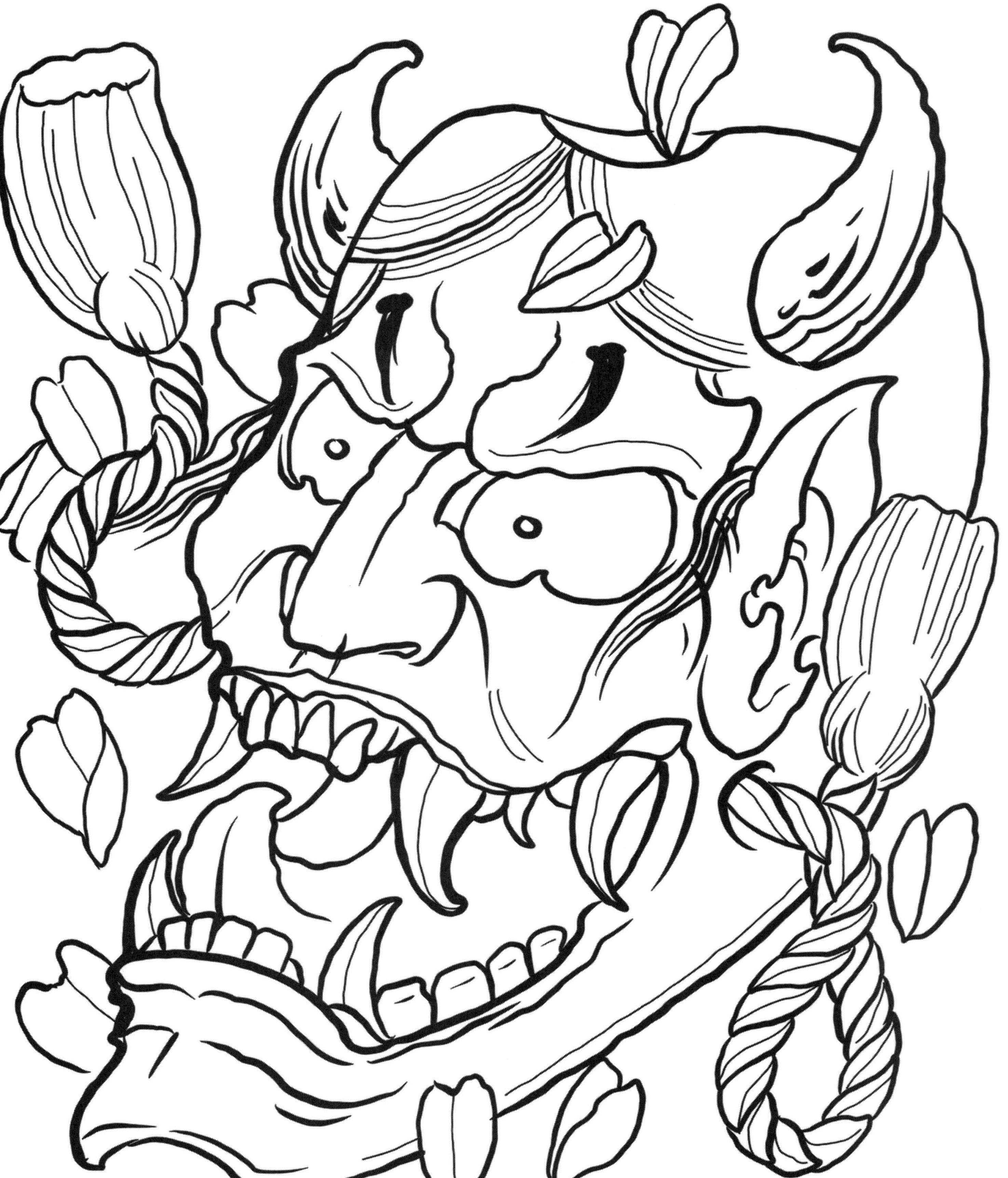

← 7

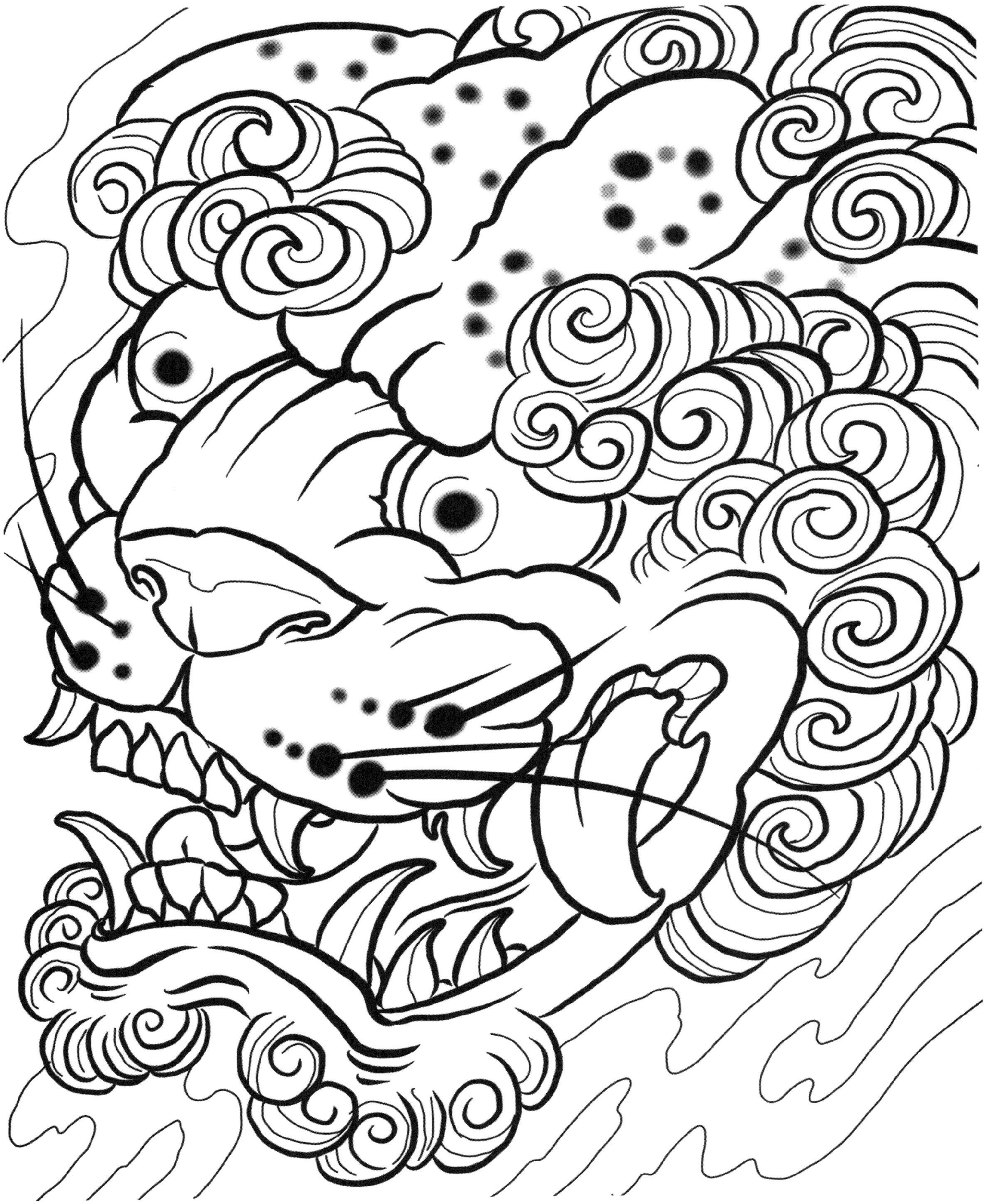

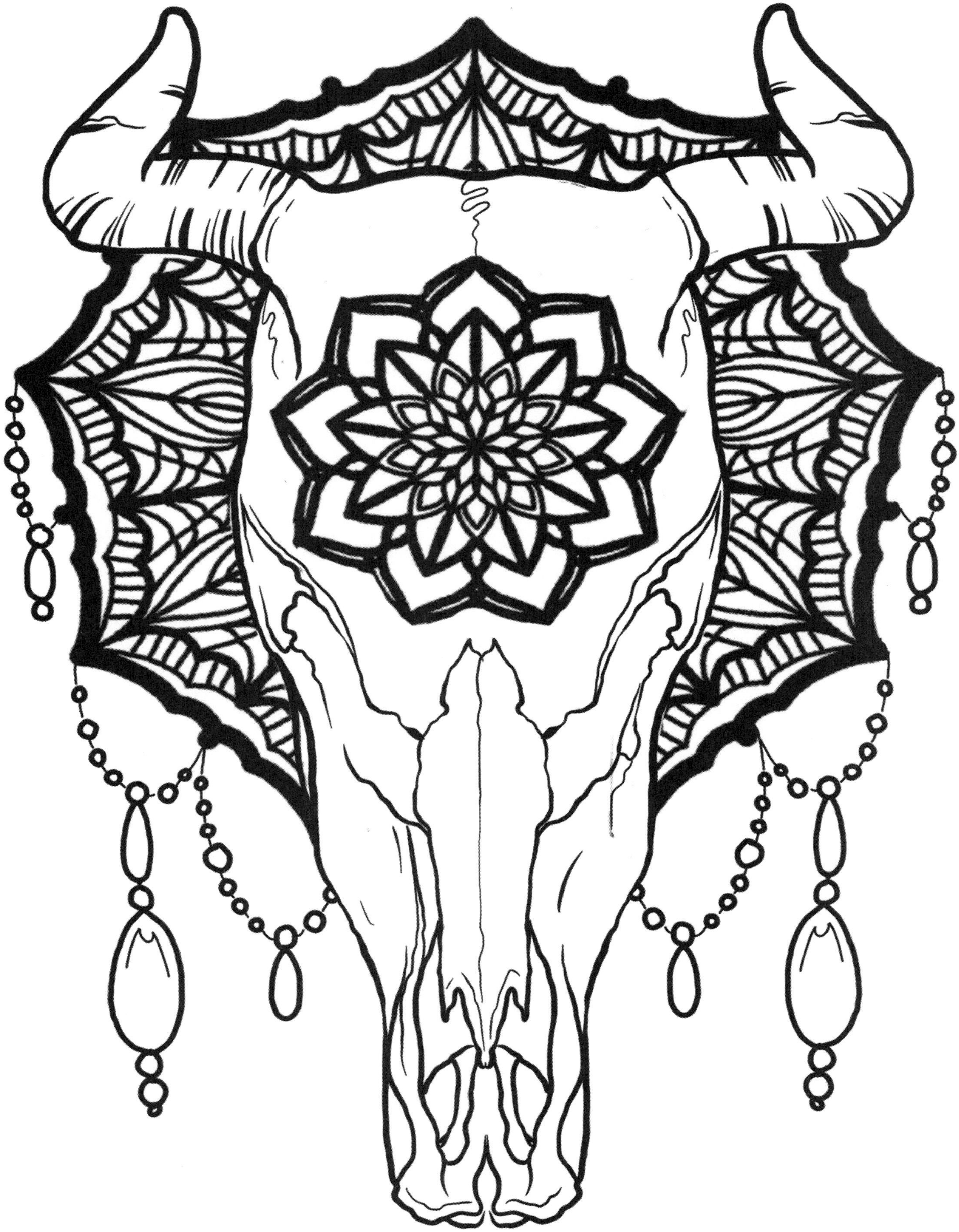

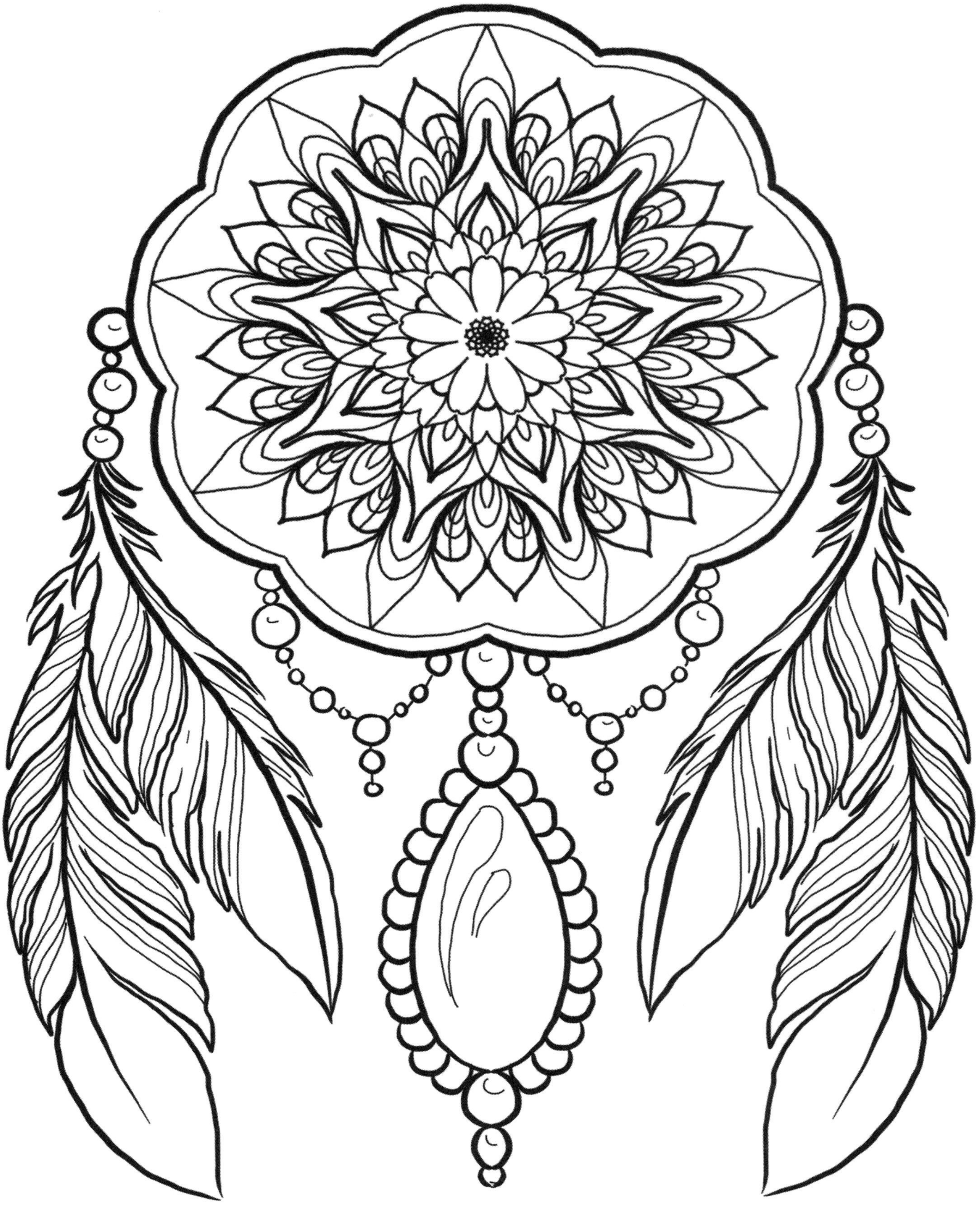

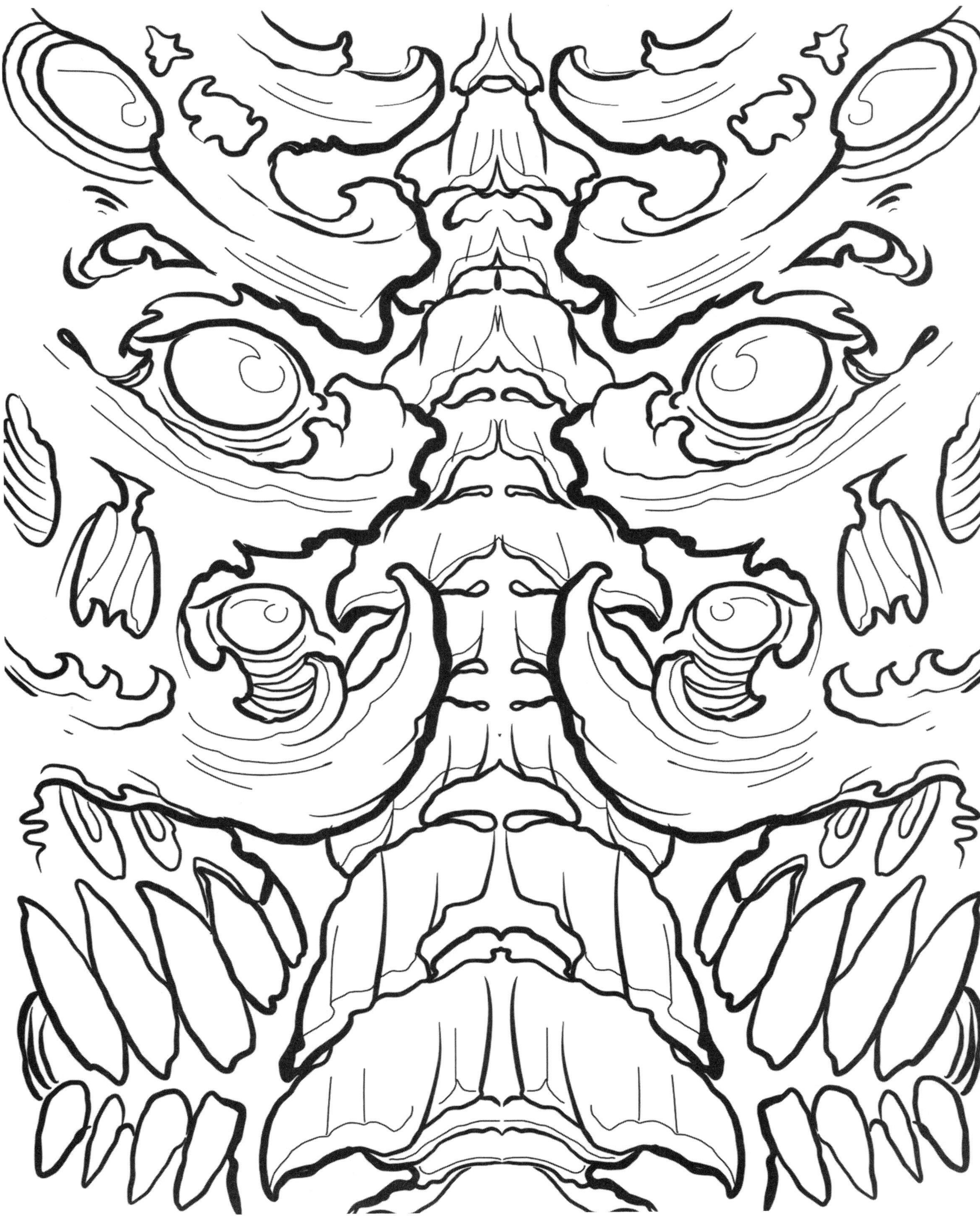

← 11

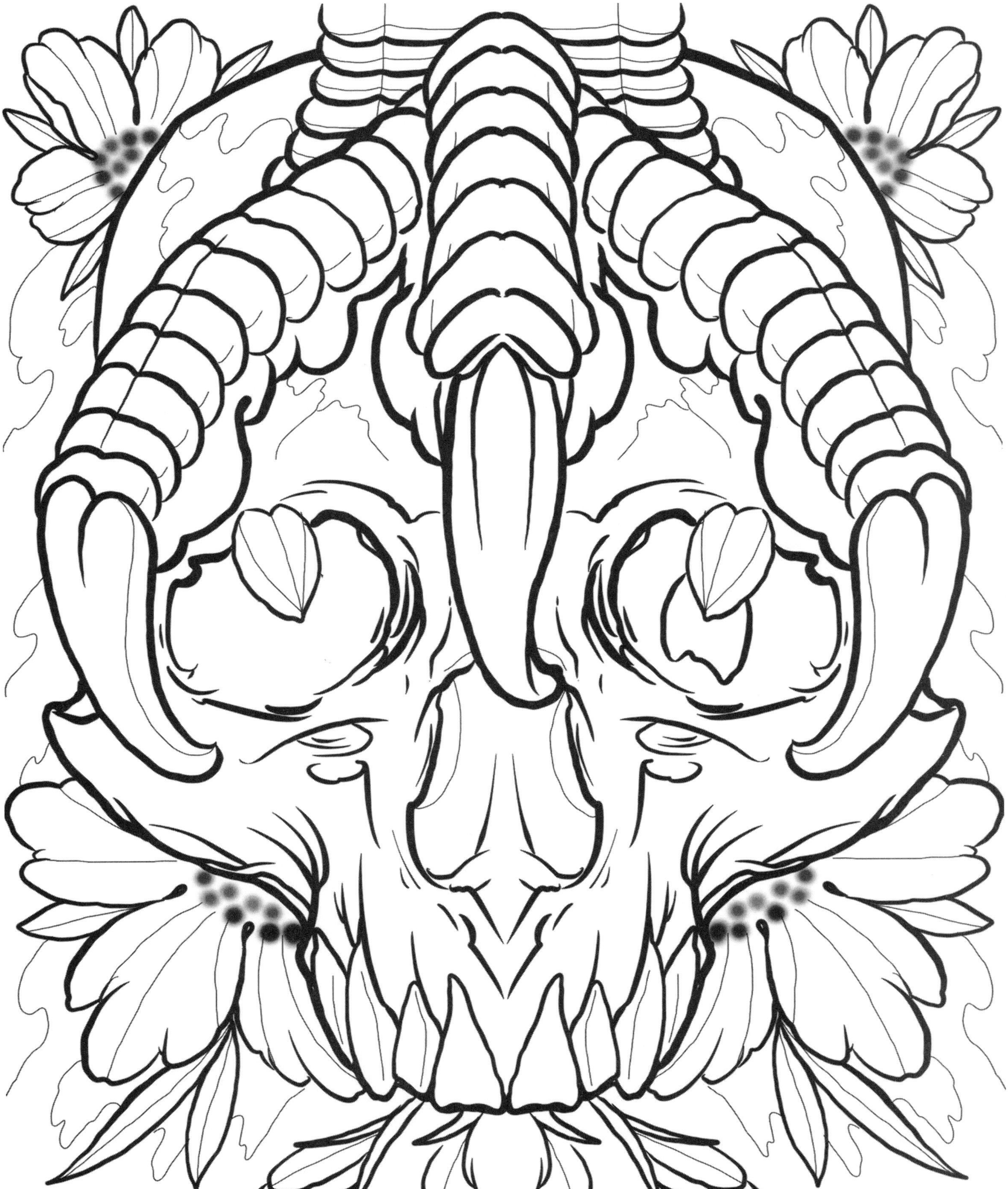

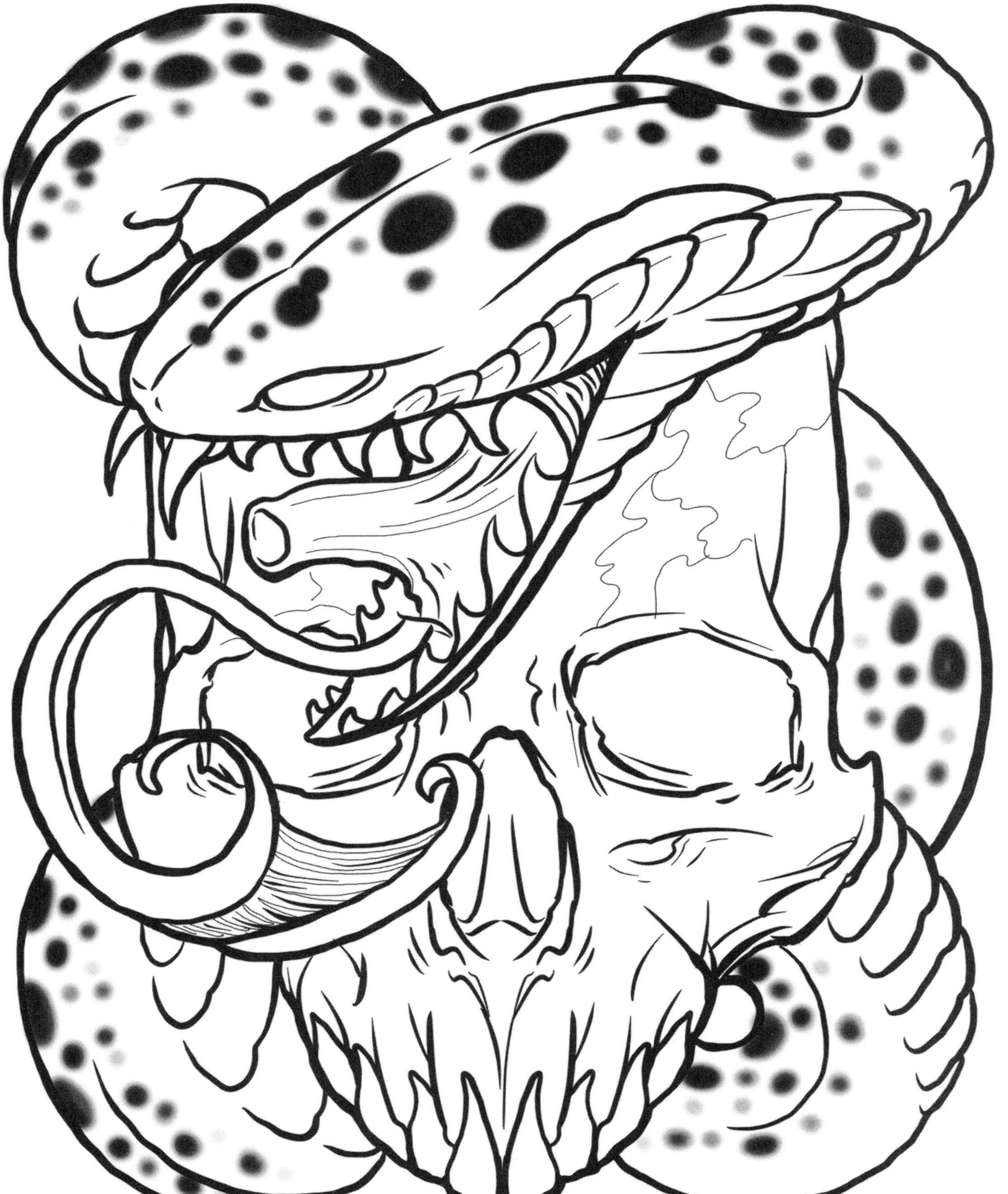

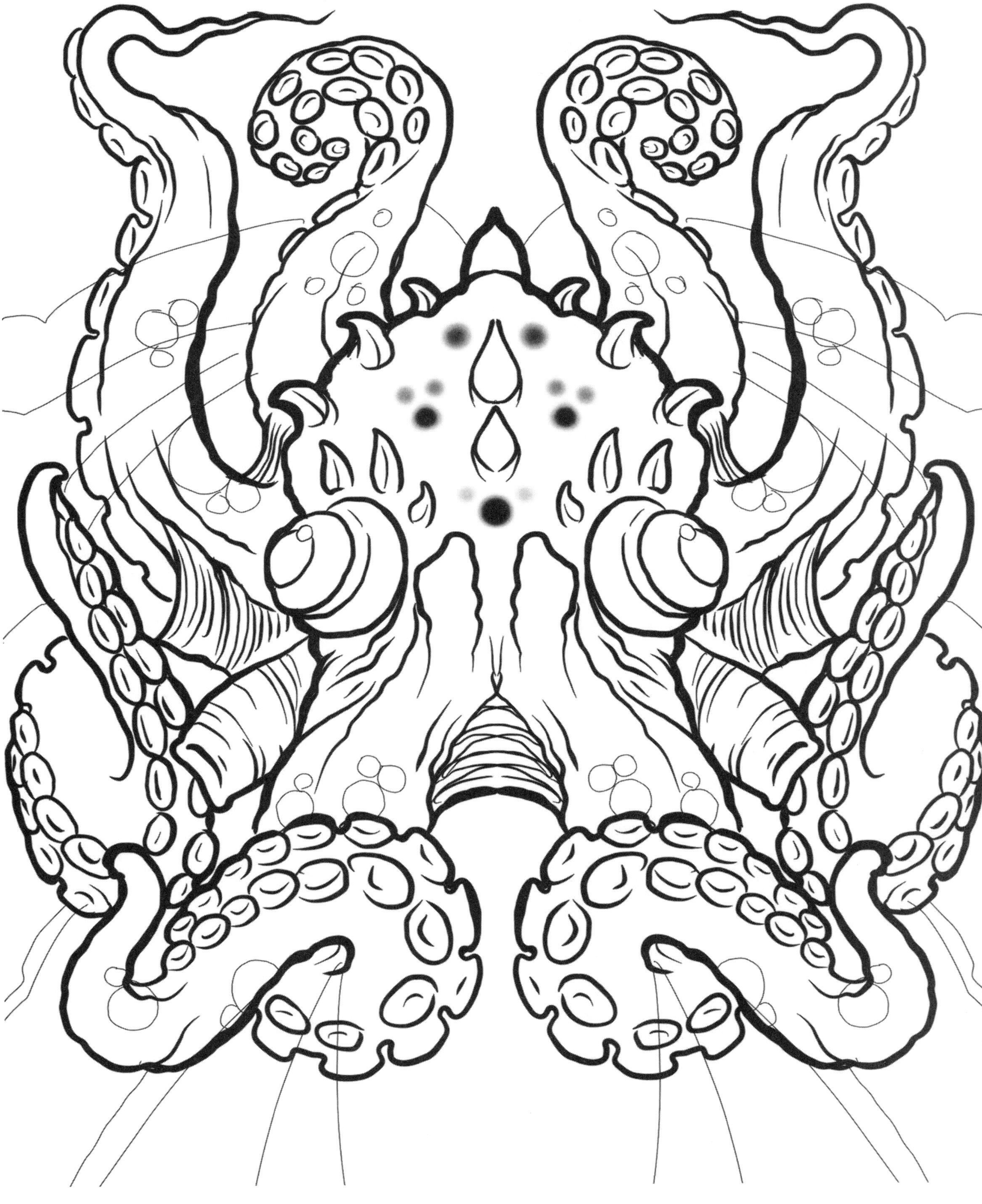

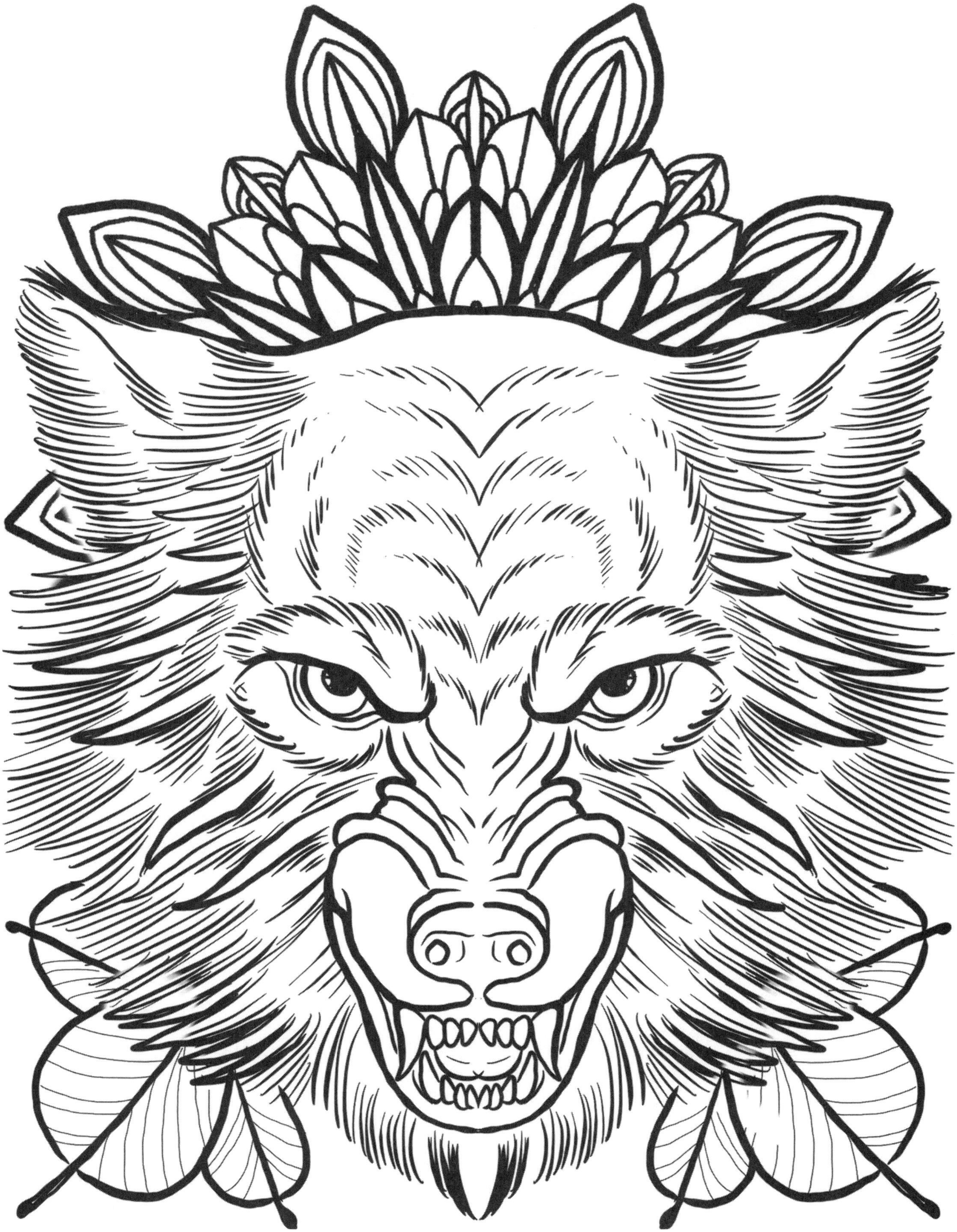

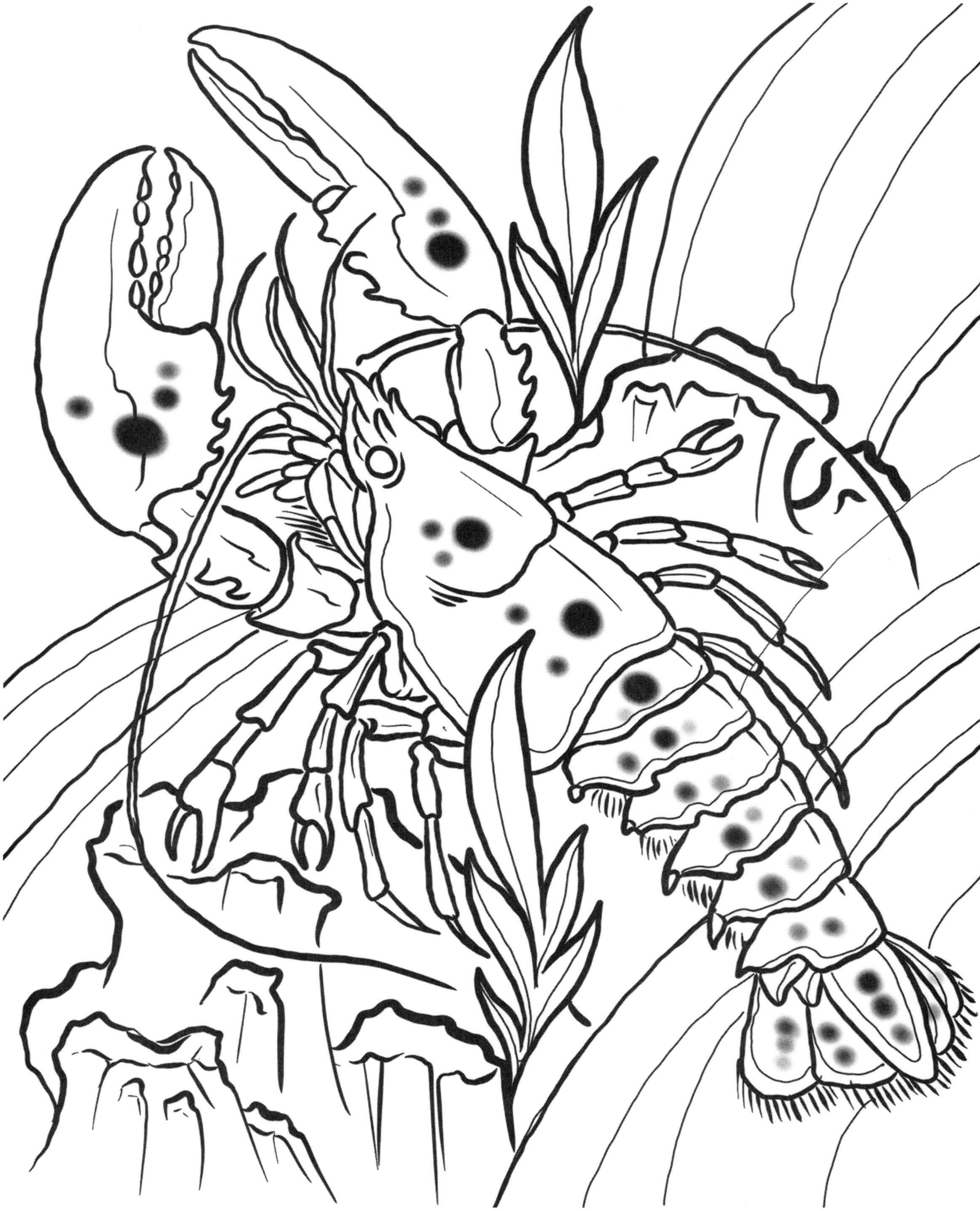

← 16

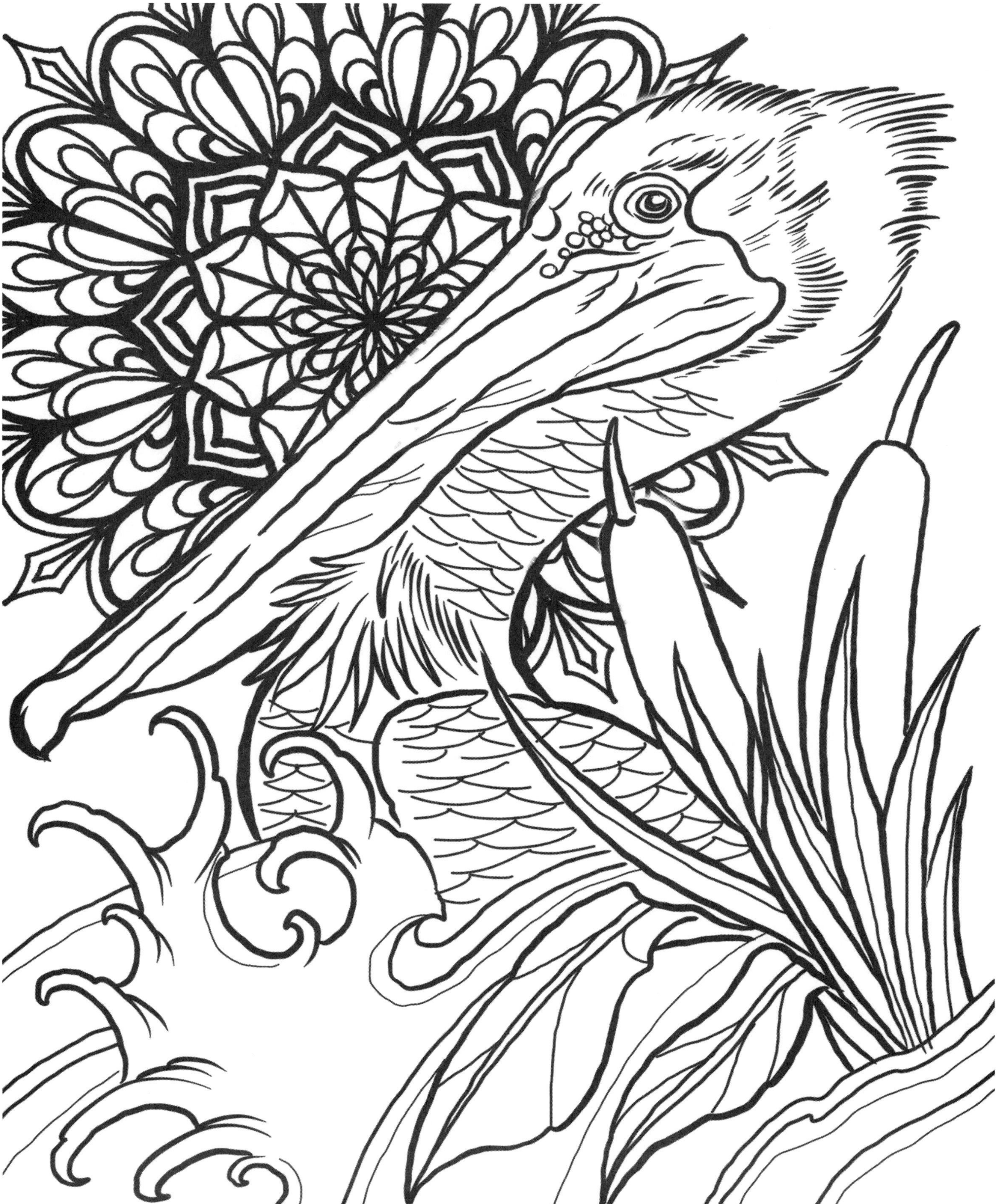

← 17

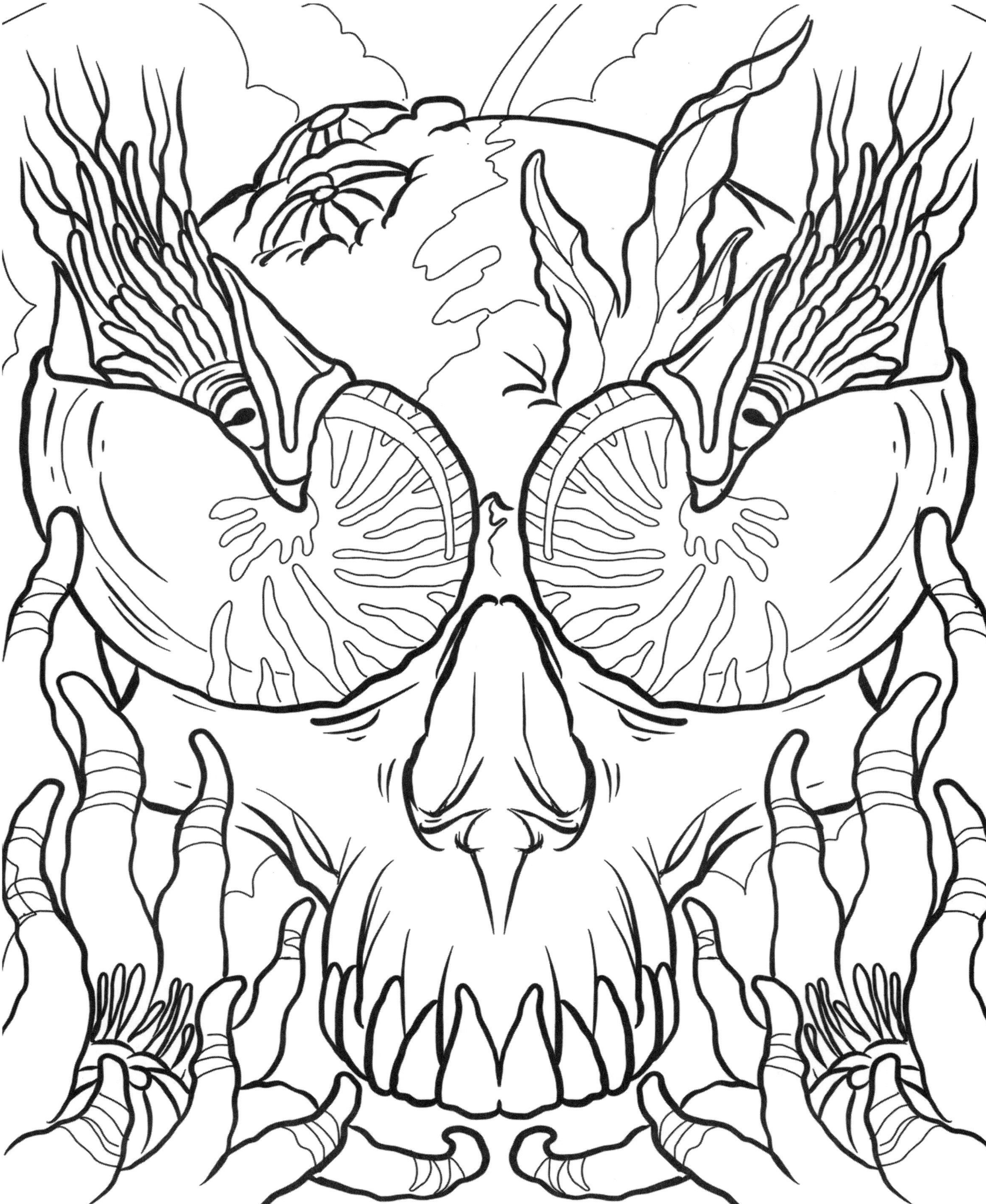

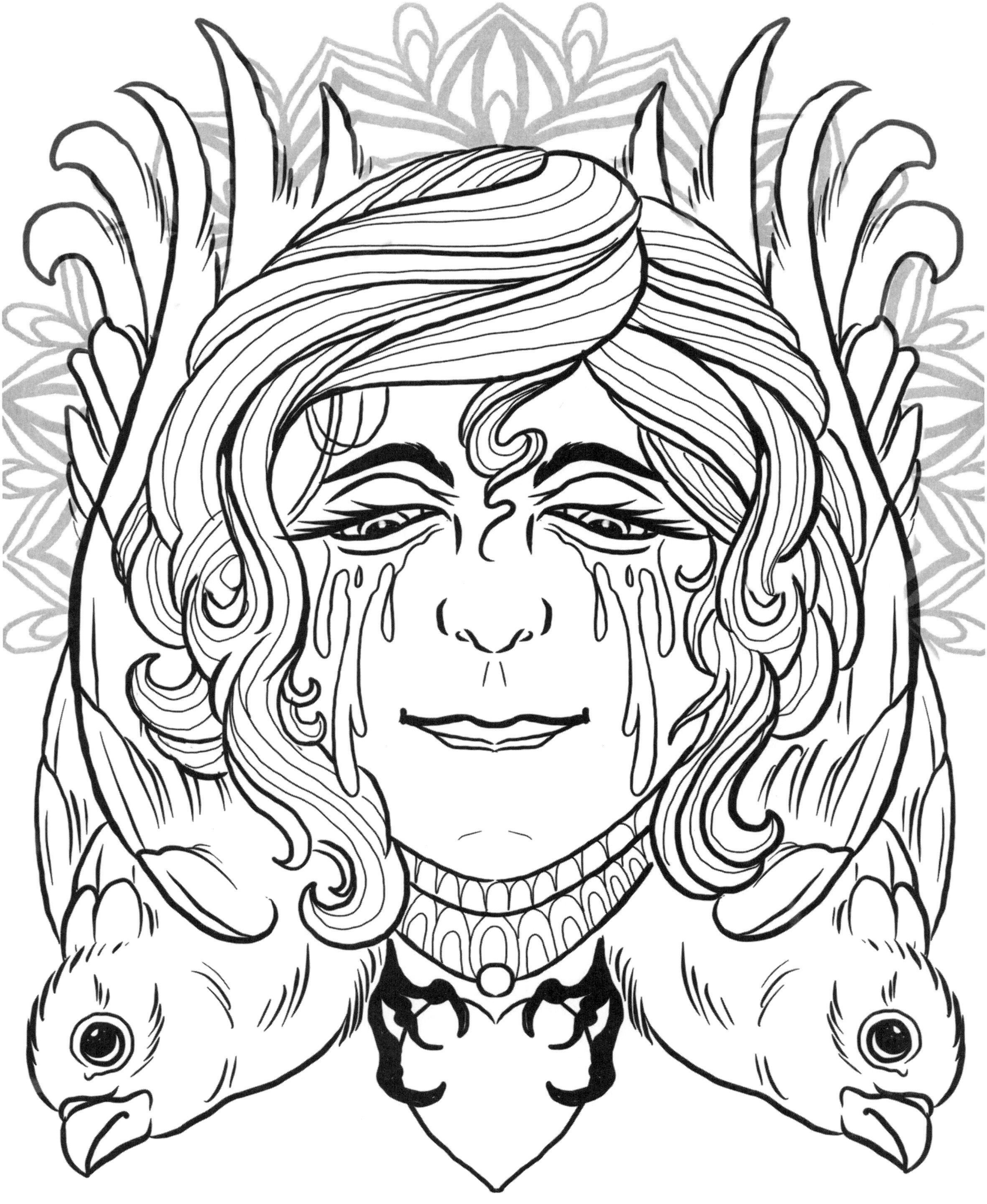

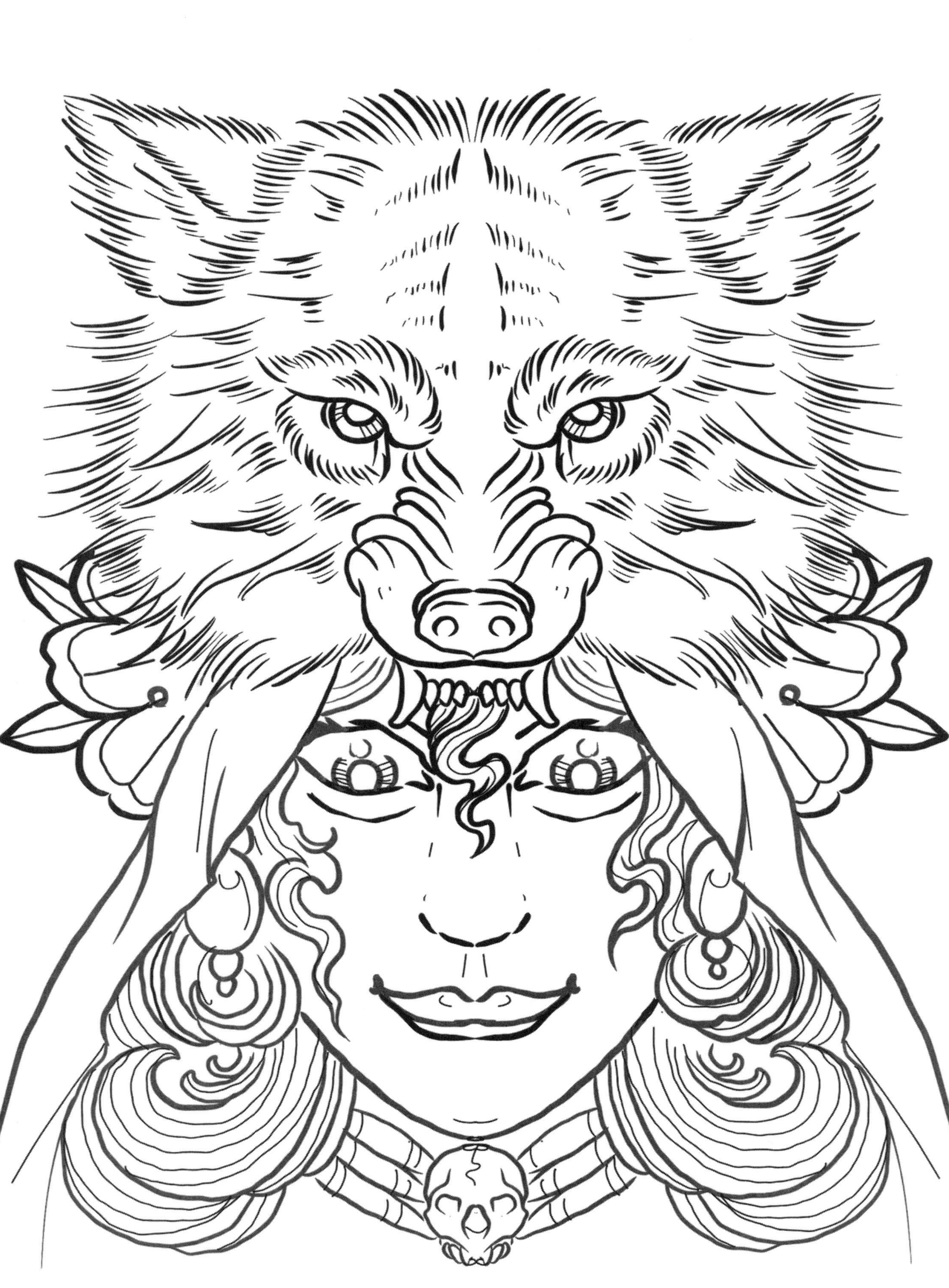

← 20

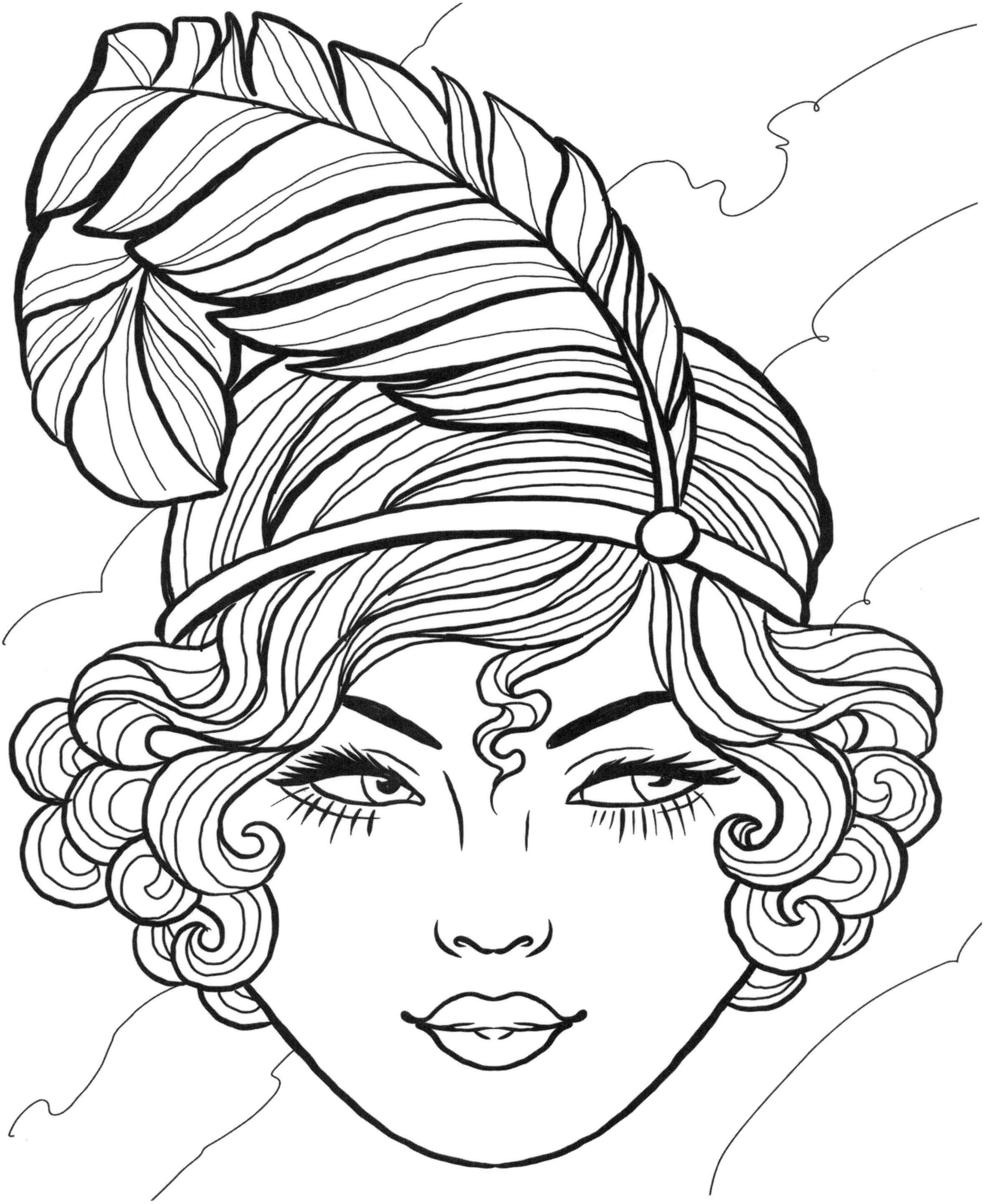

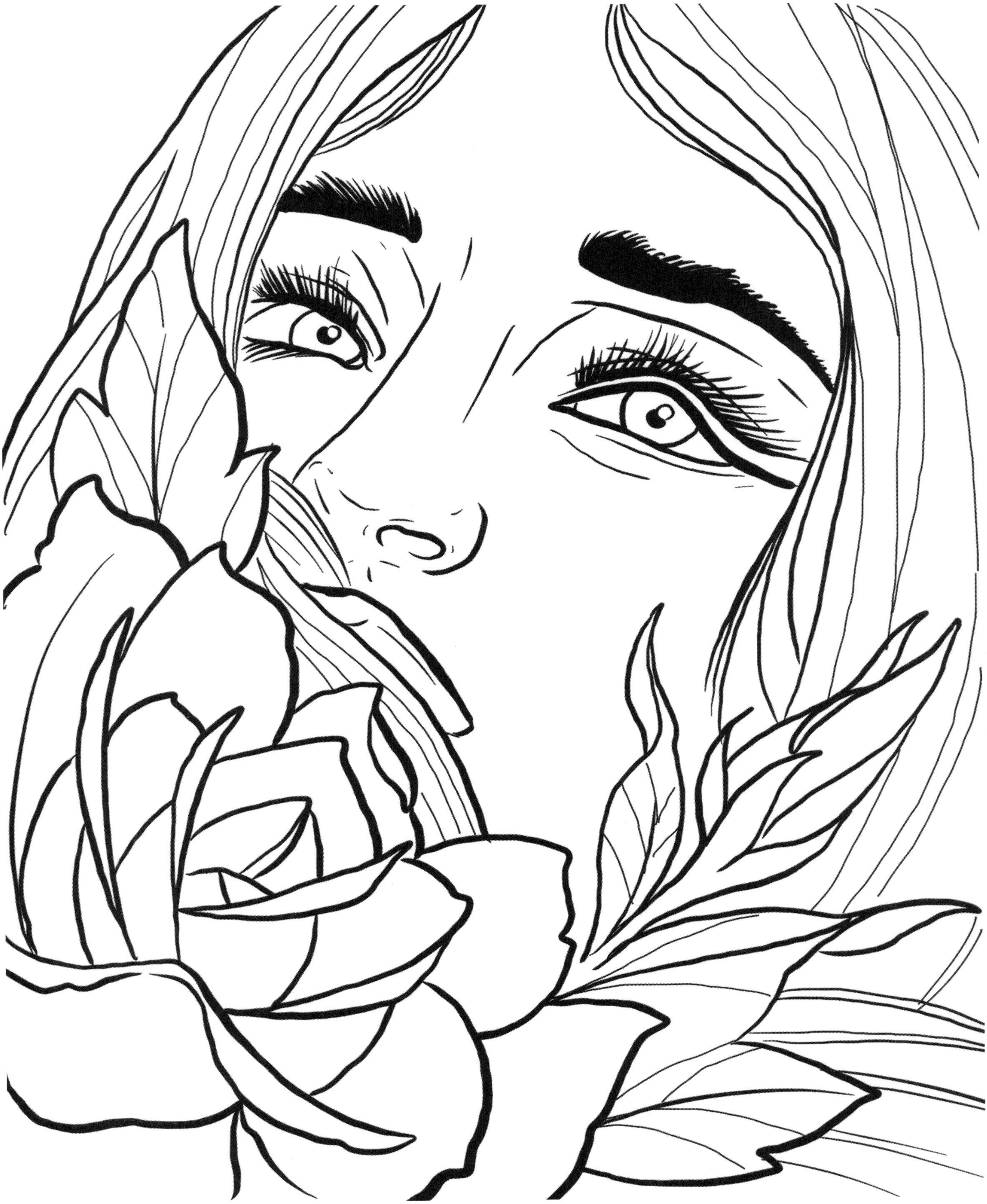

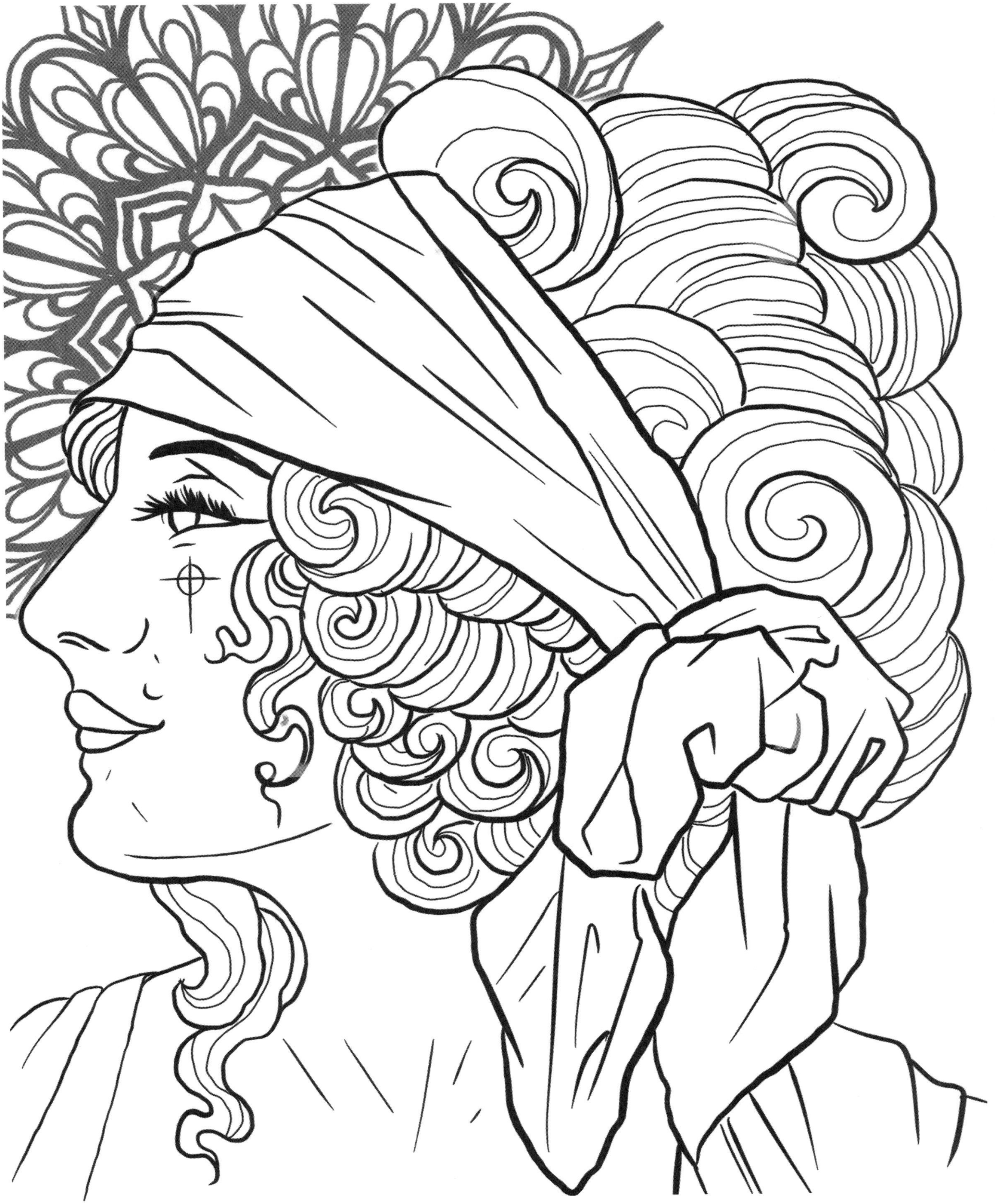

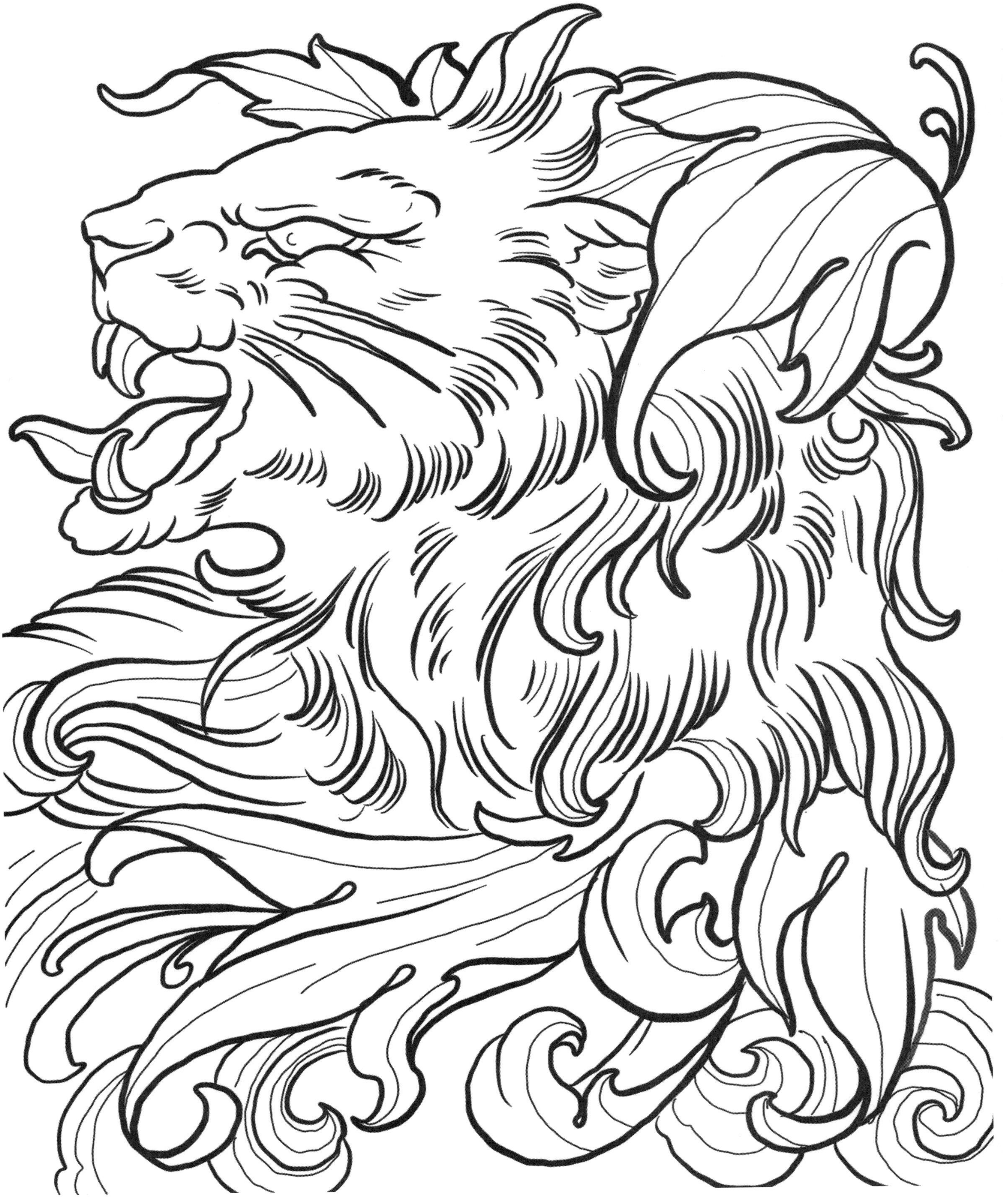

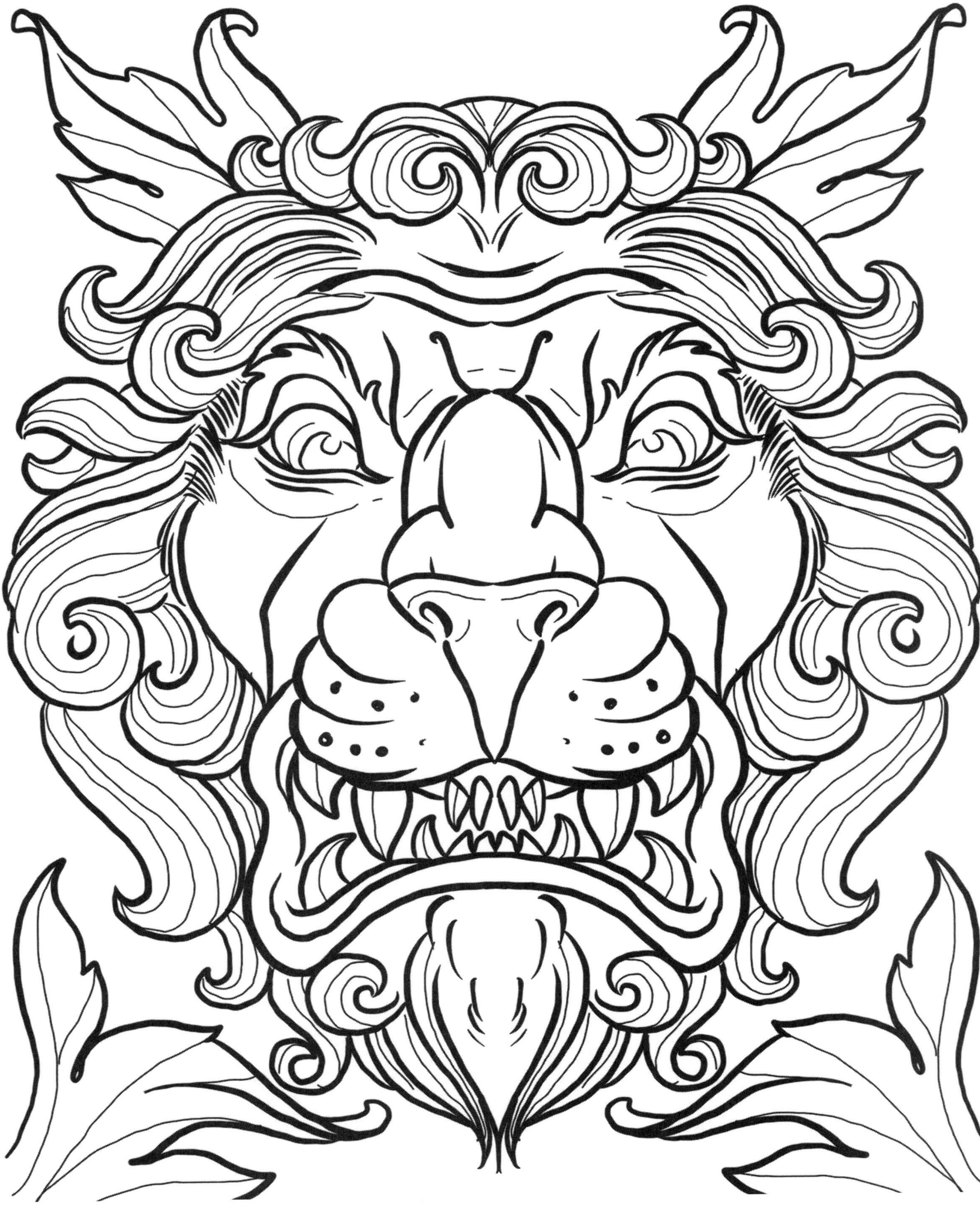

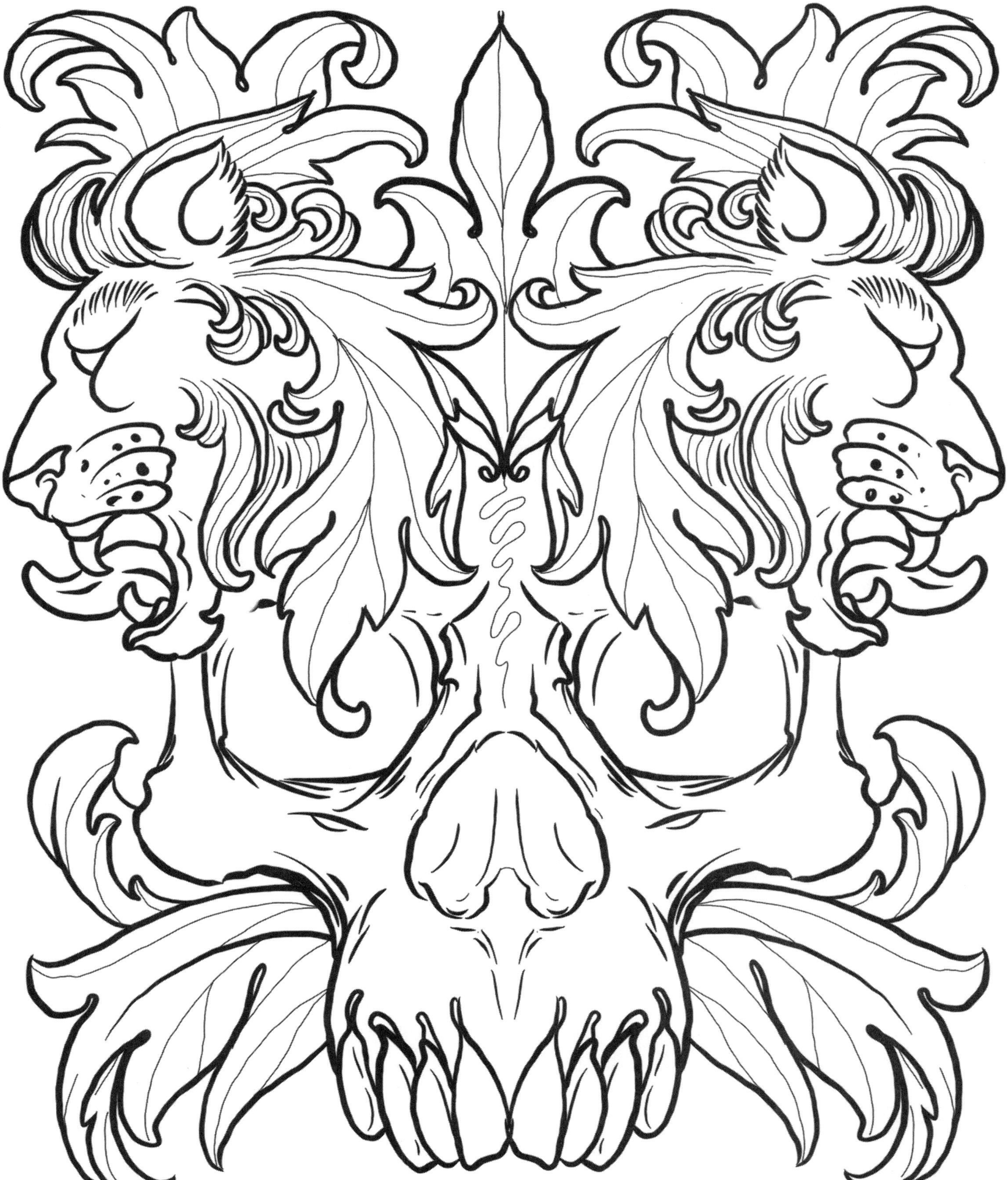

← 26

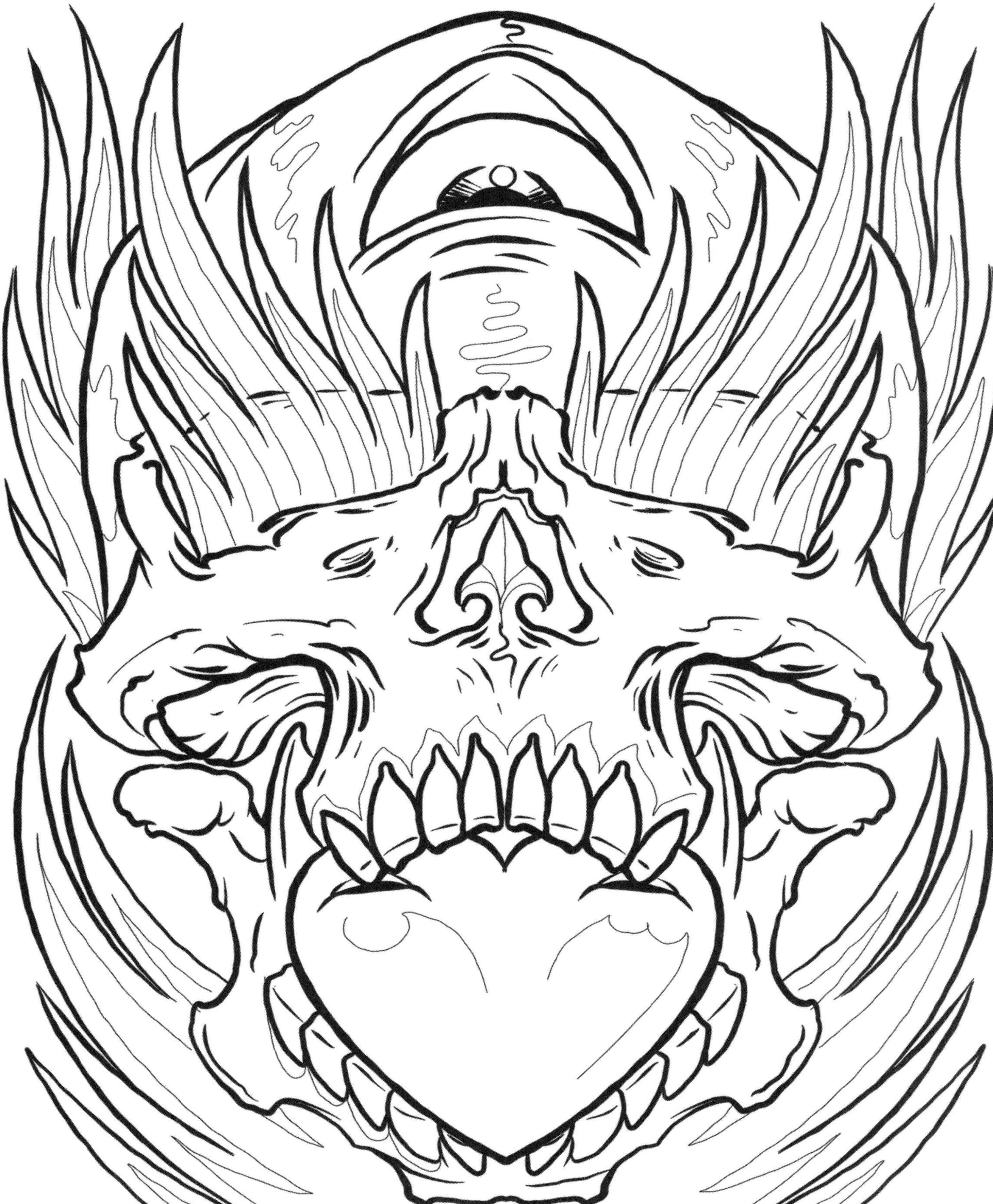

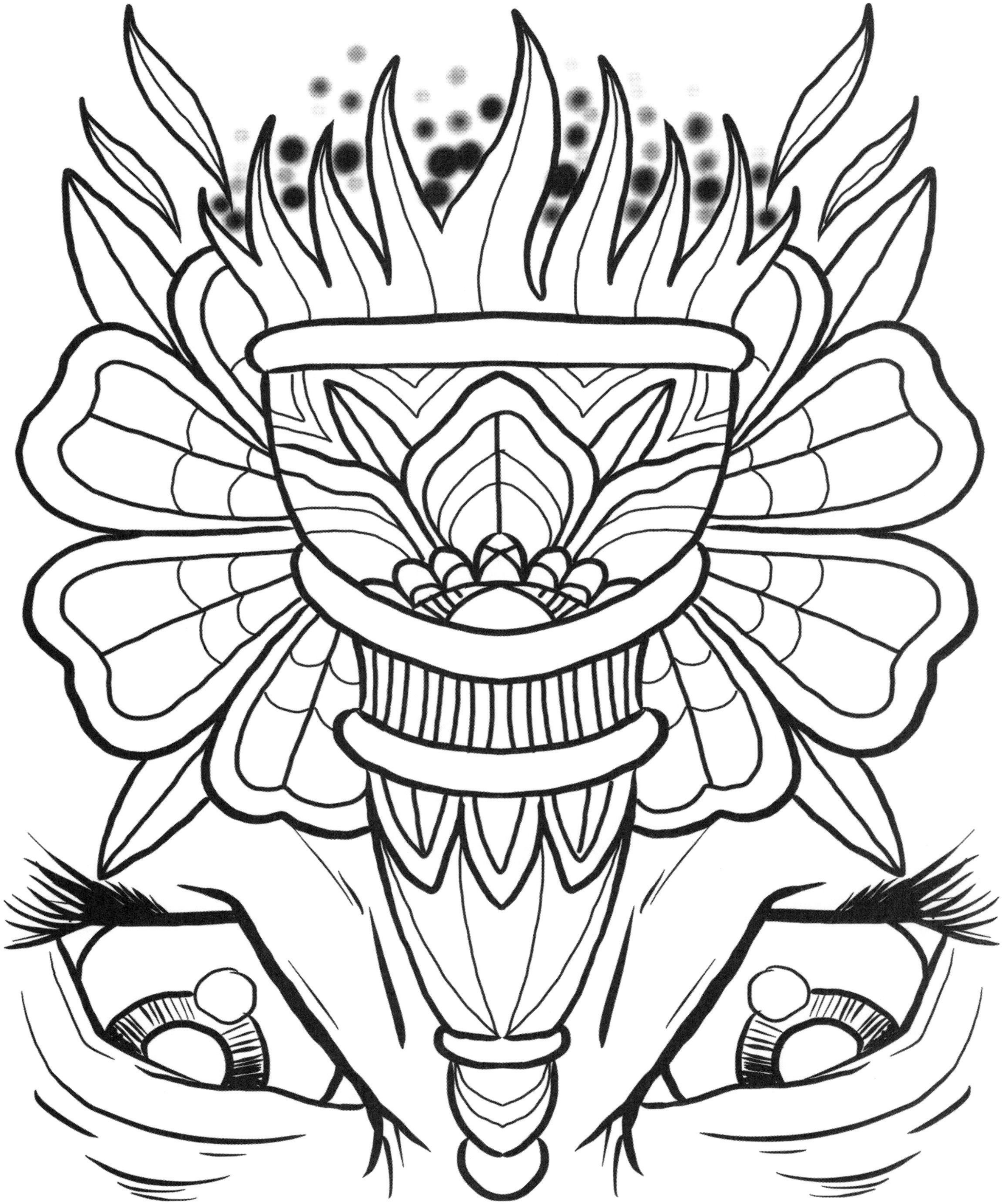

← 28

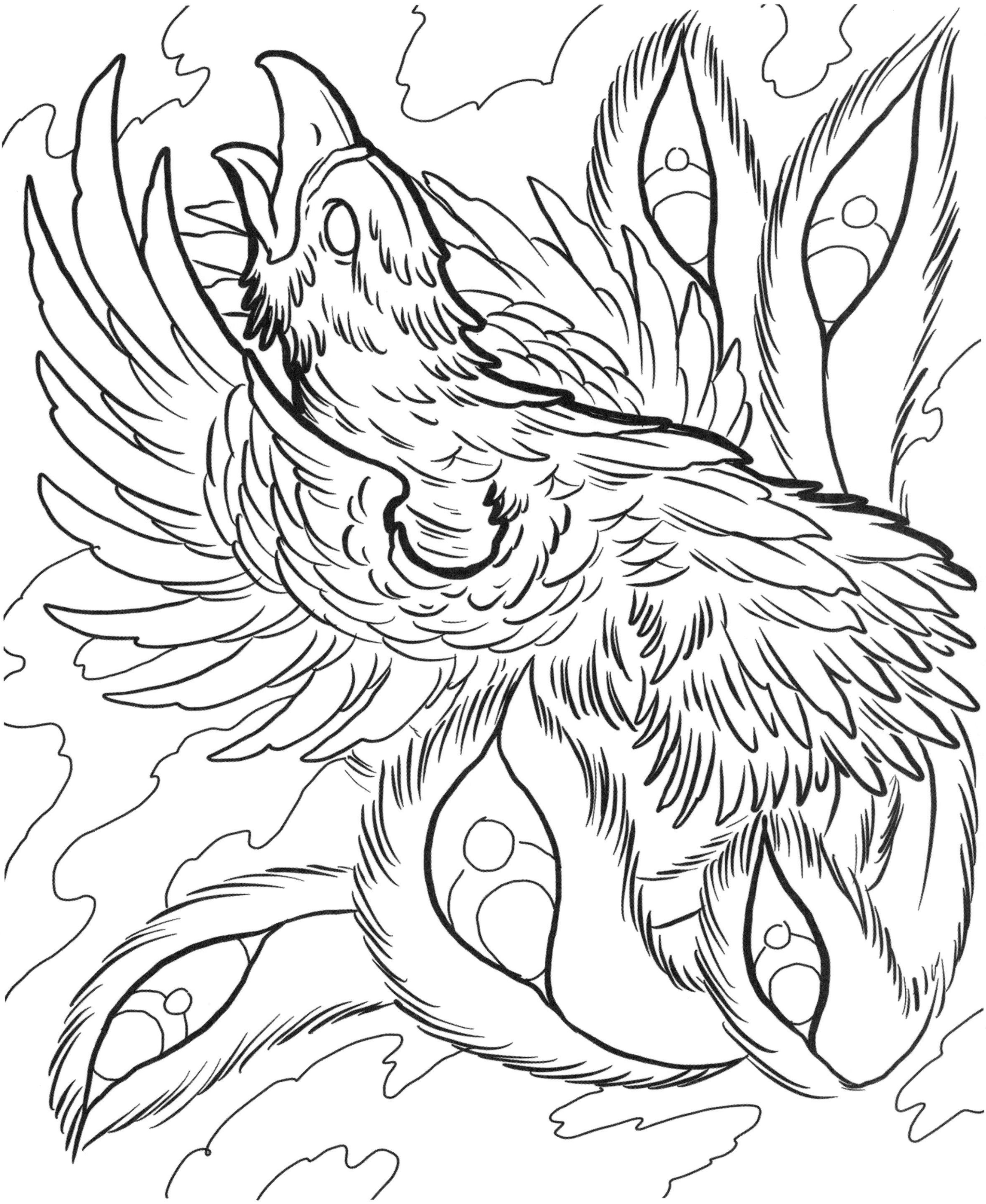

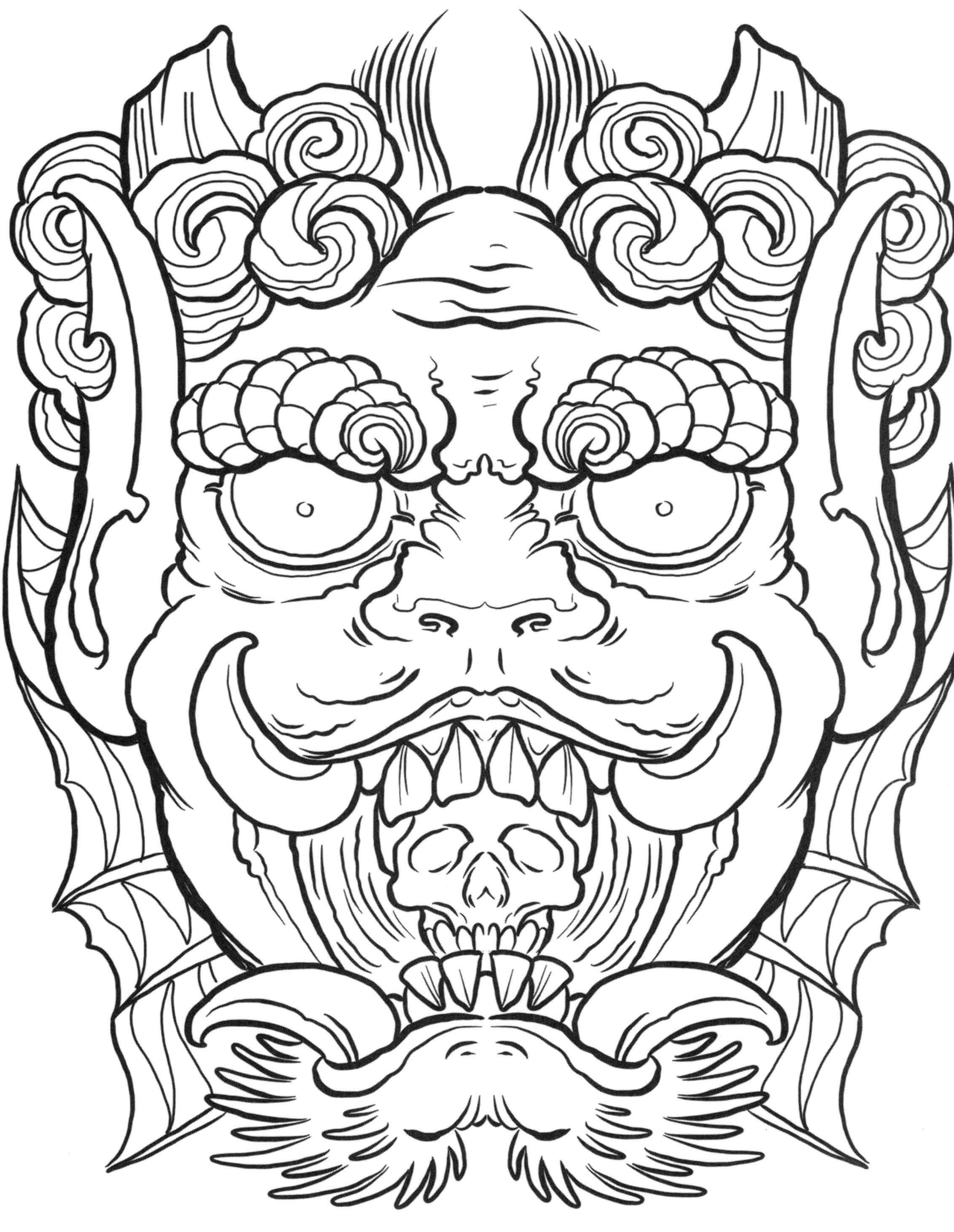

← 30

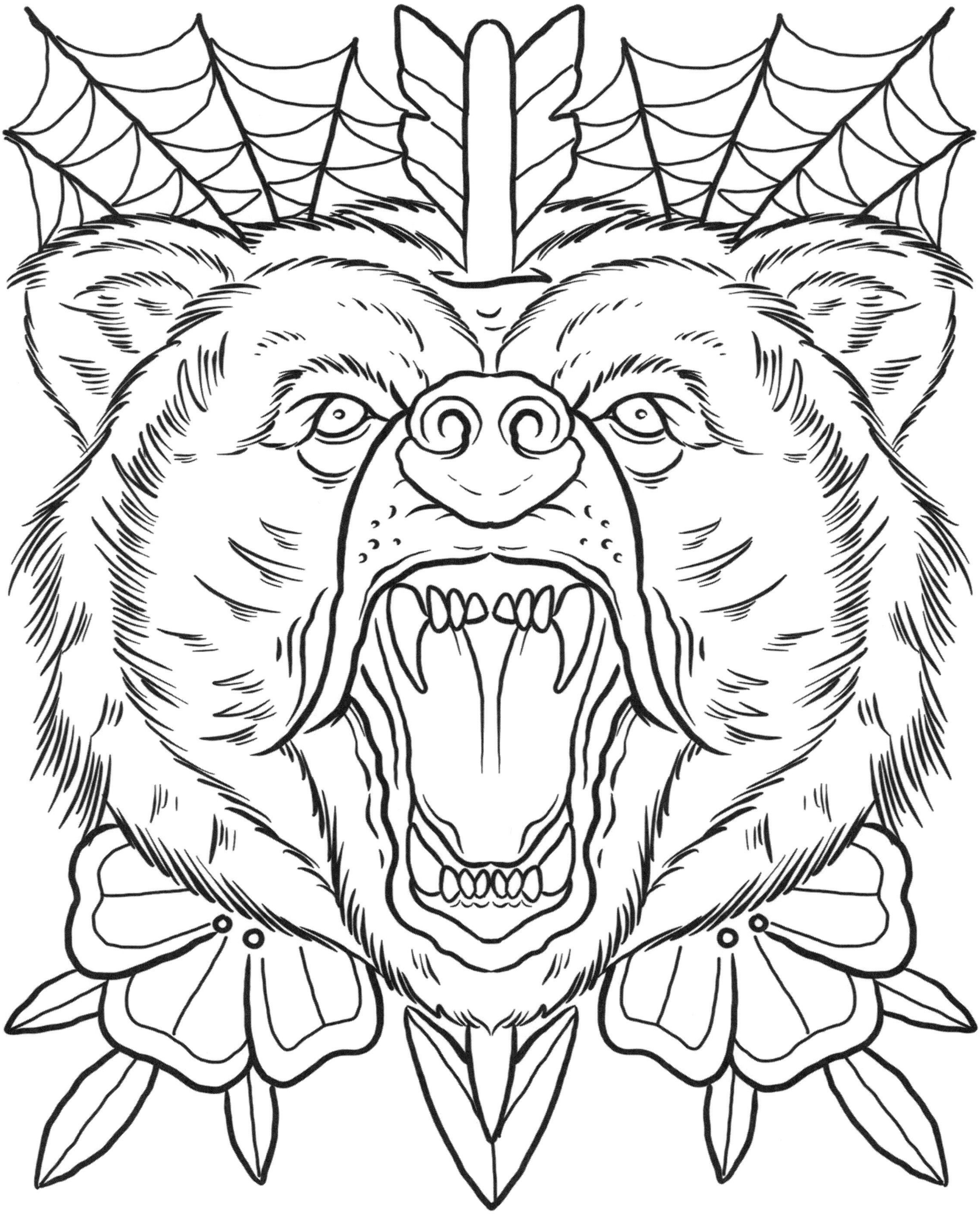

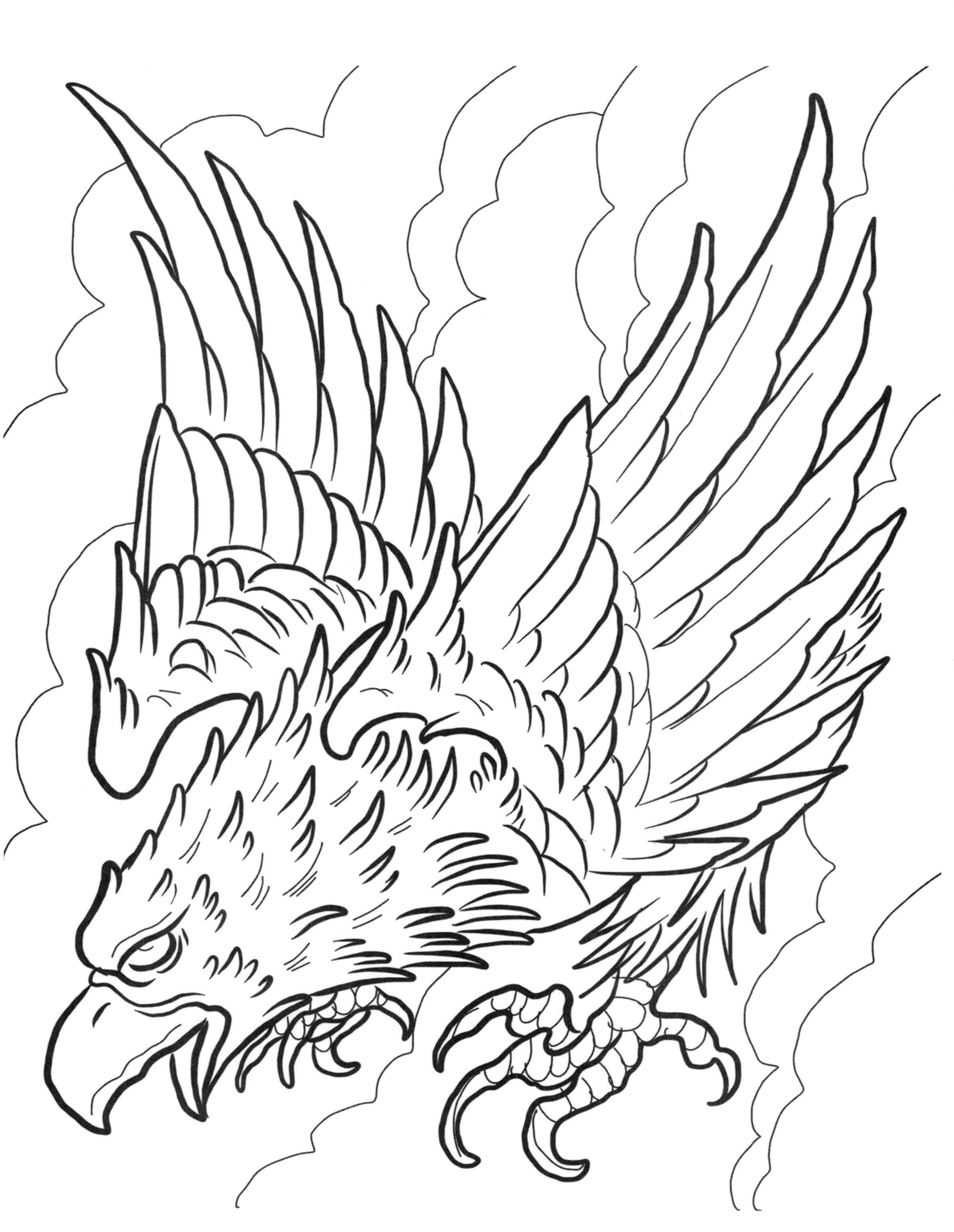

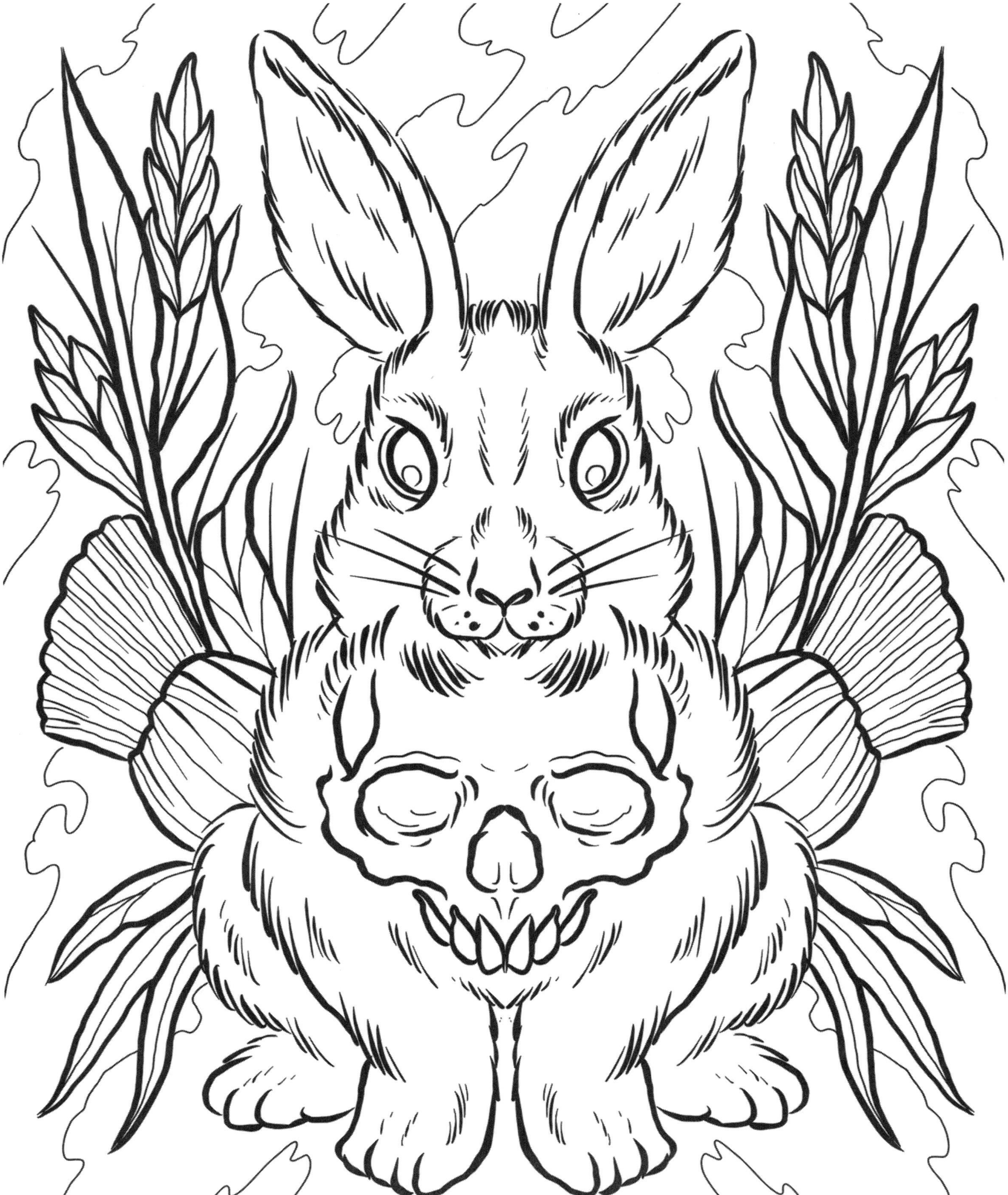

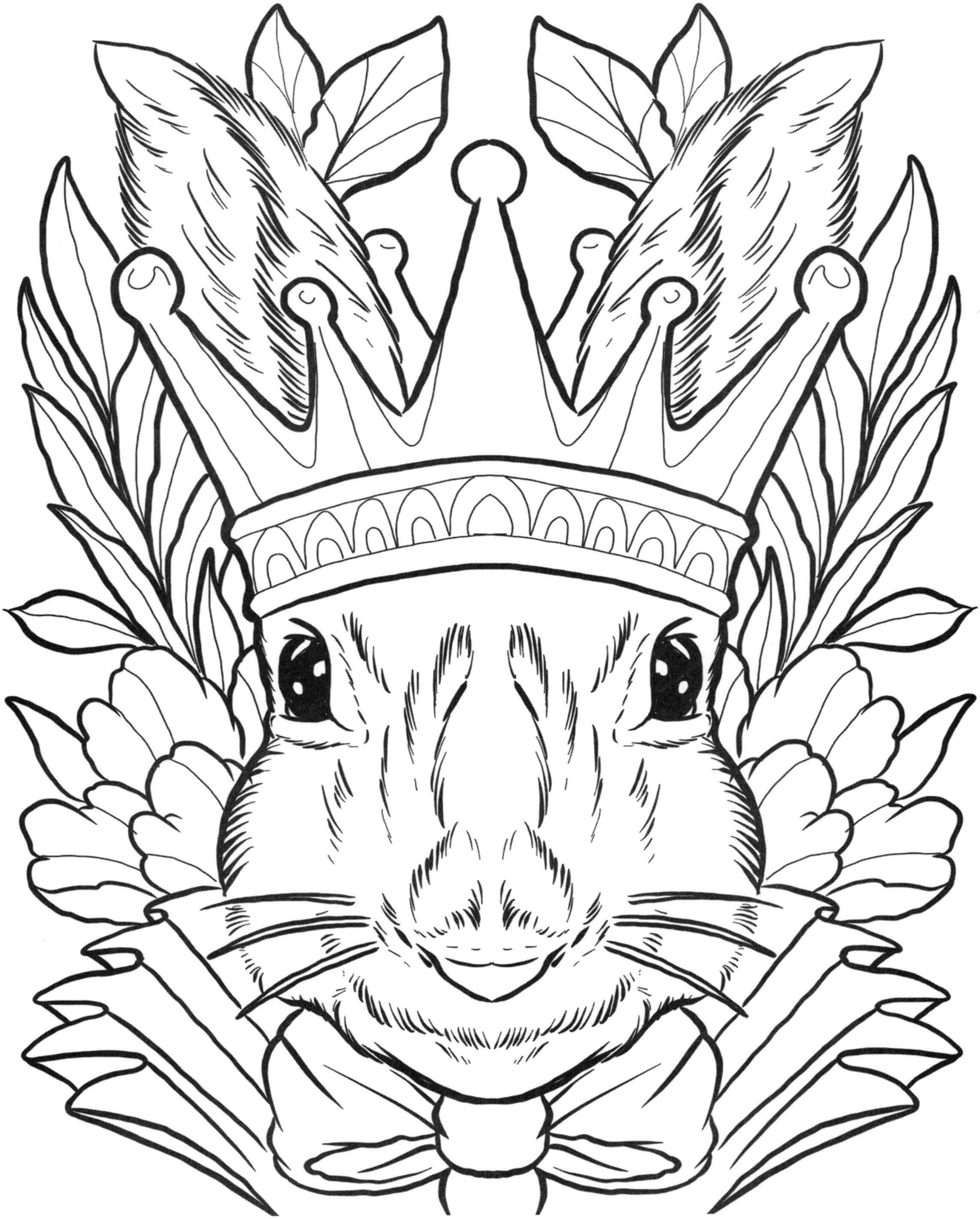

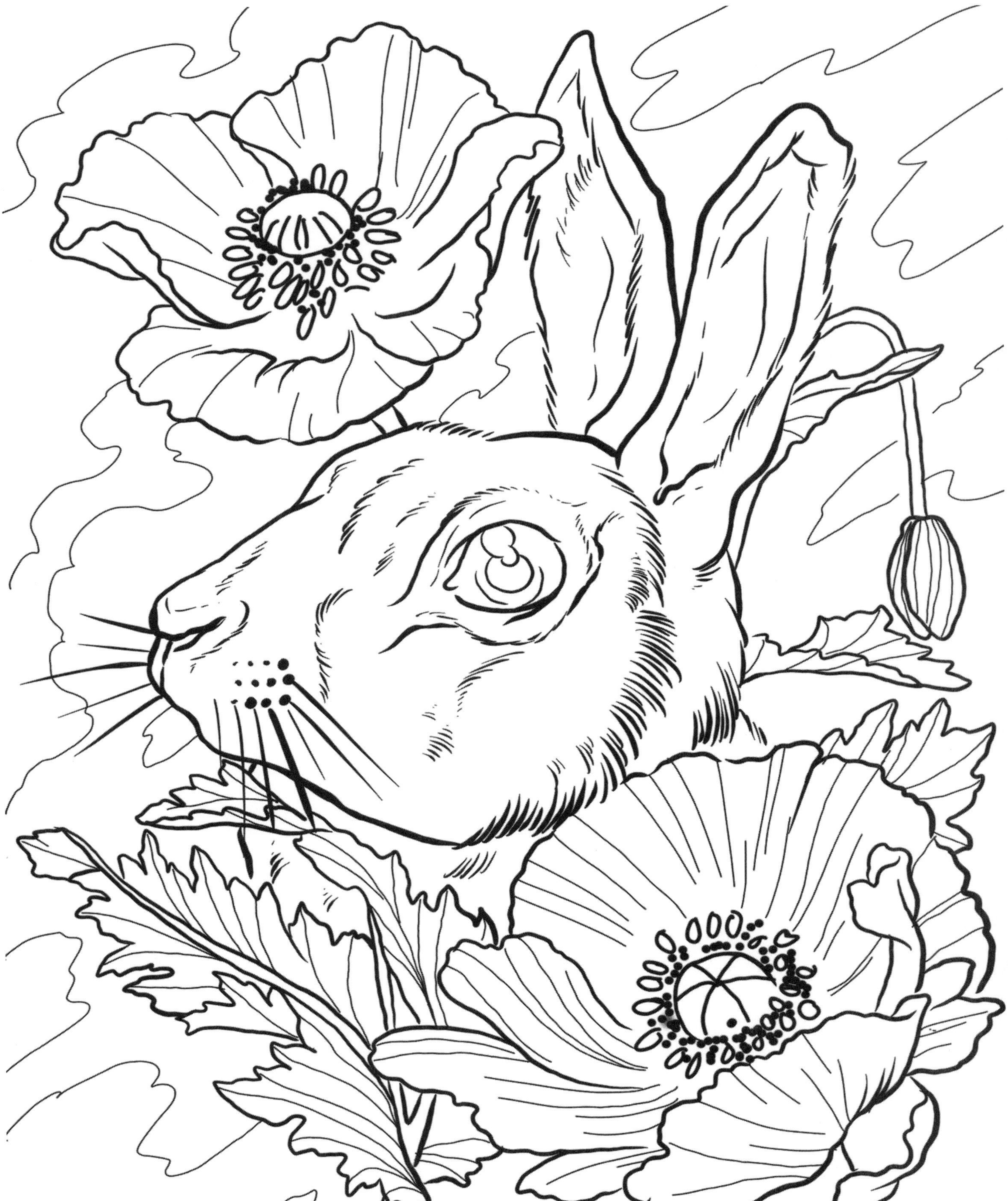

← 35

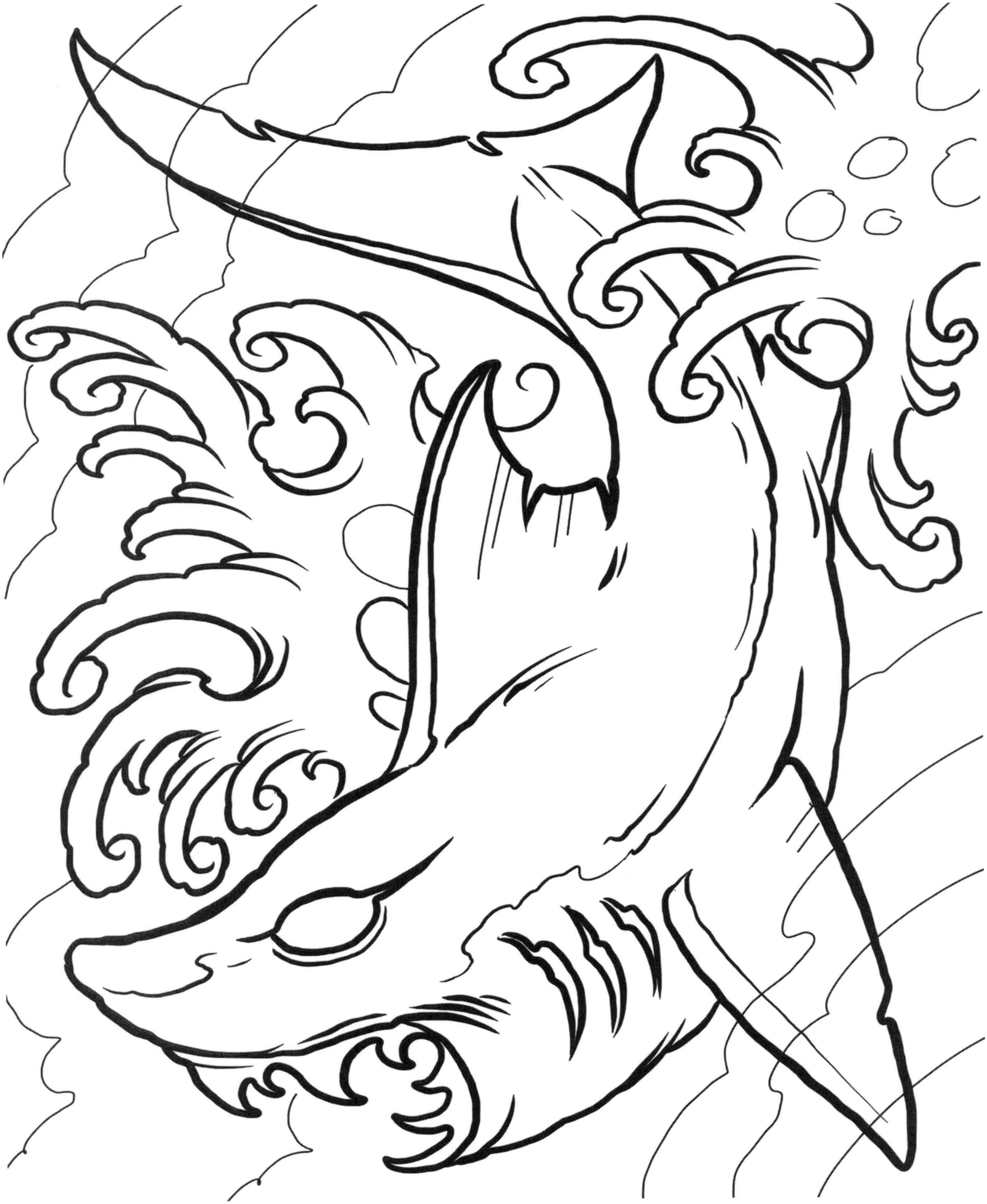

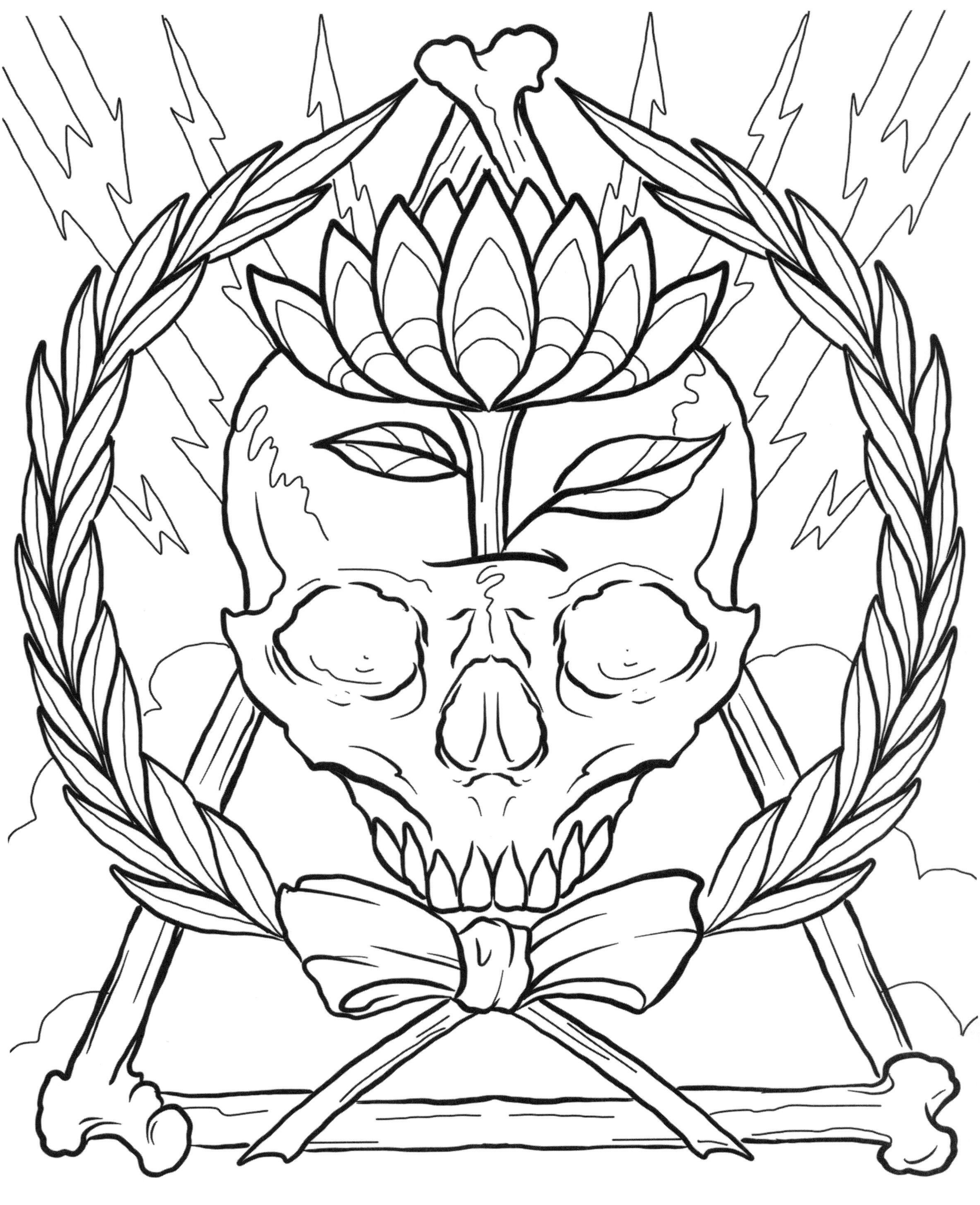

⟵ 37

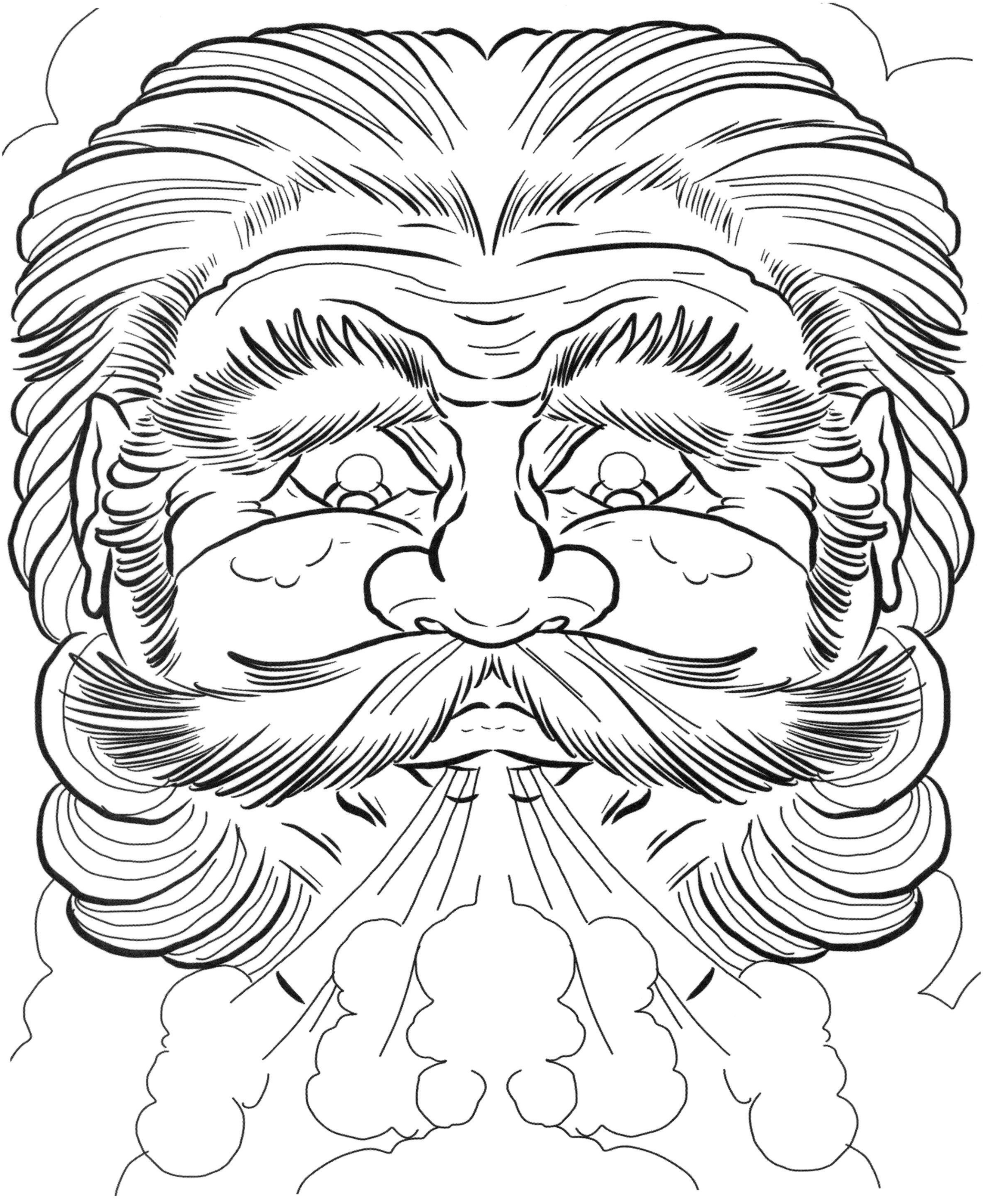

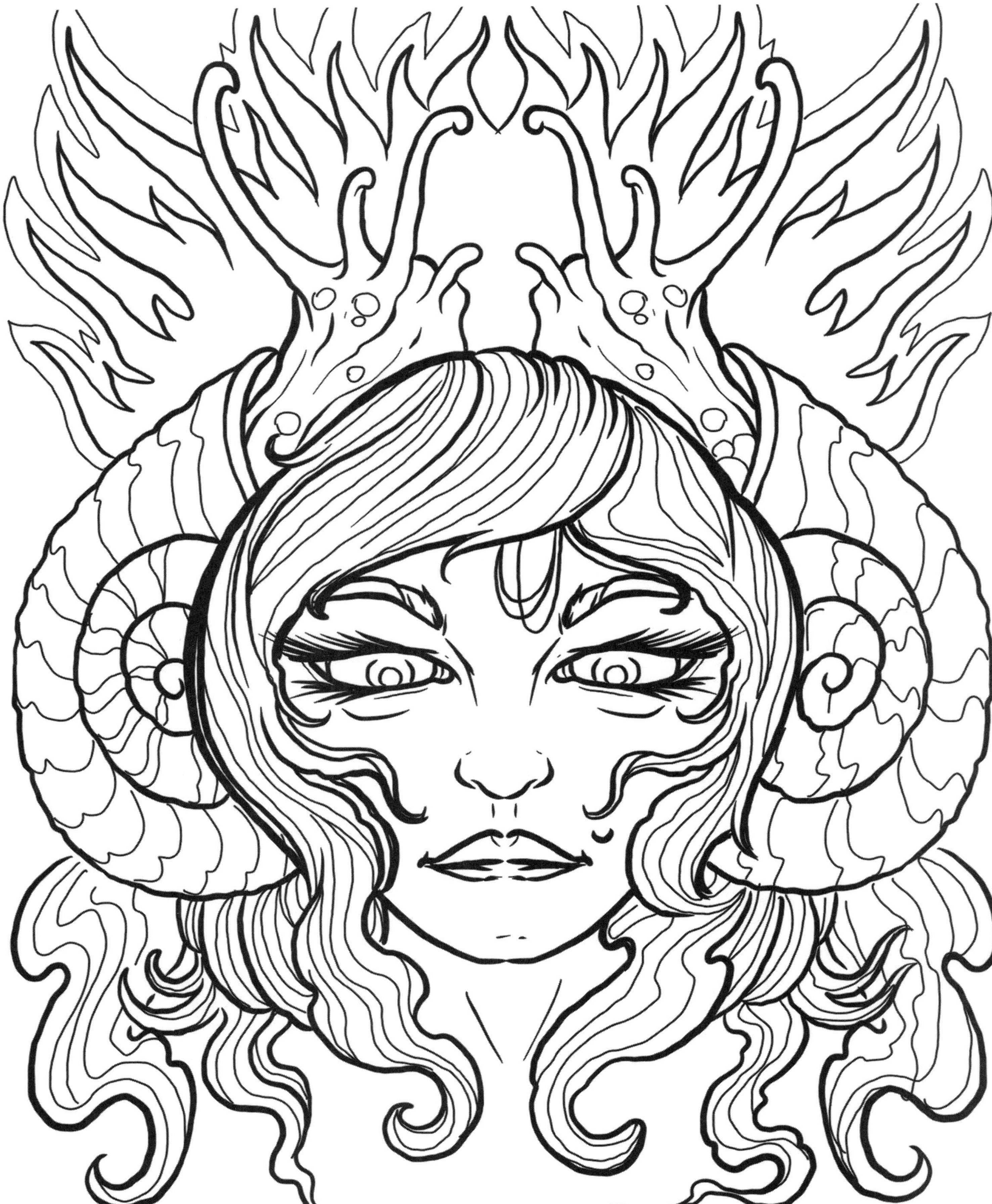

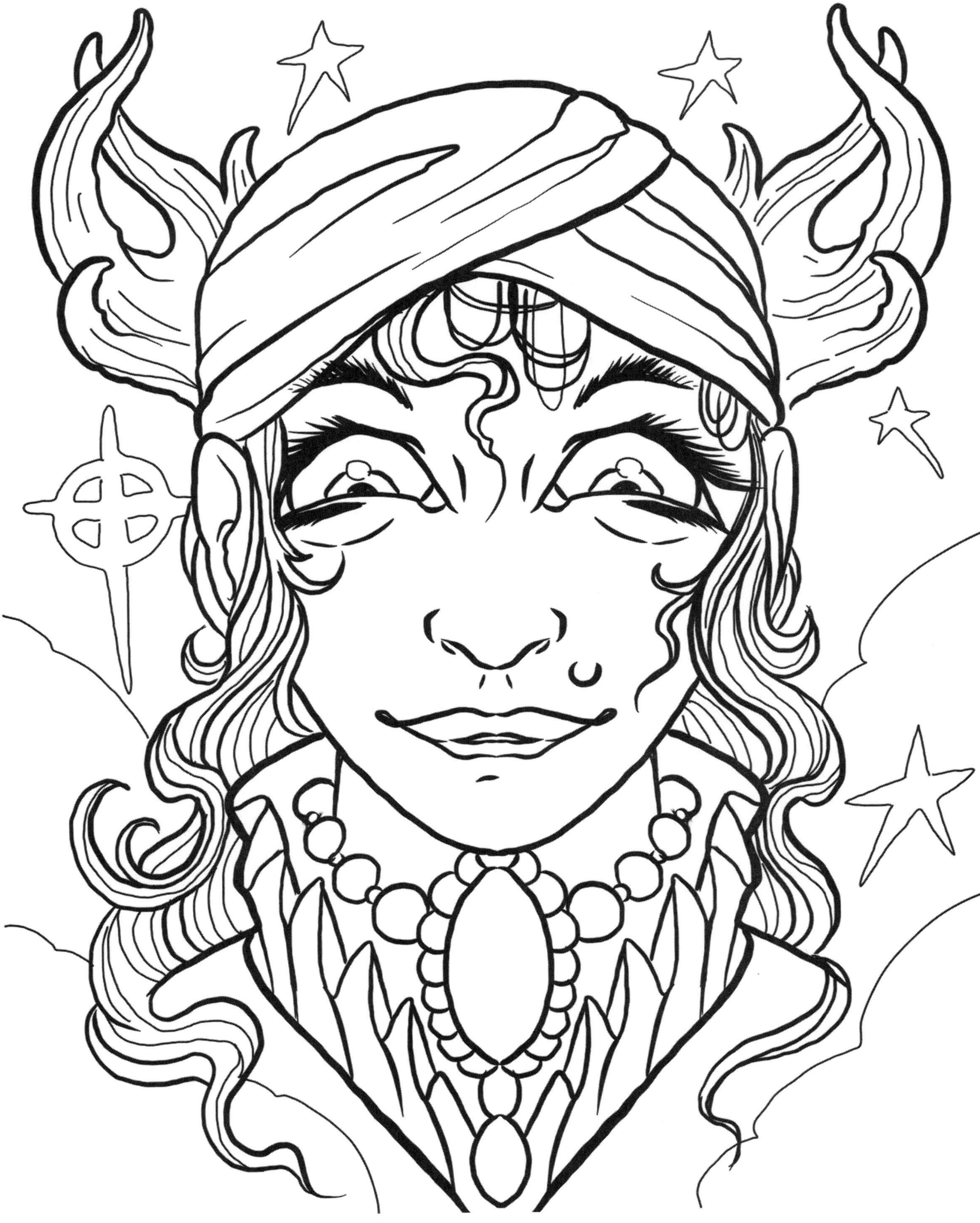

← 40

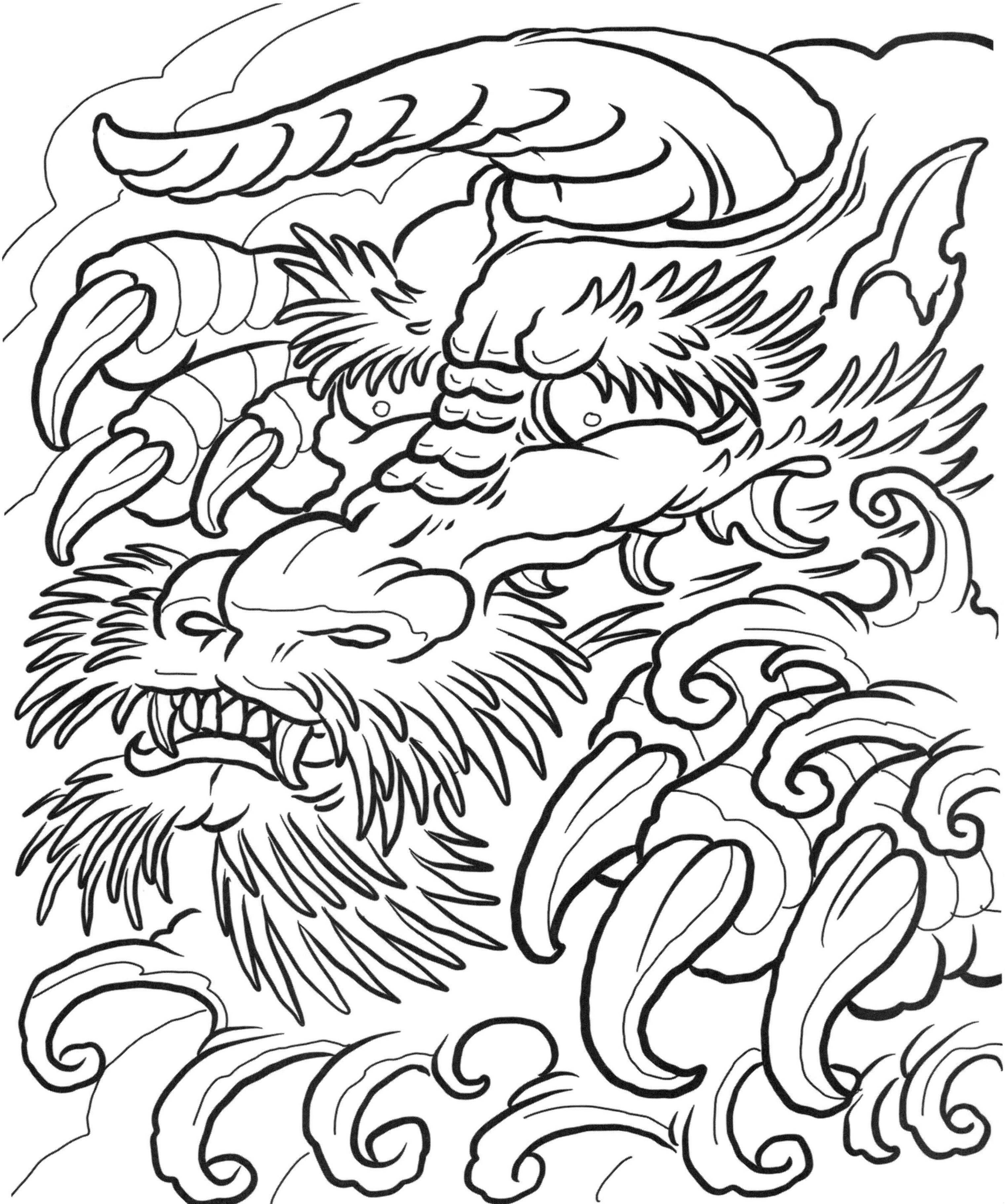

← 41

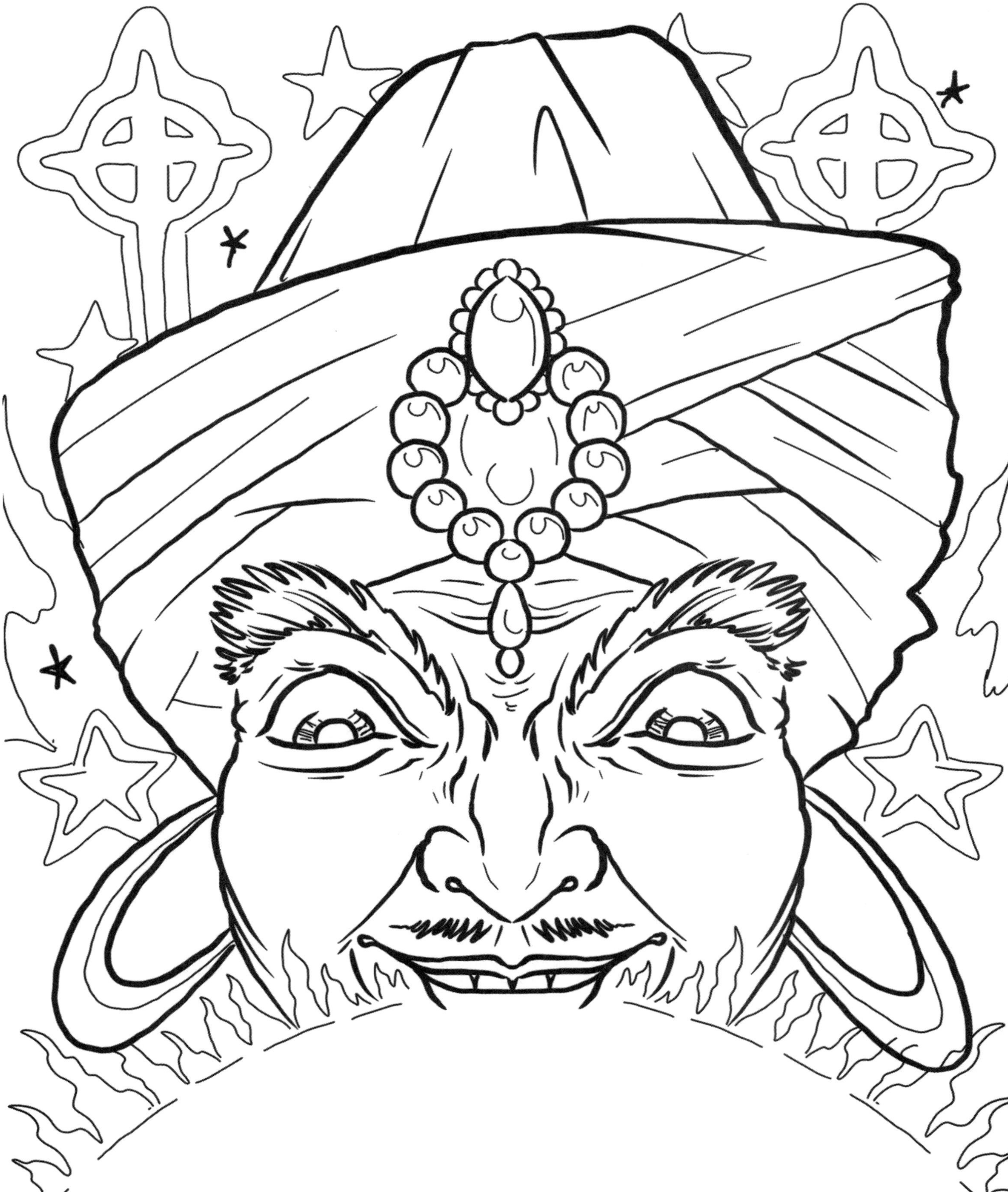

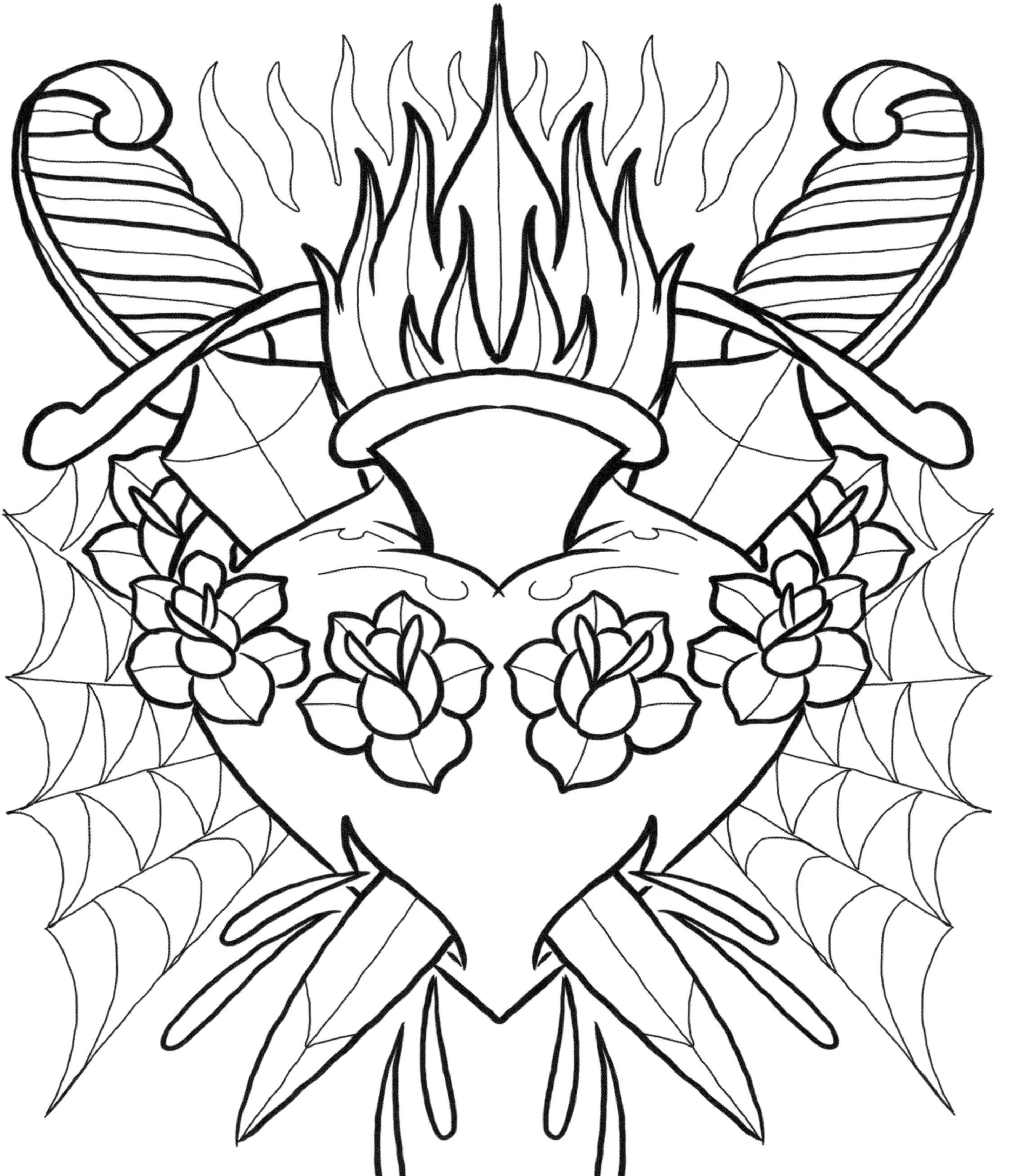

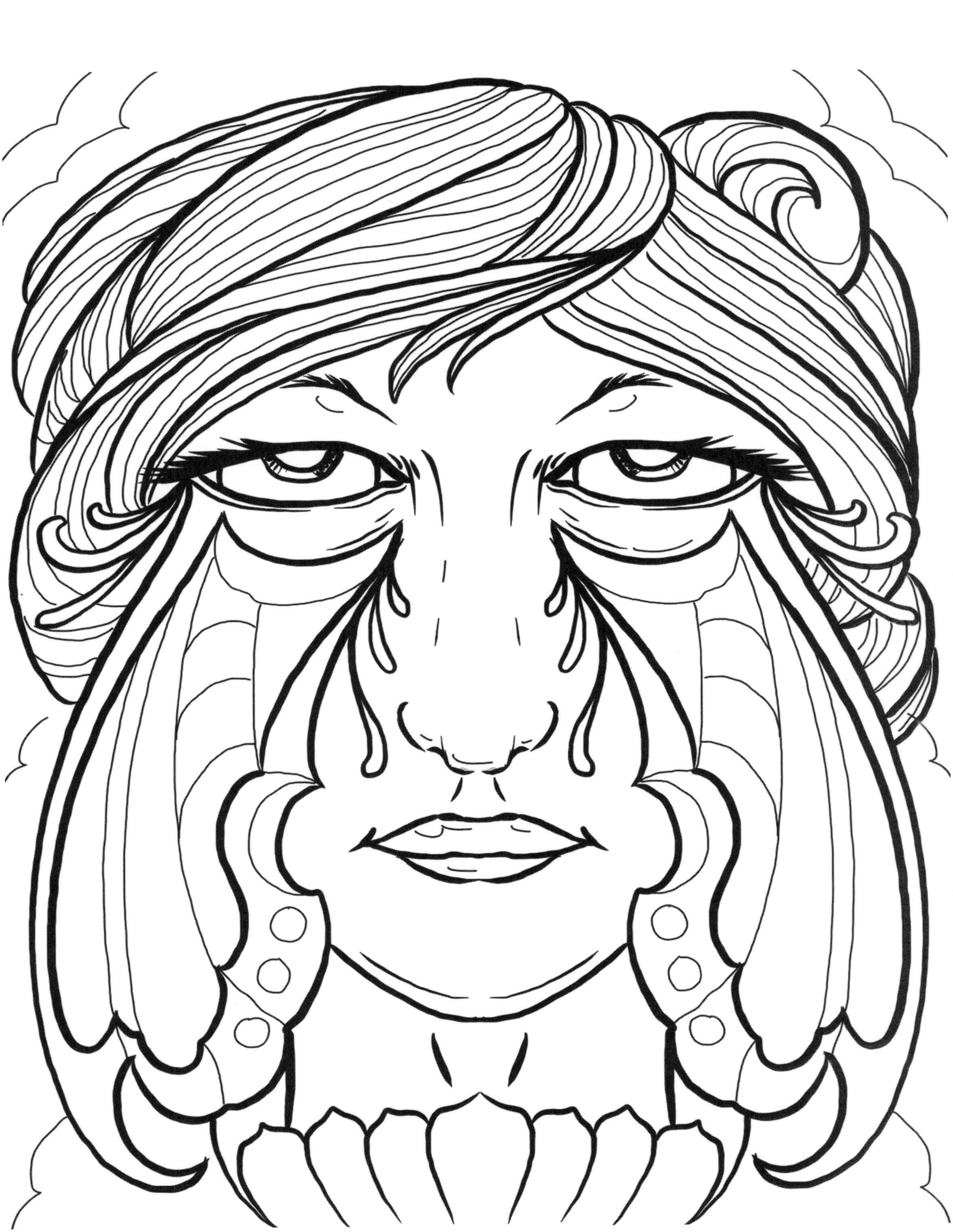

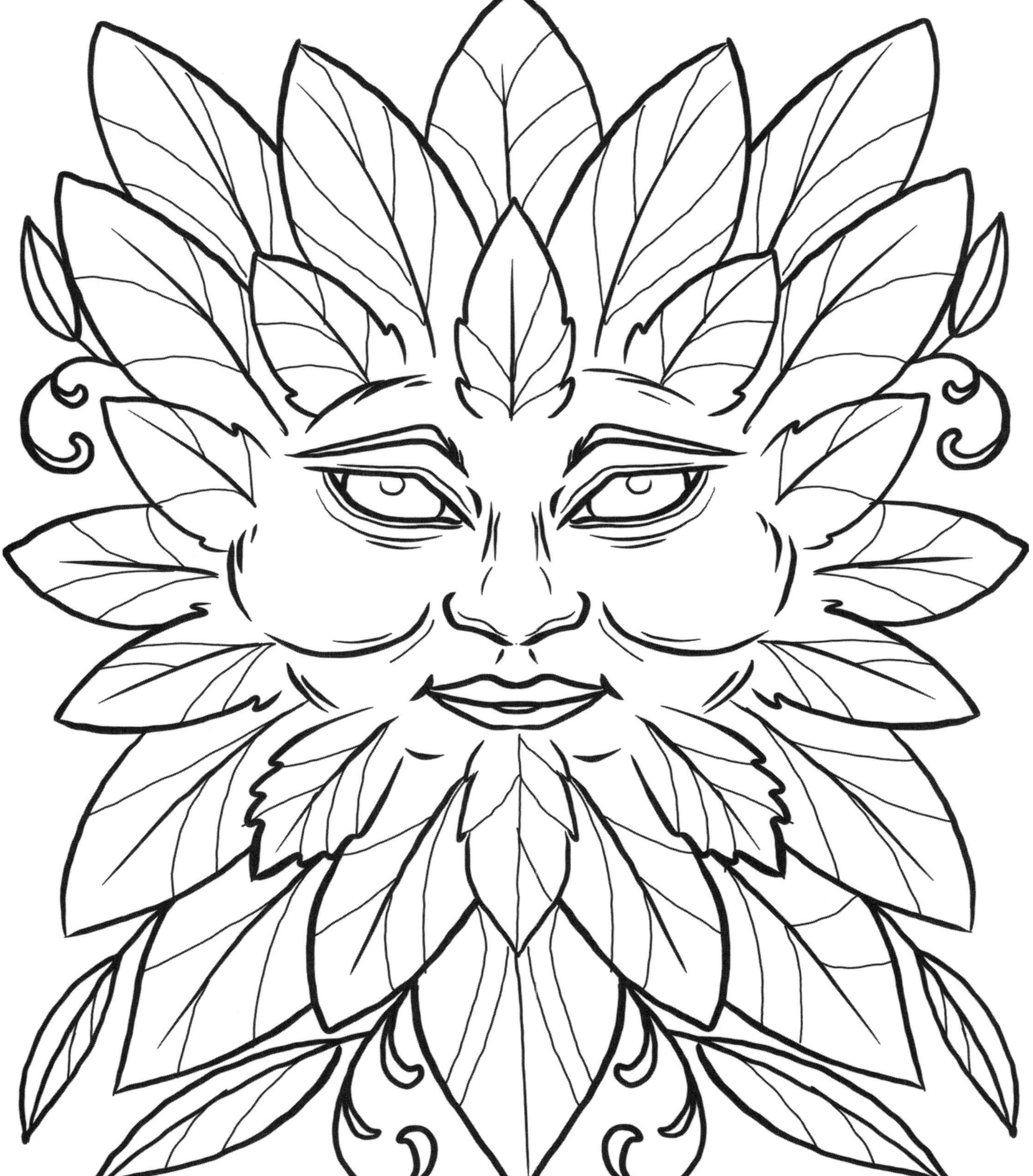

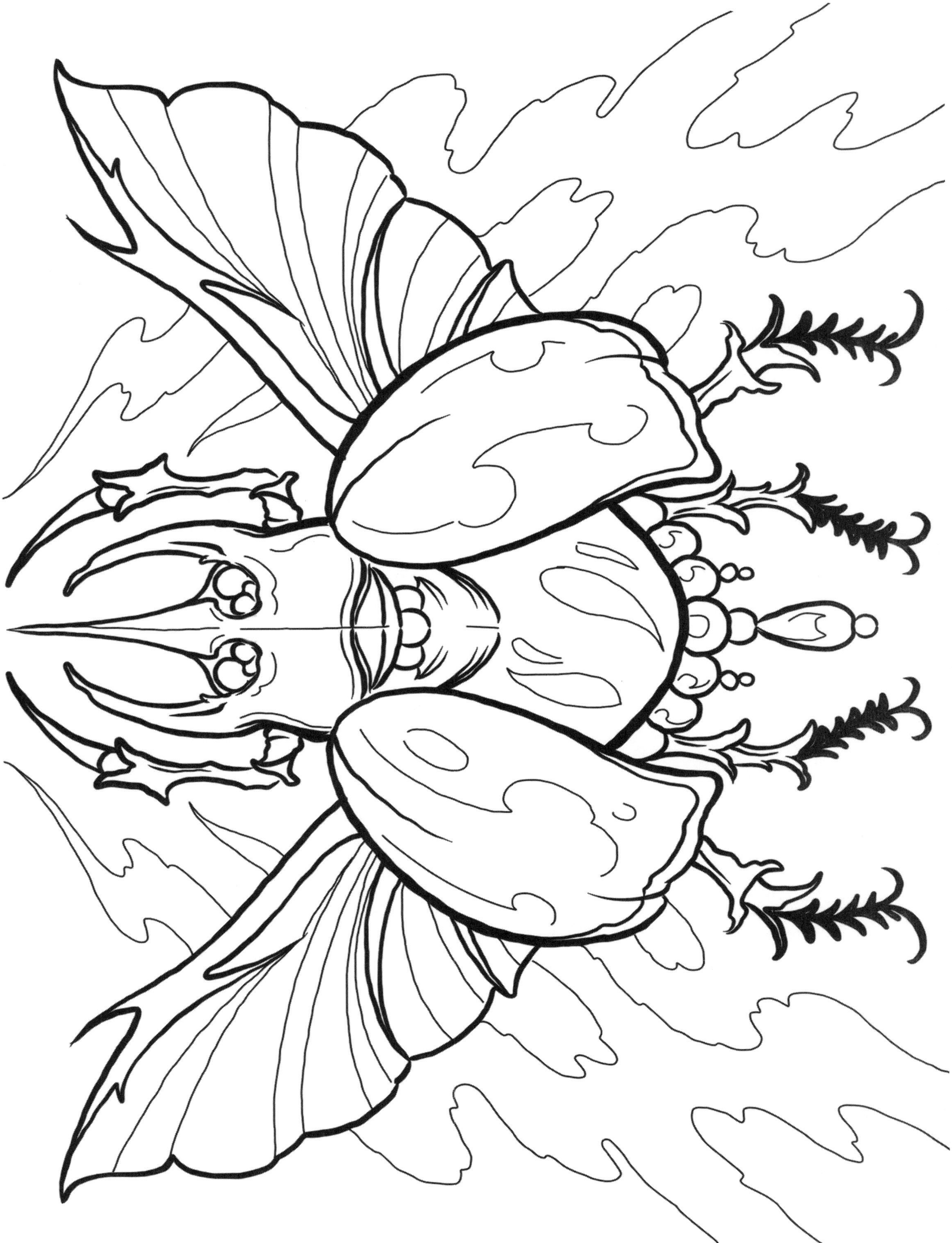

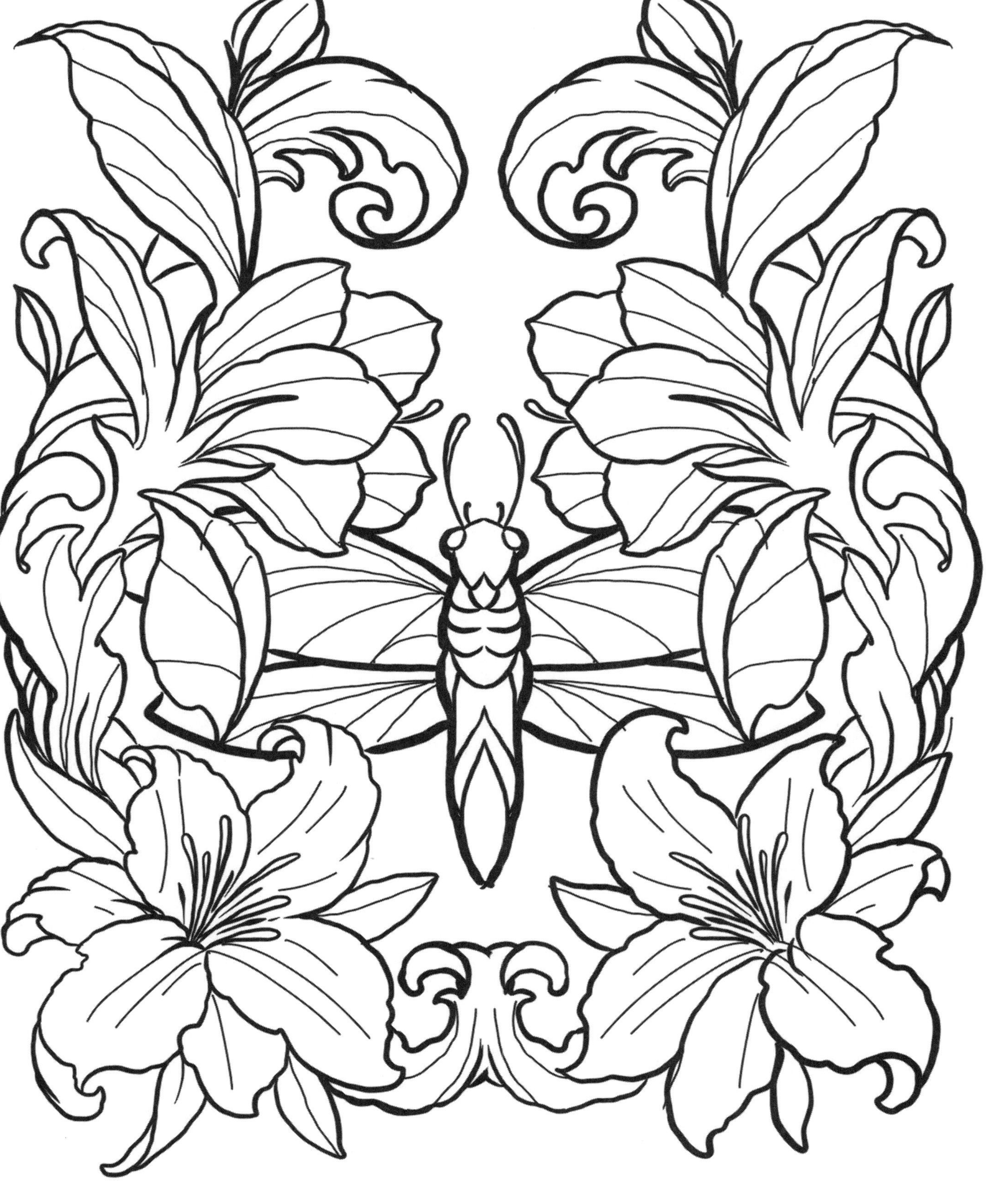

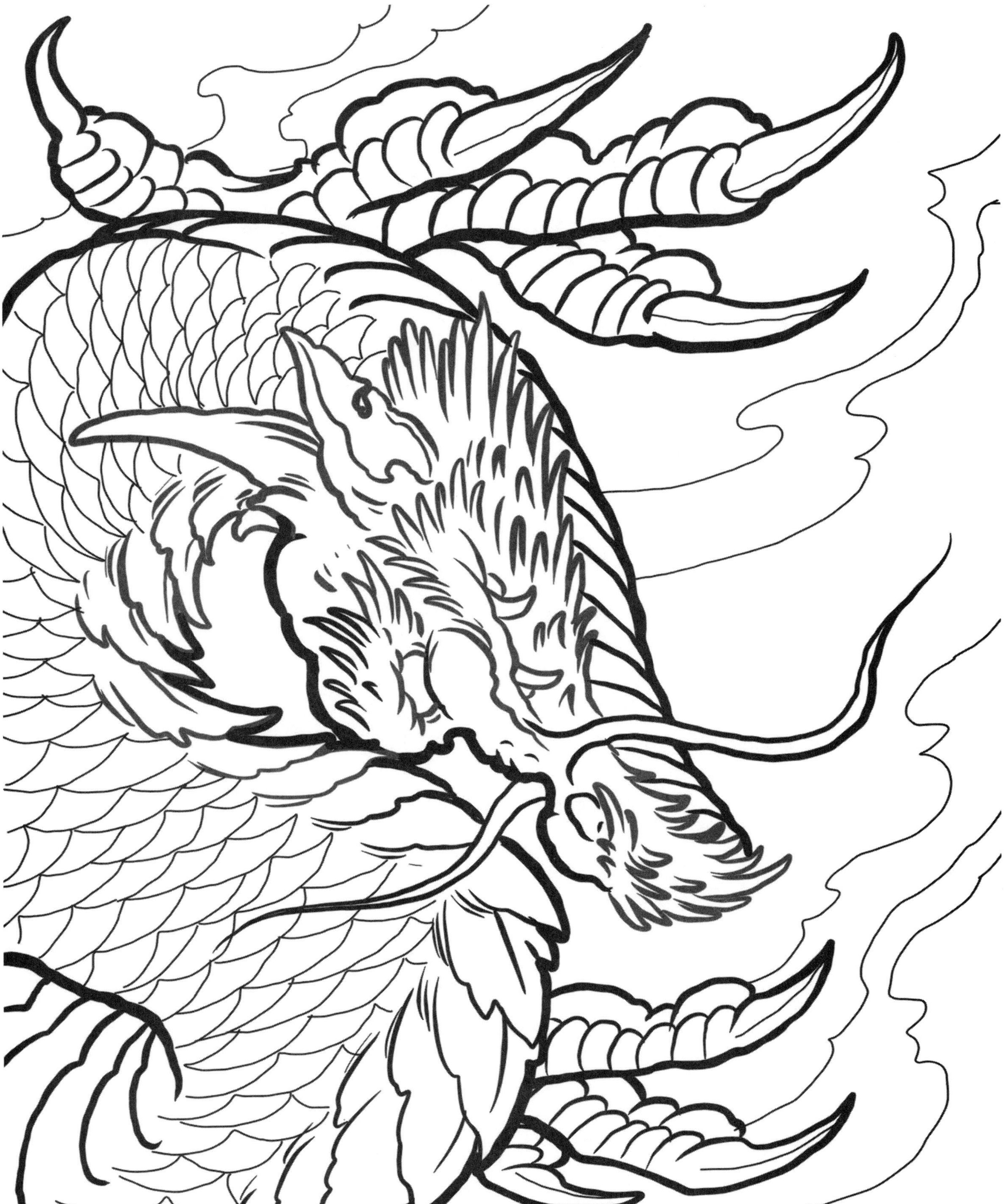

← 48

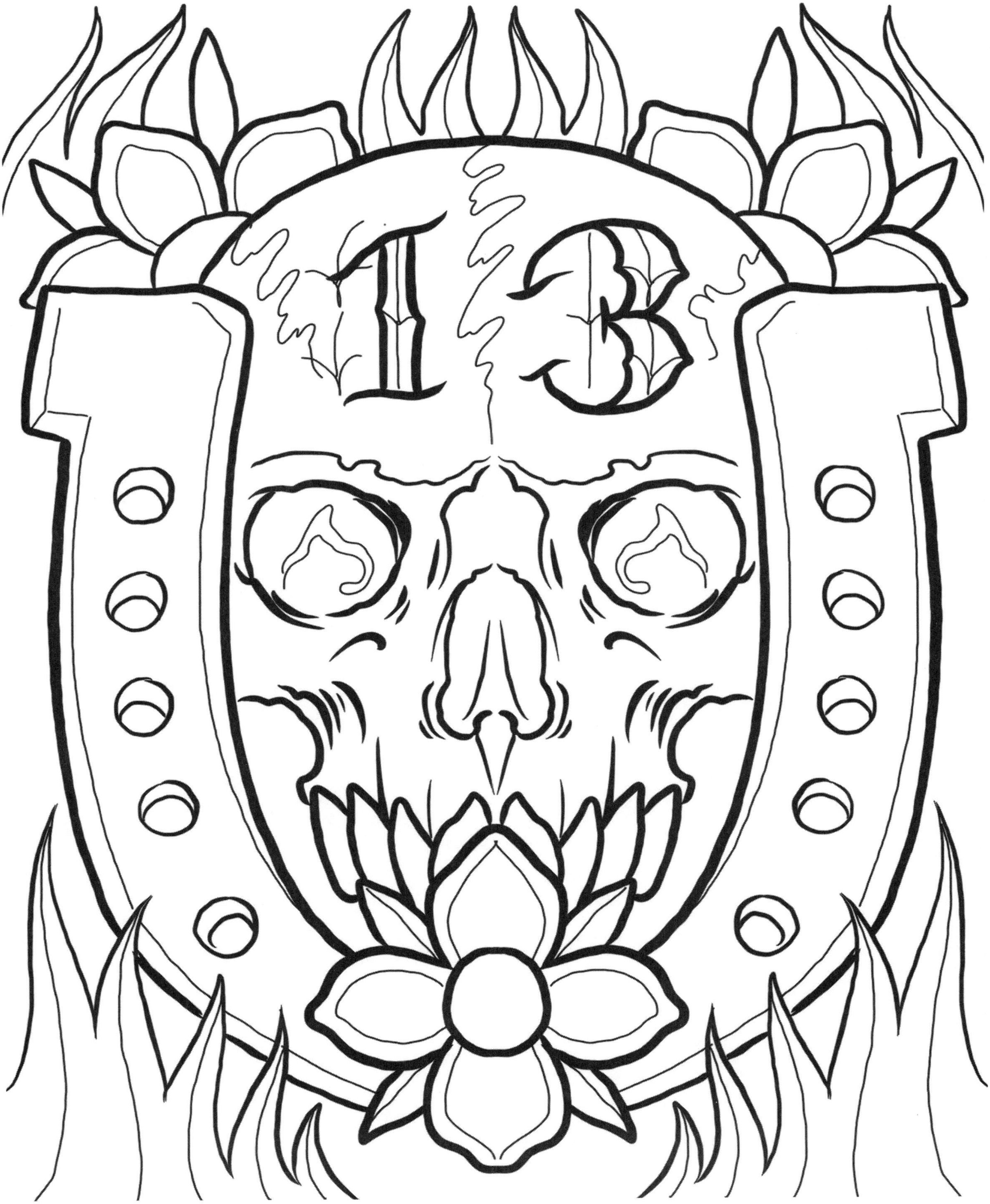
13

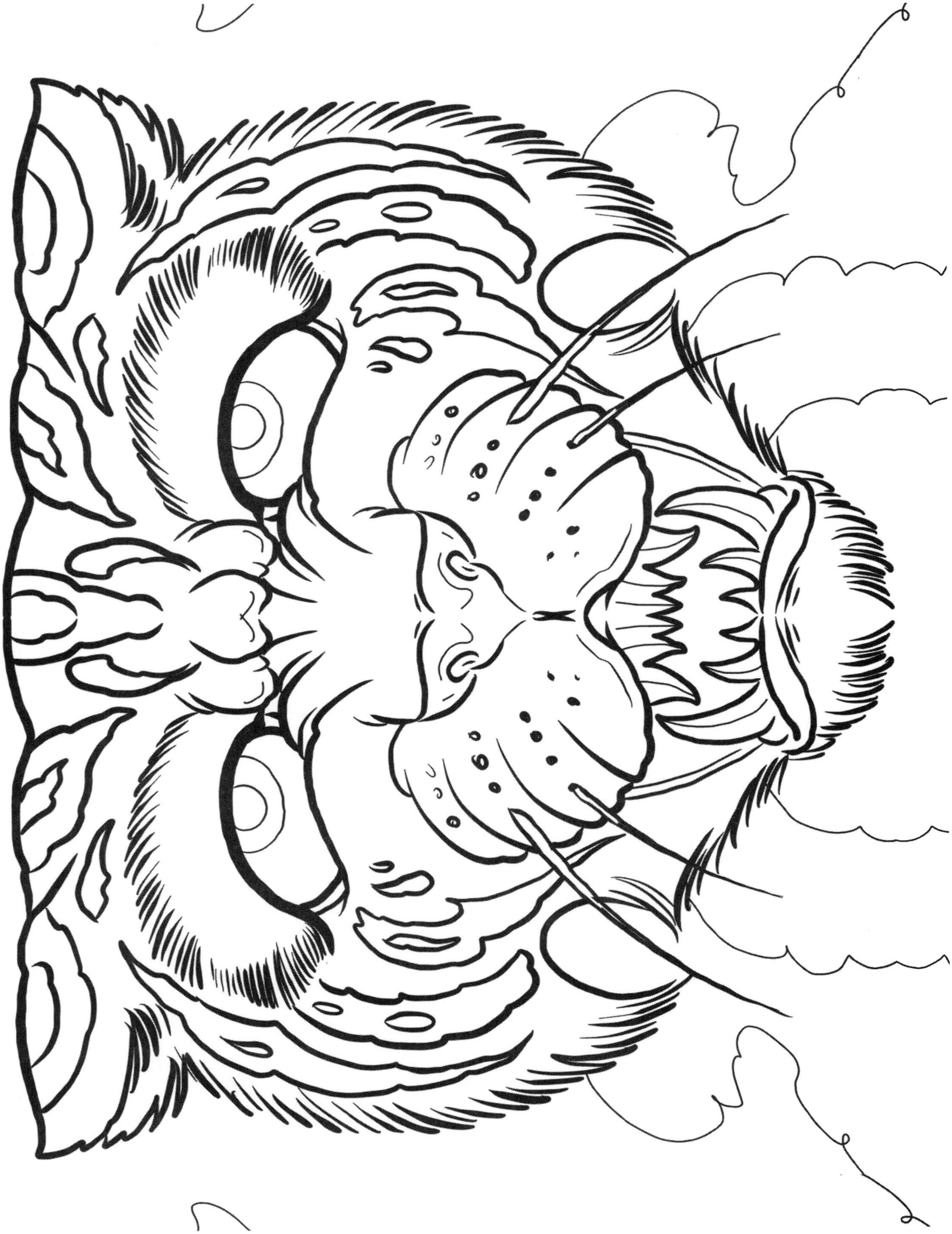

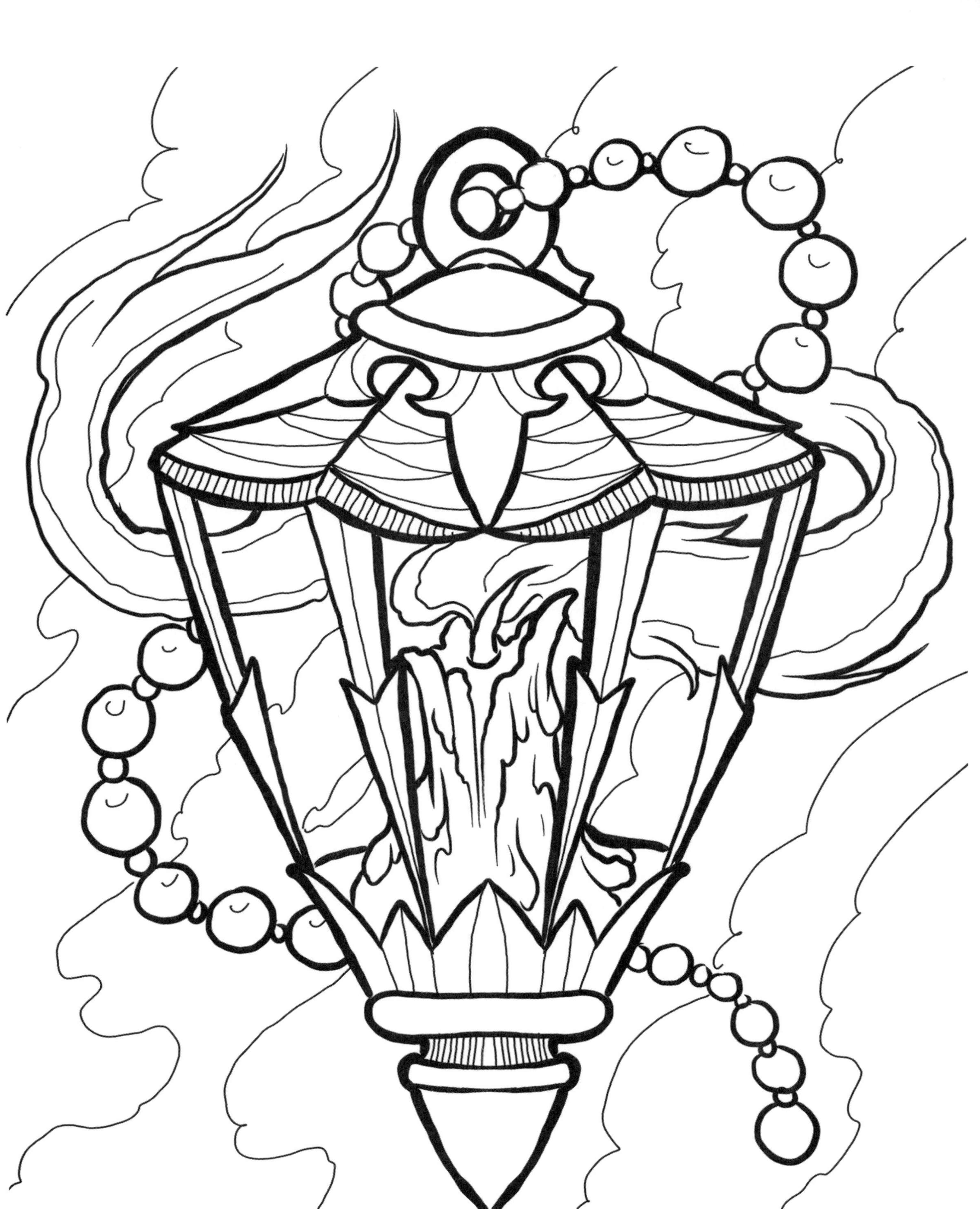

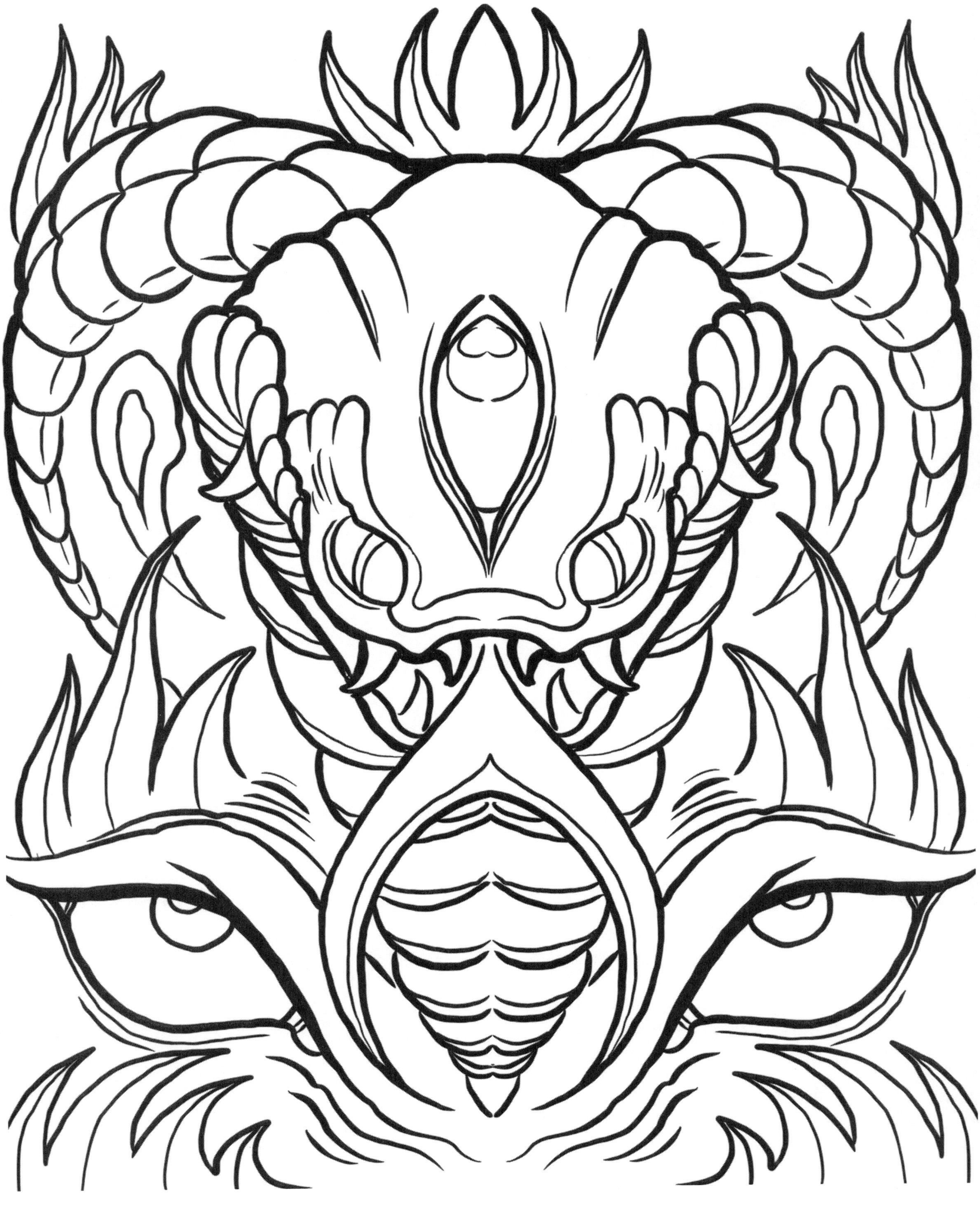

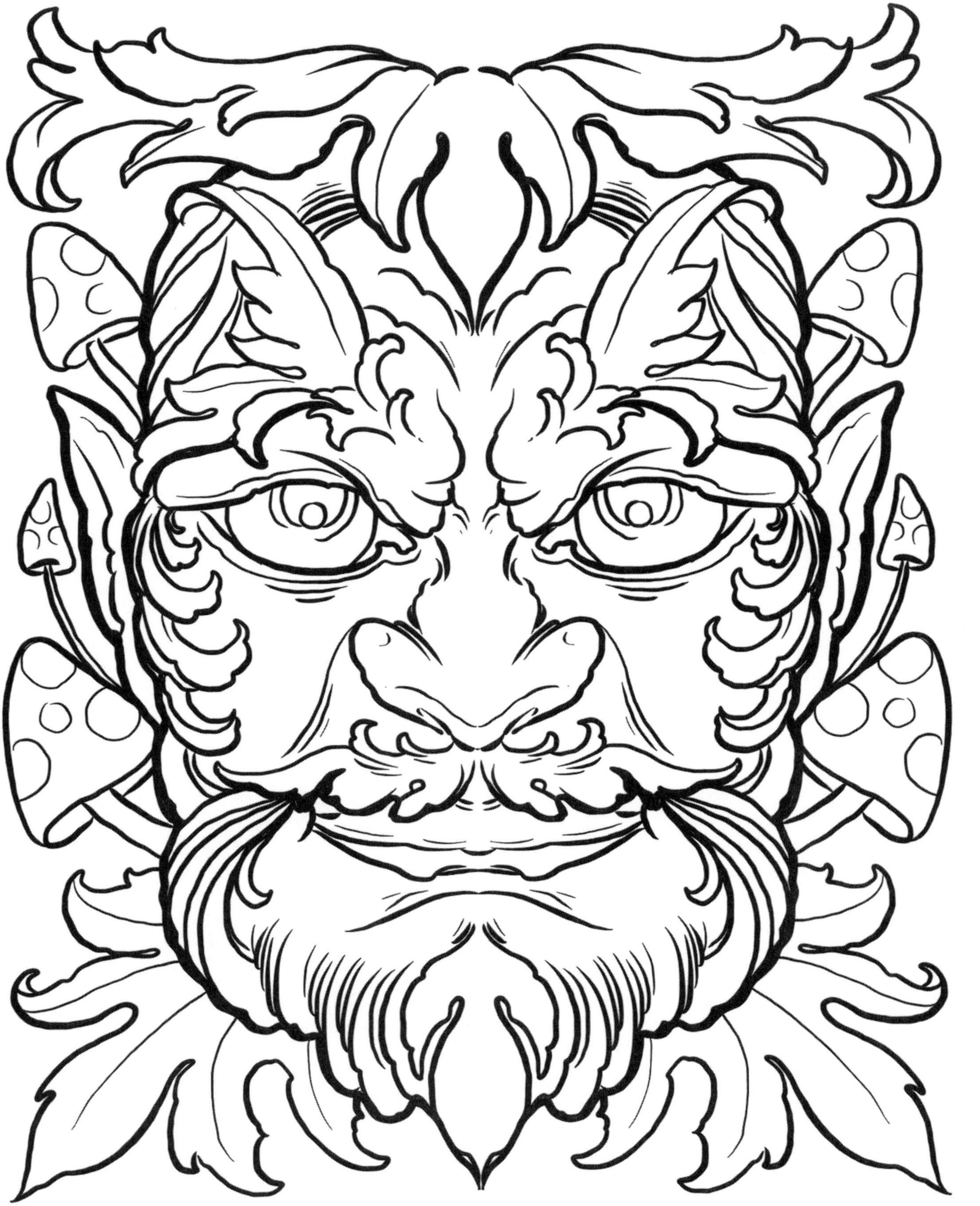

← 53

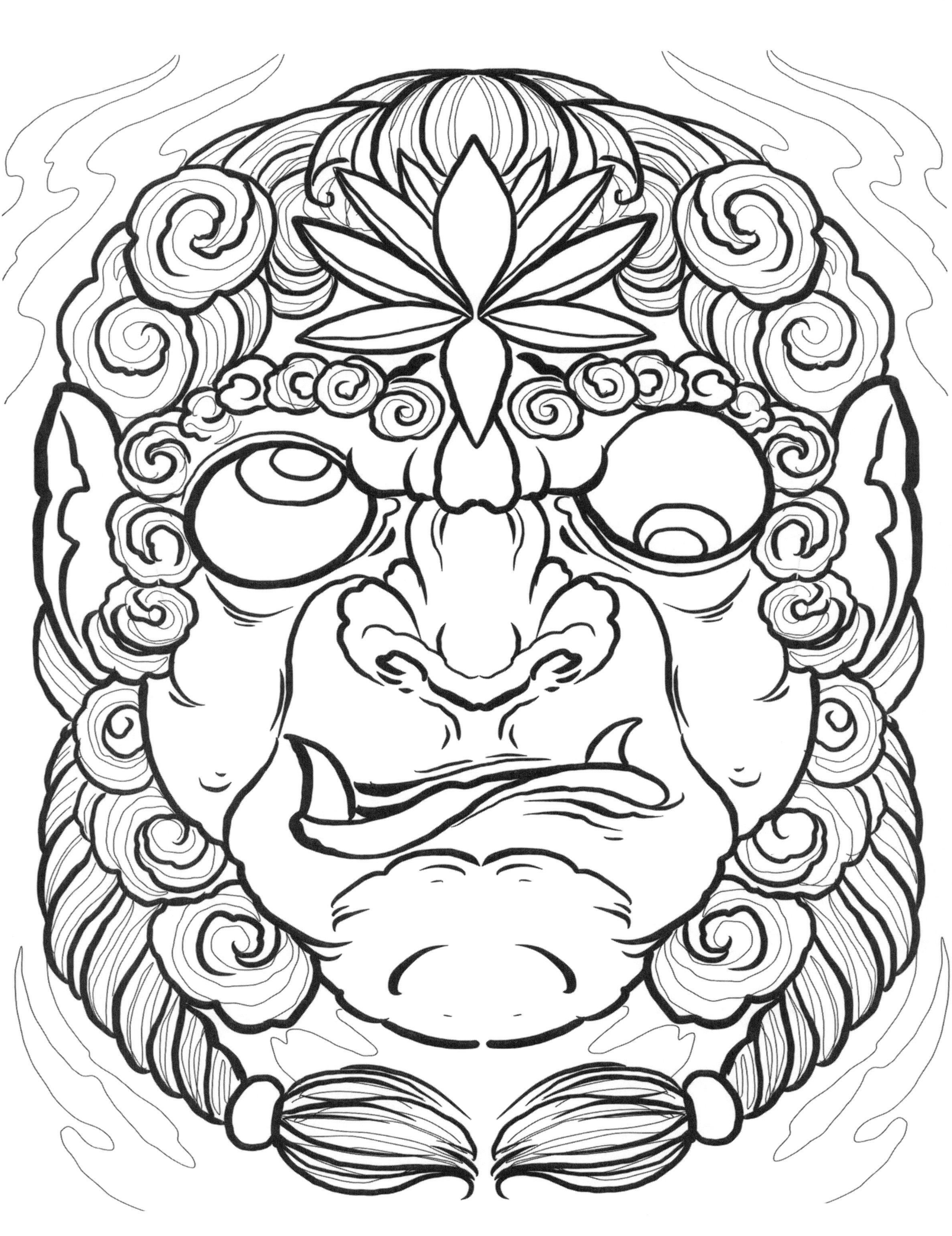

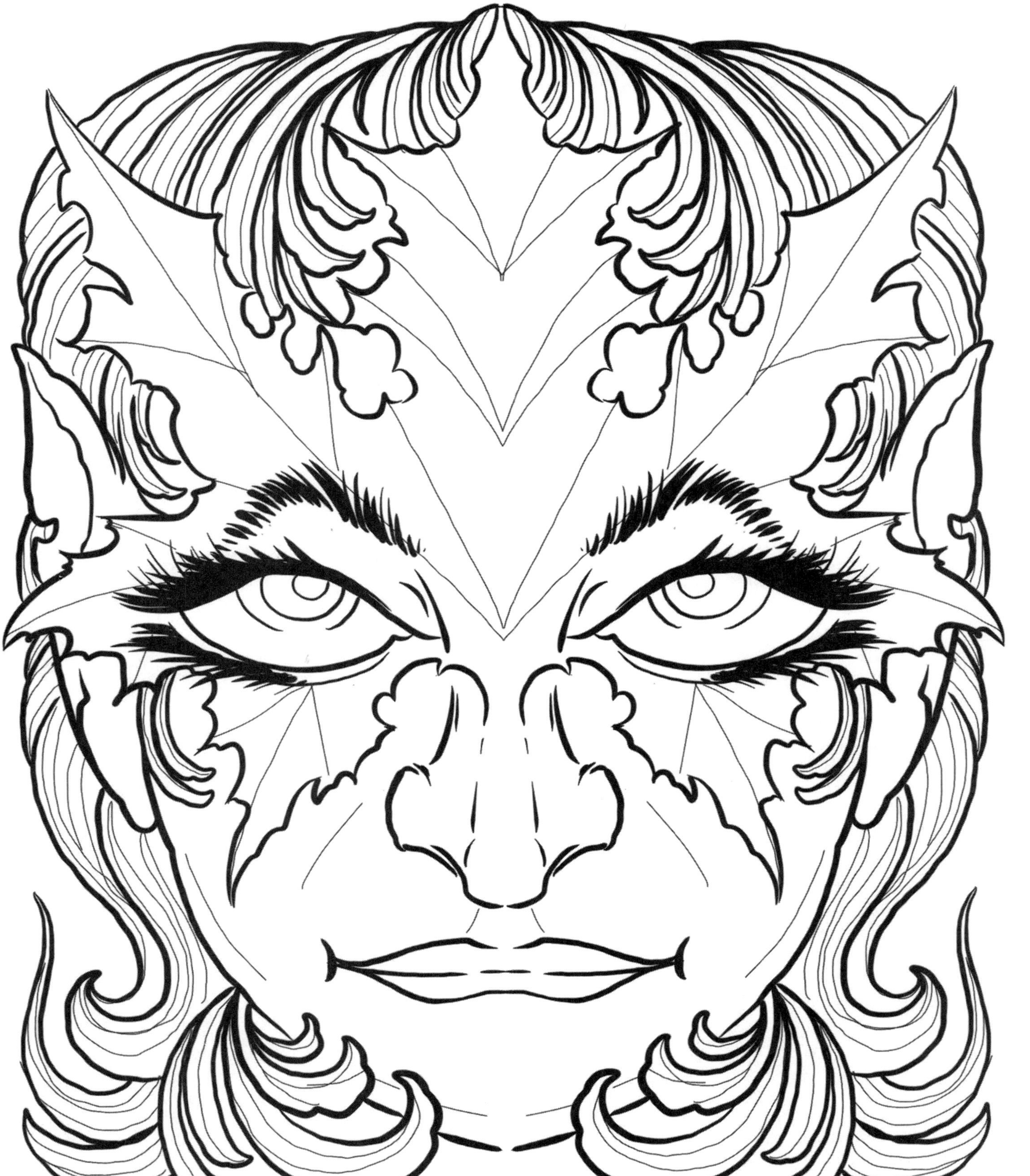

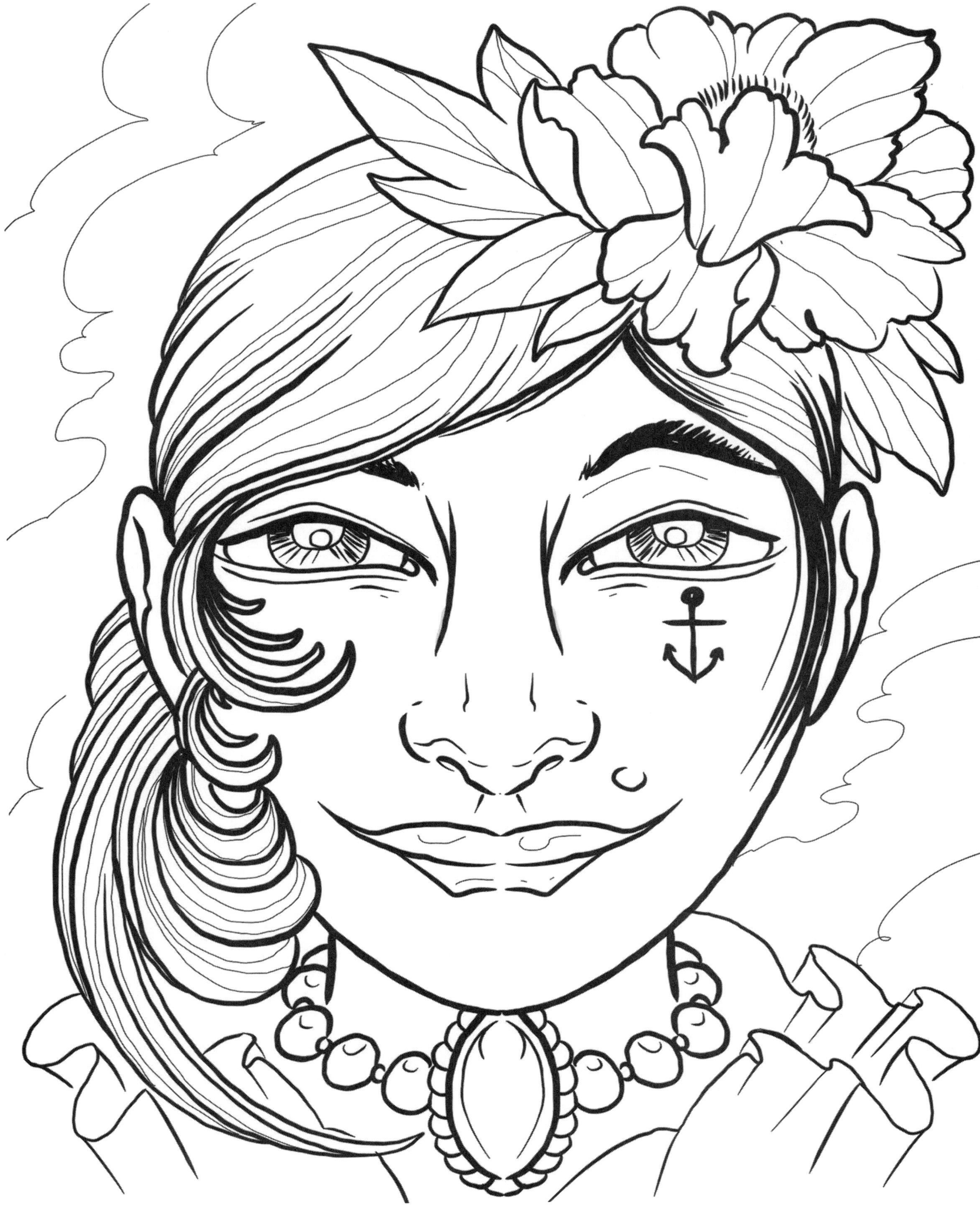

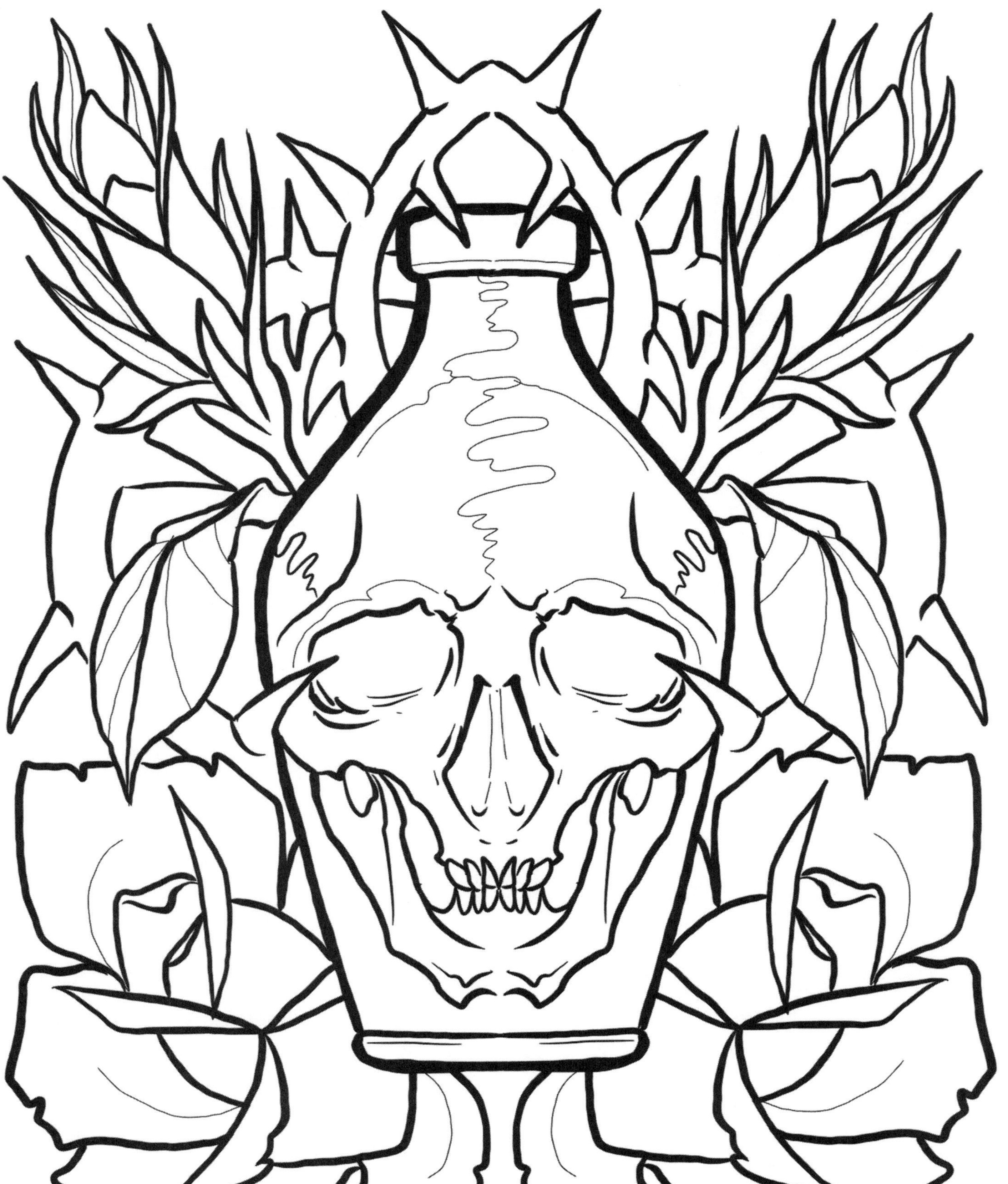

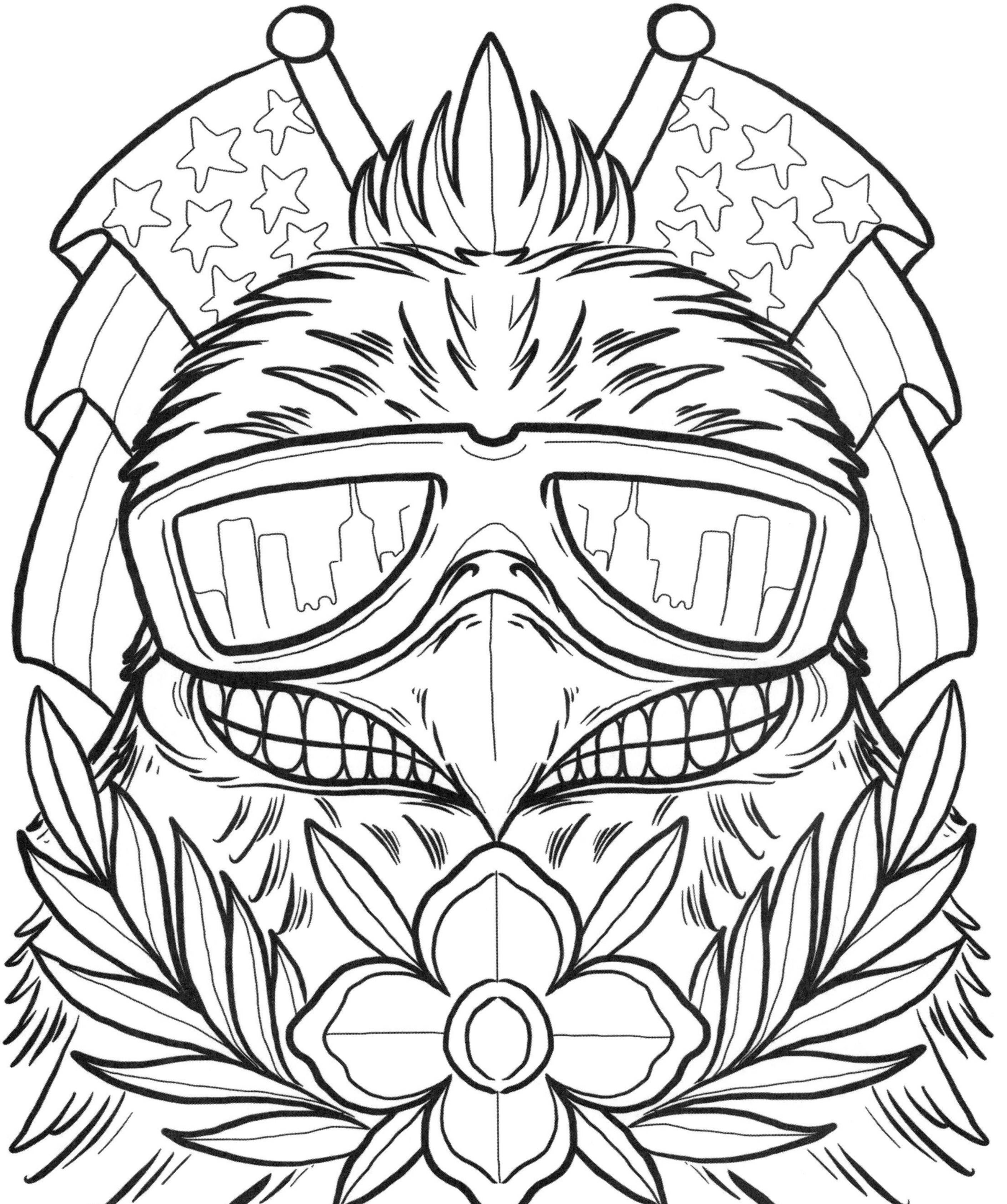

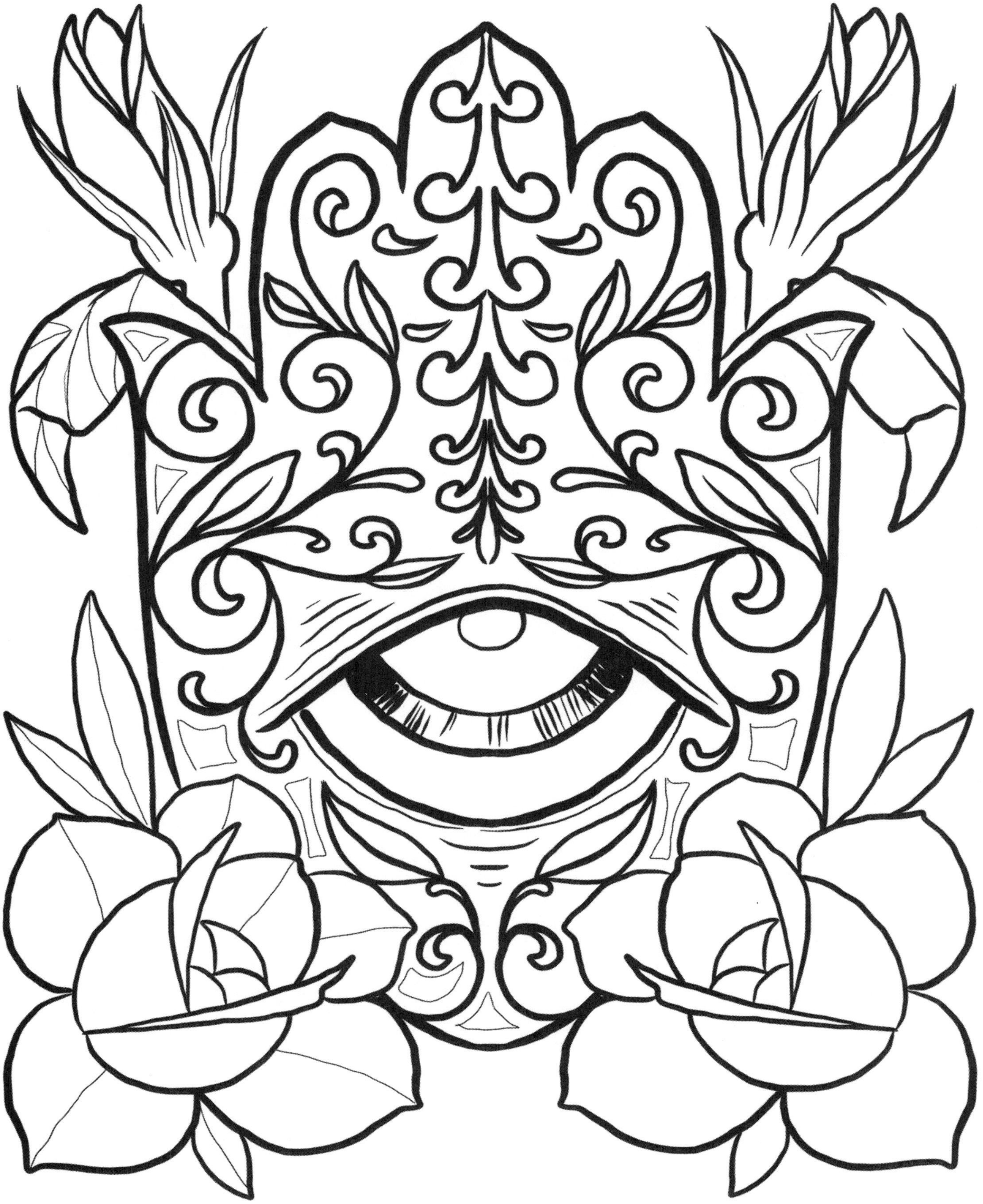

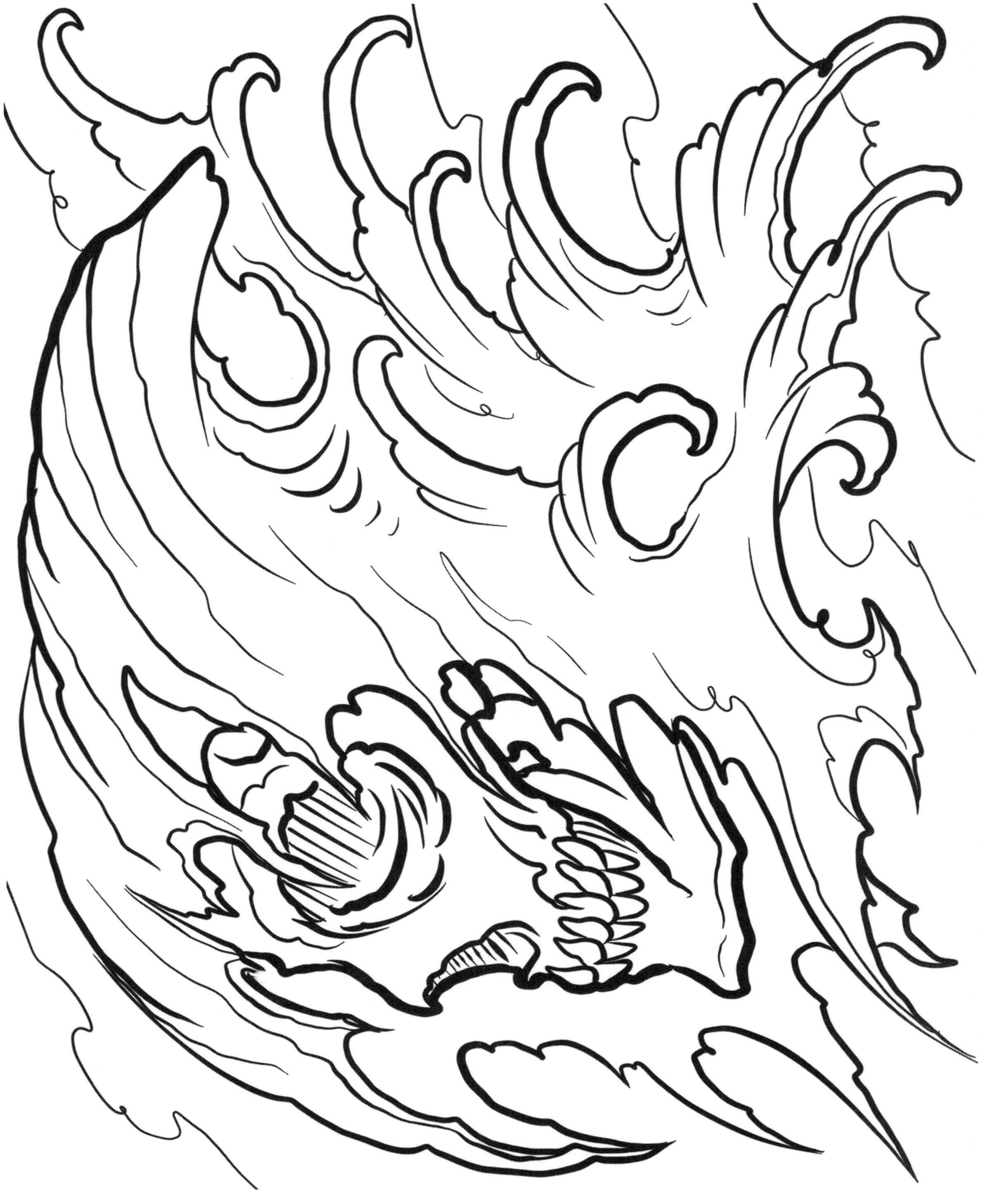

← 60

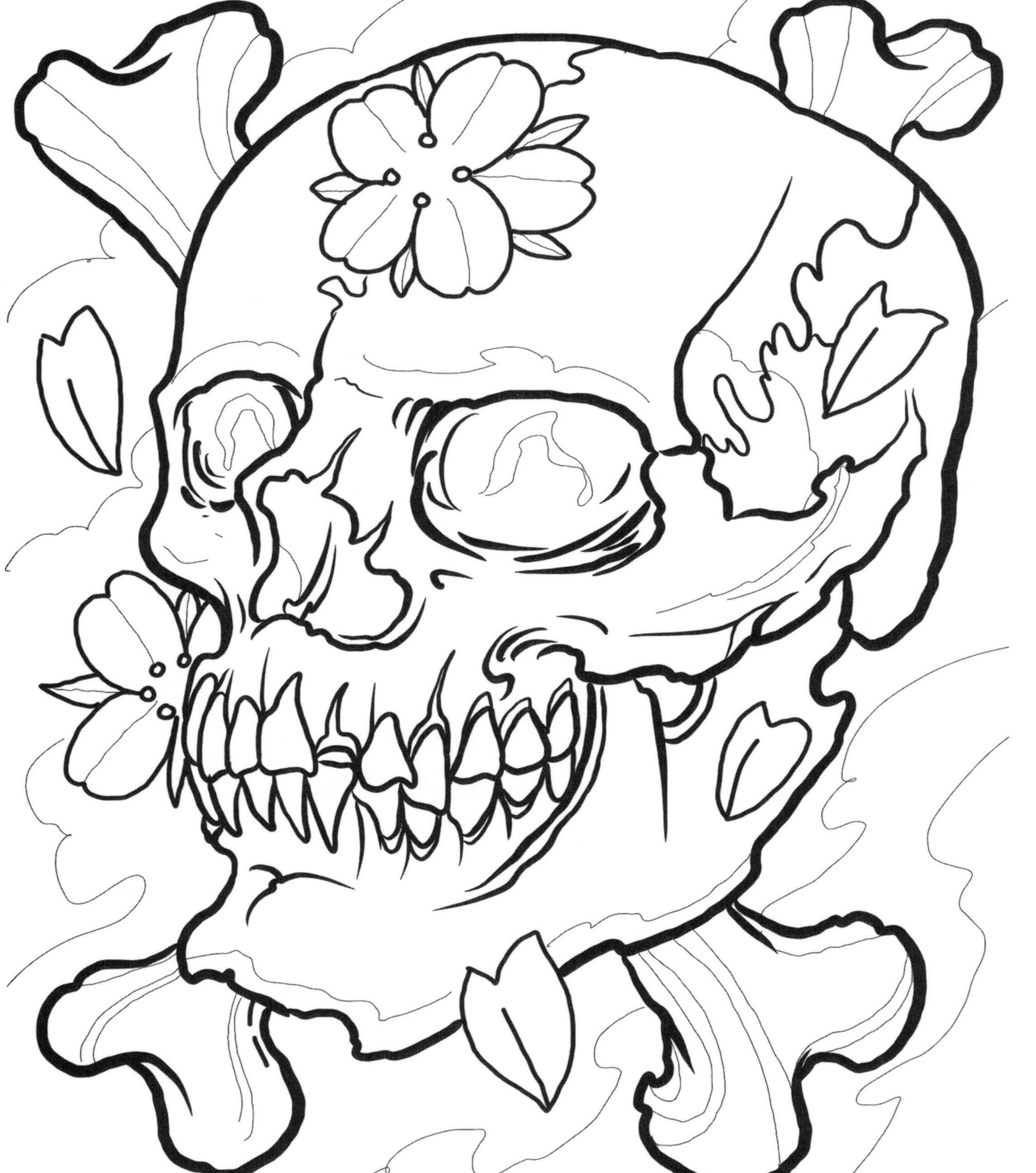

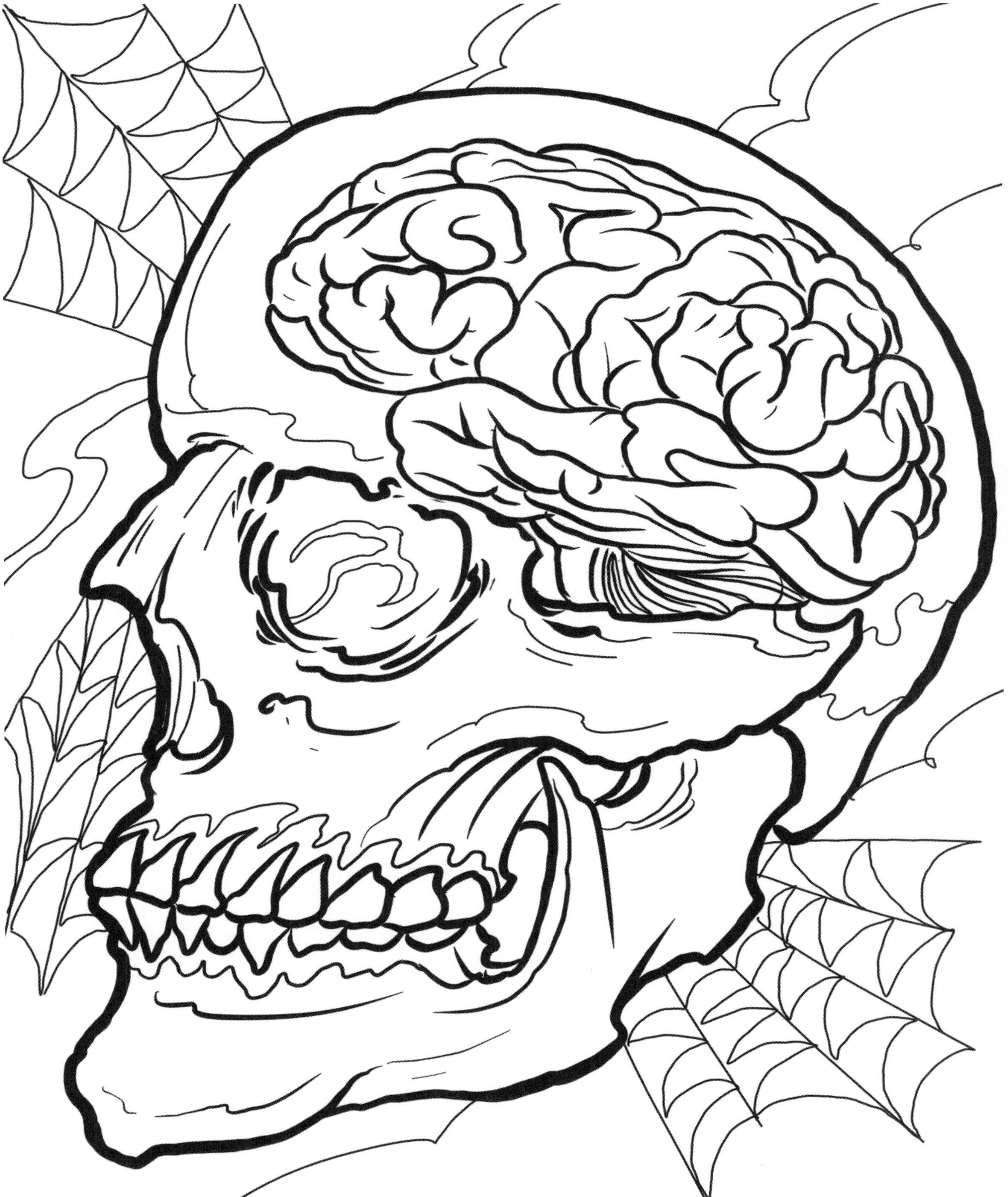

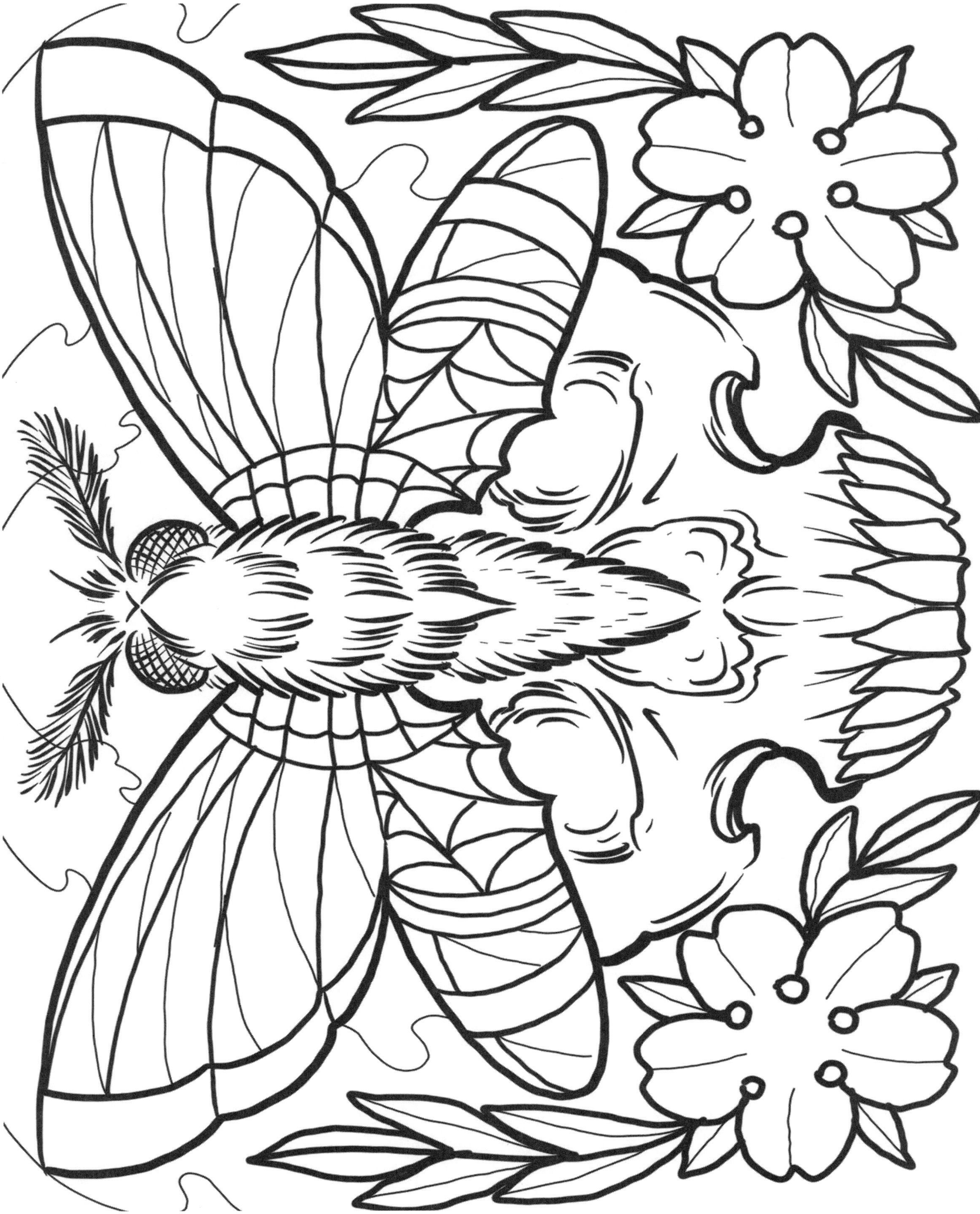

← 63

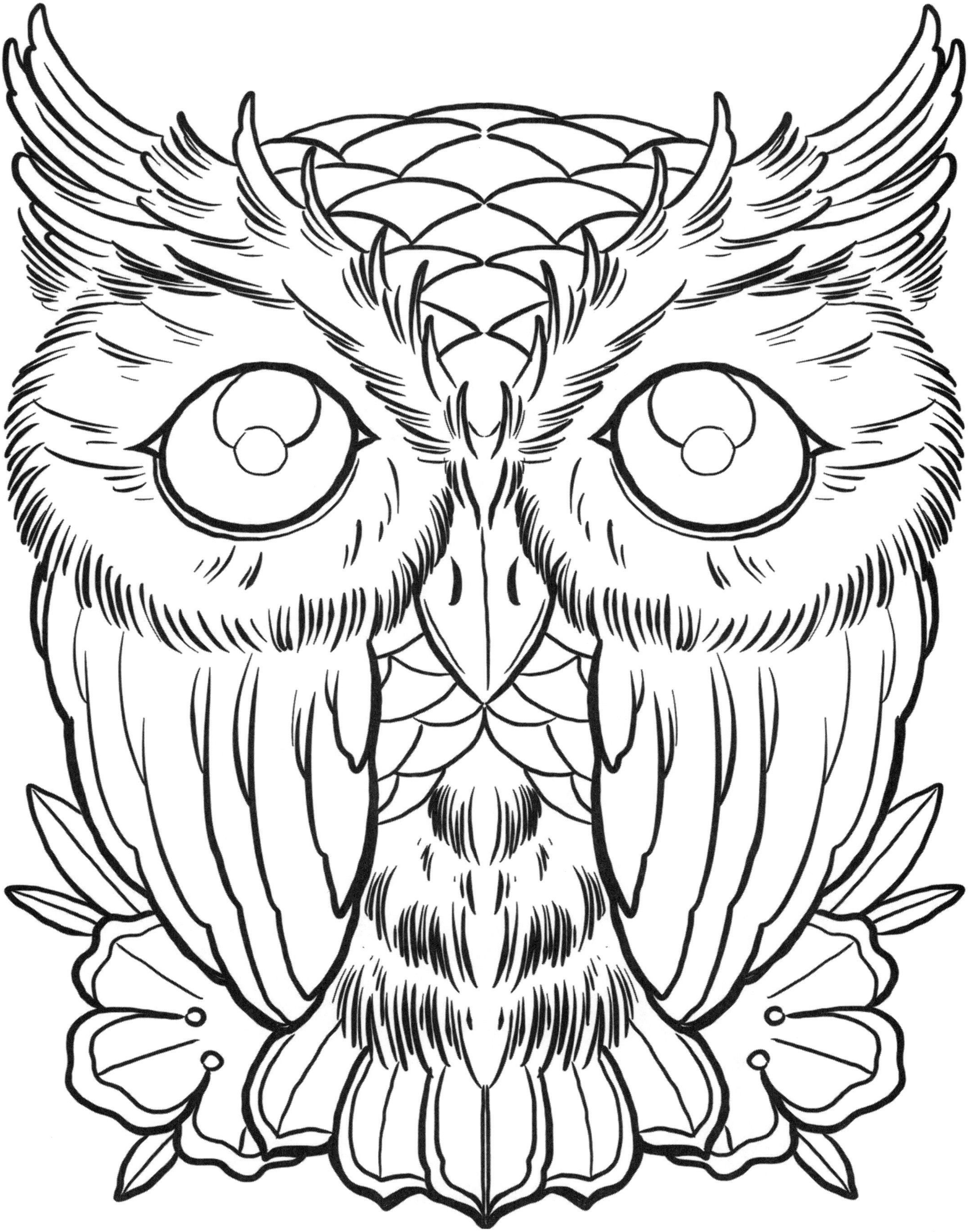

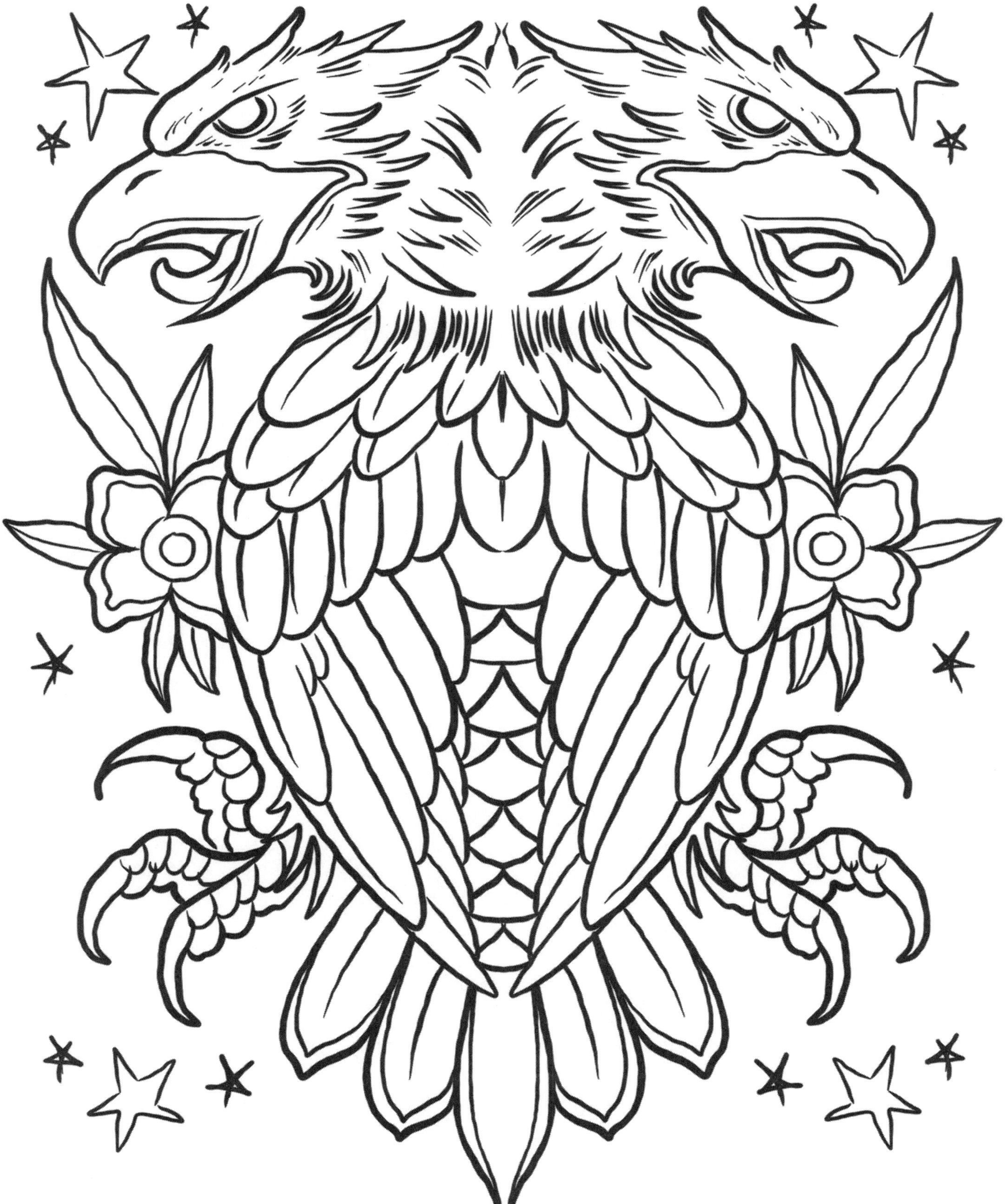

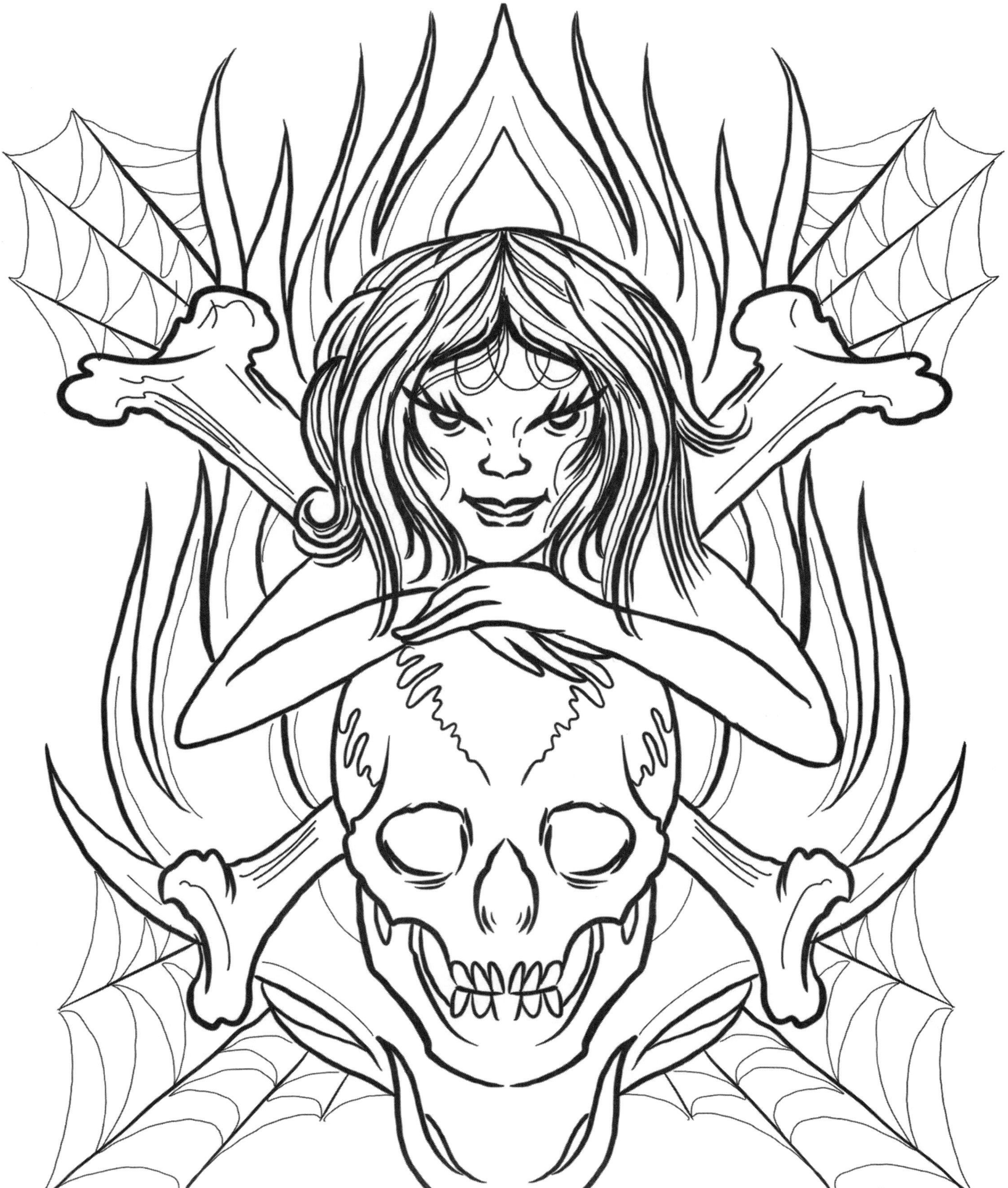

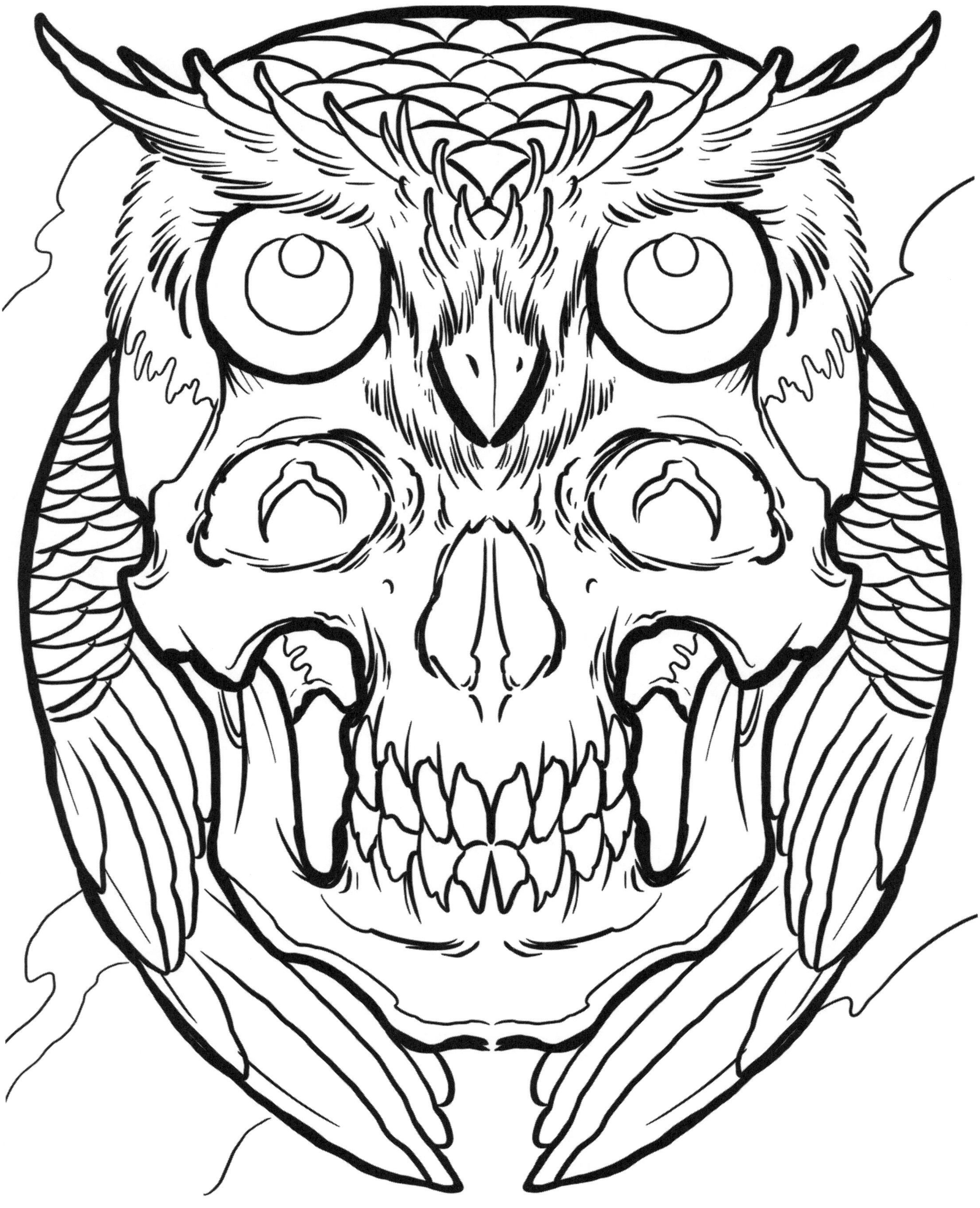

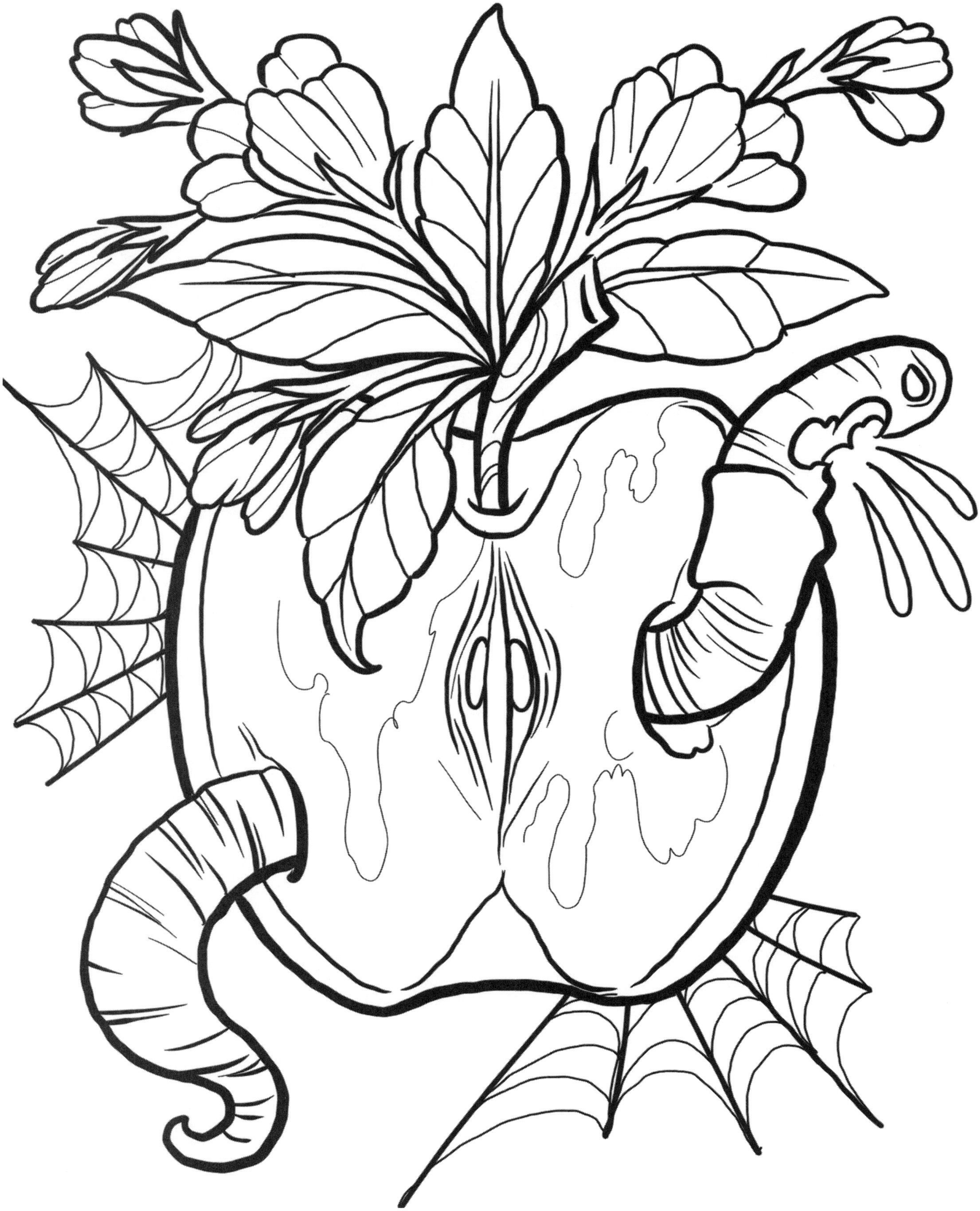

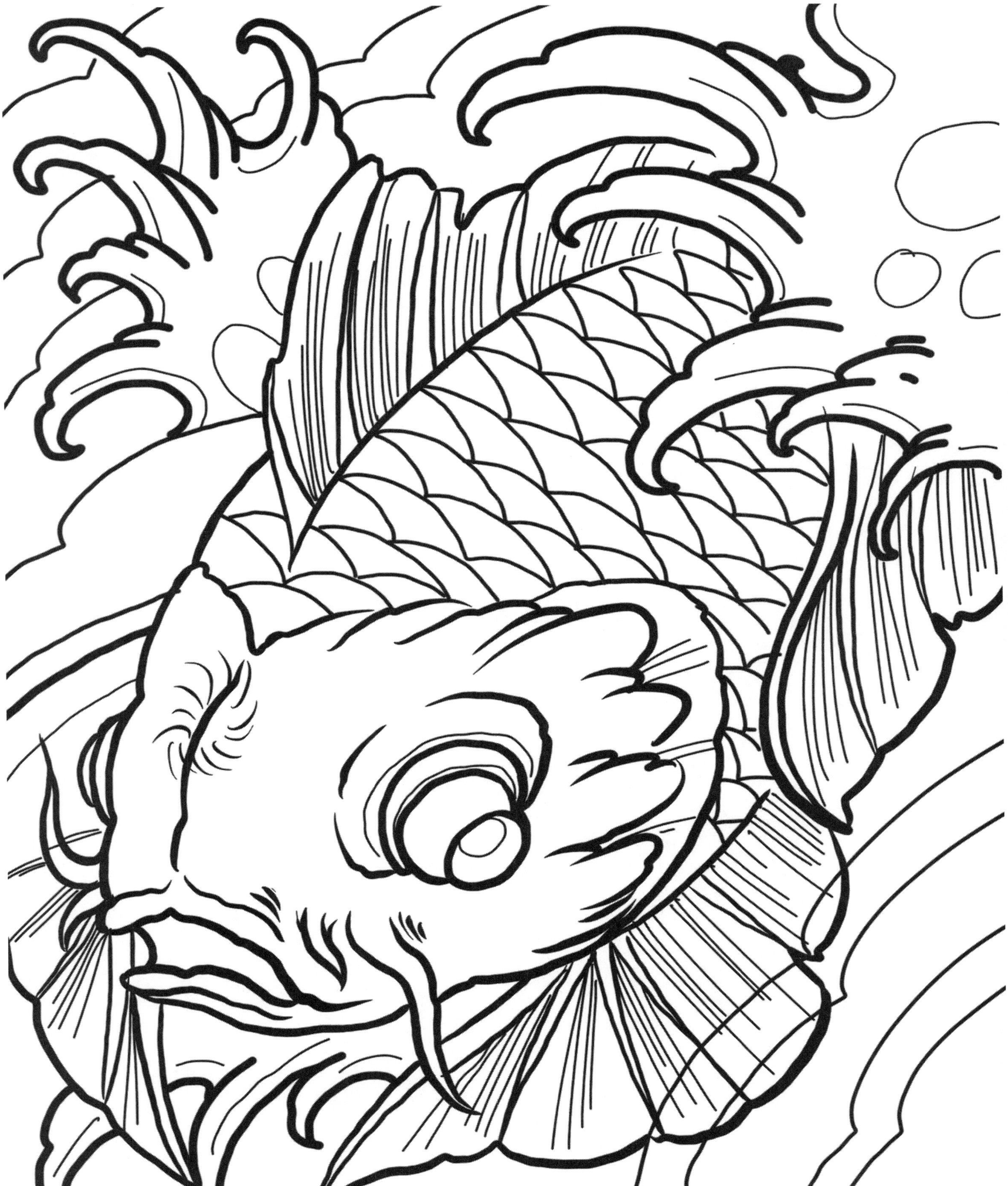

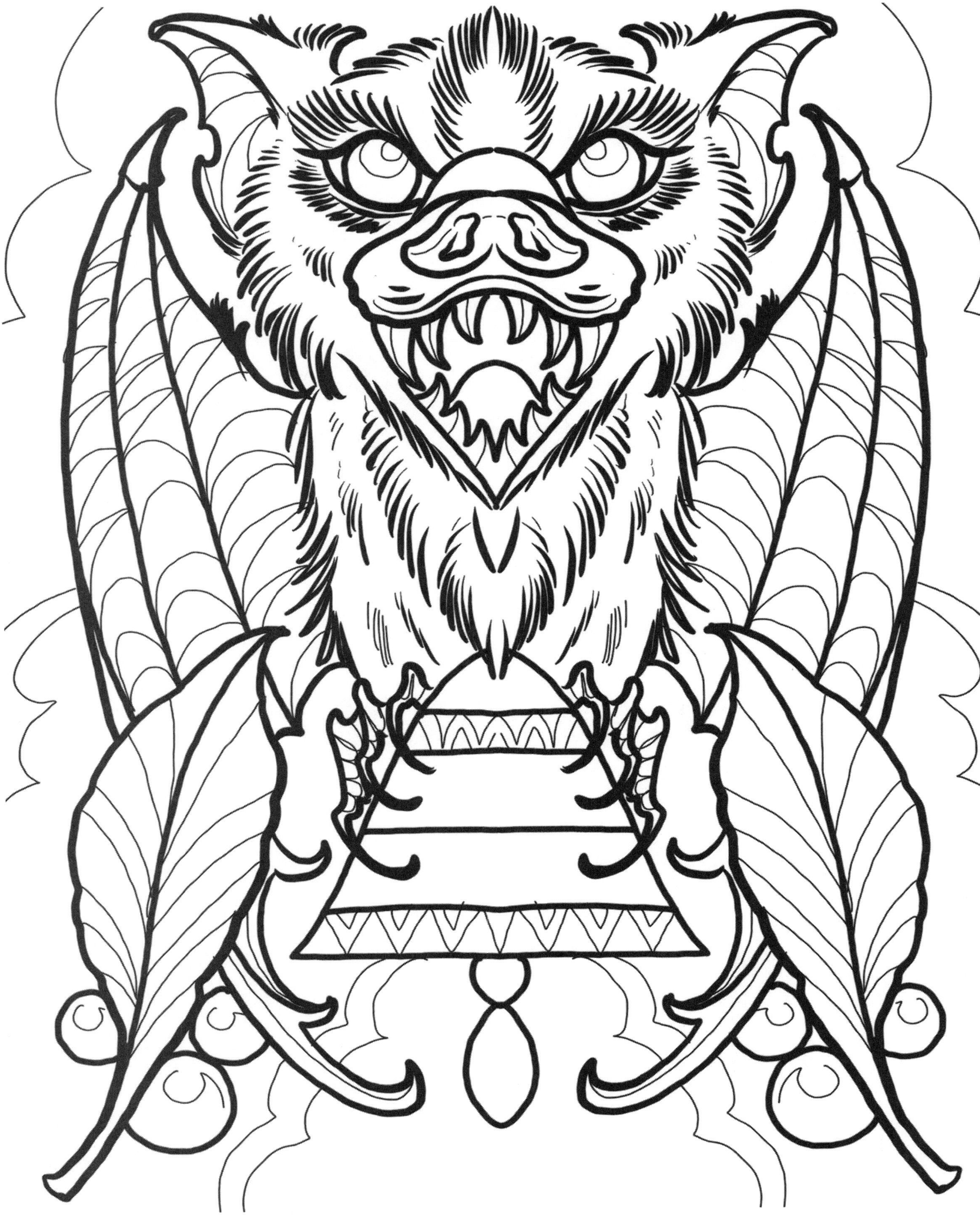

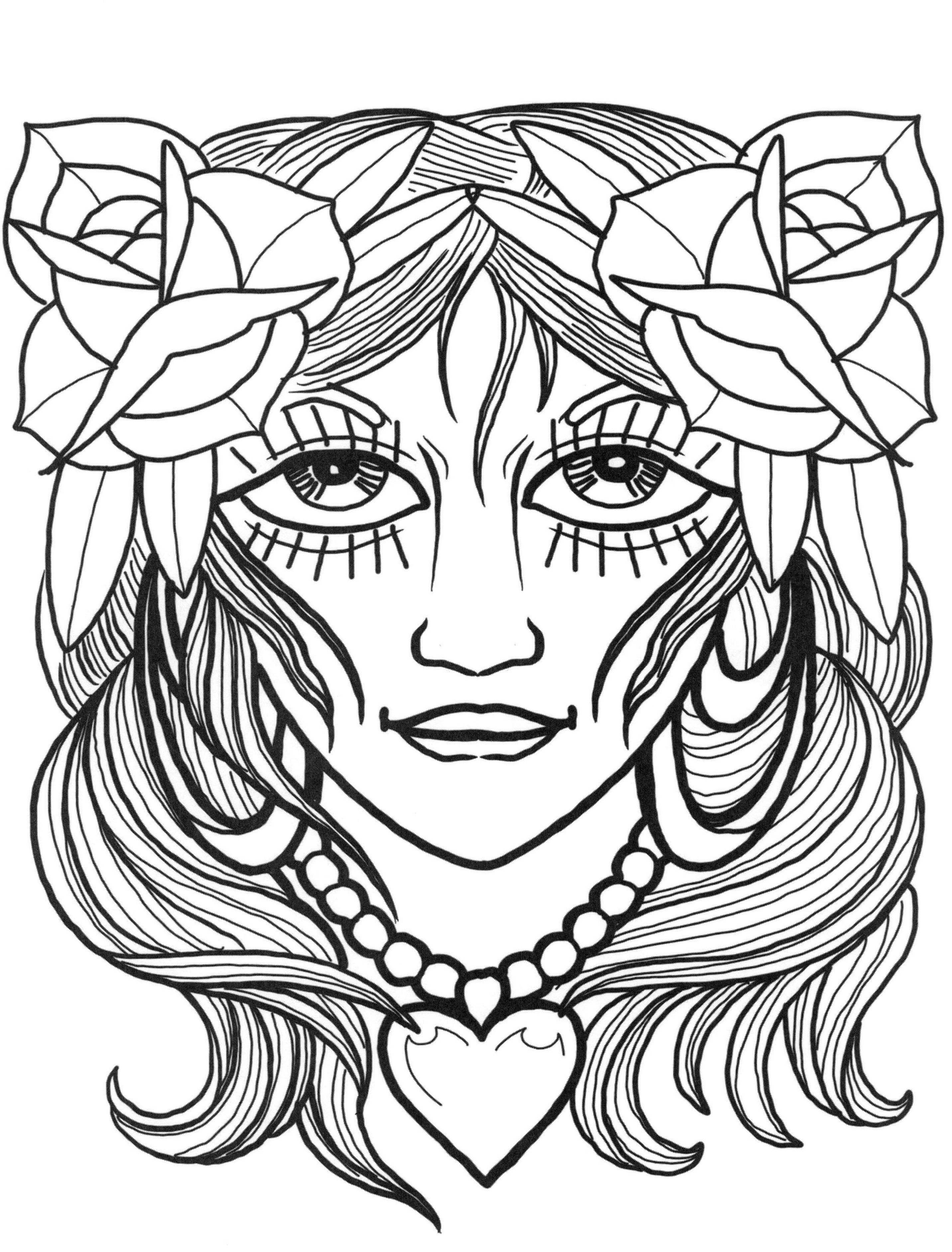

← 71

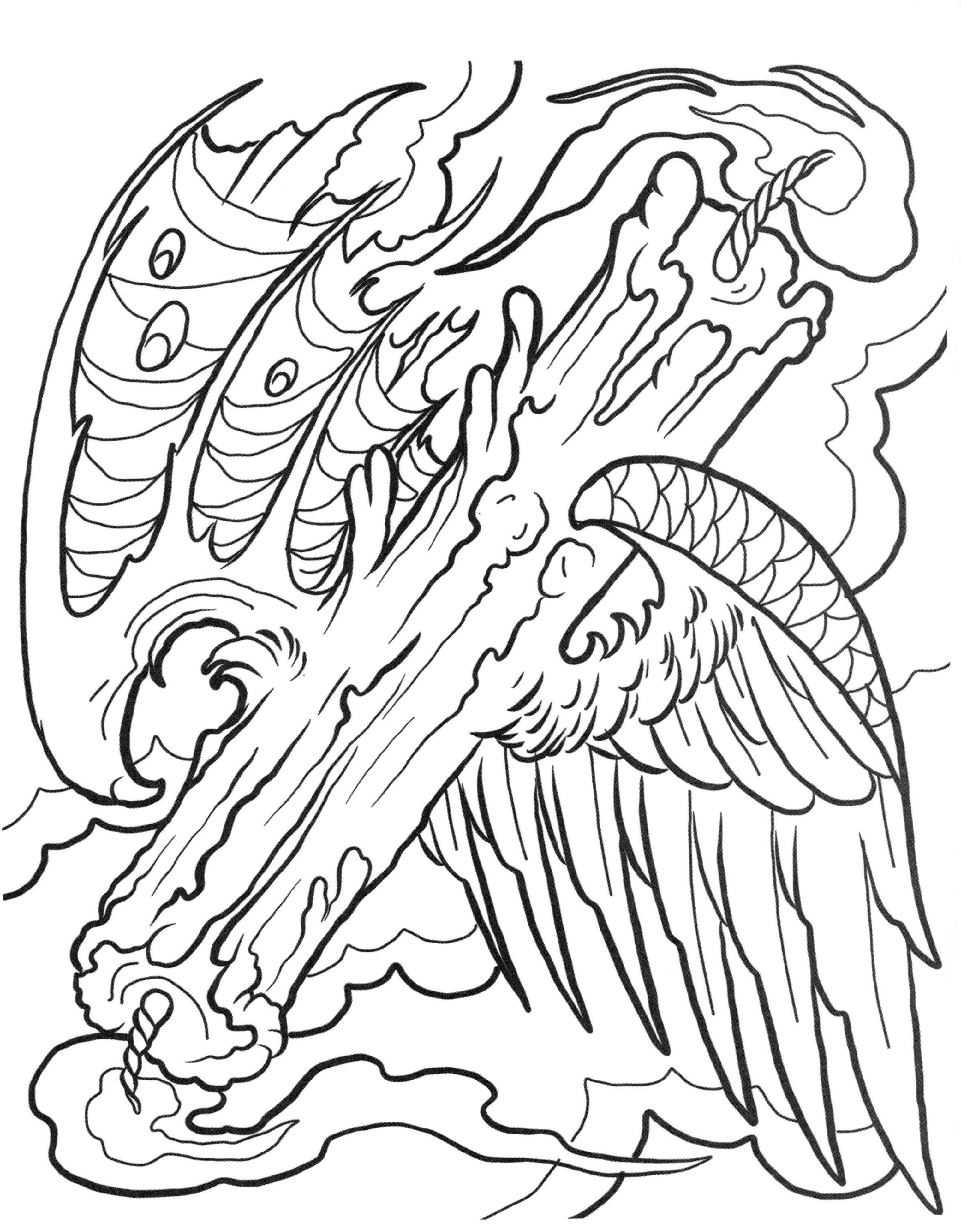

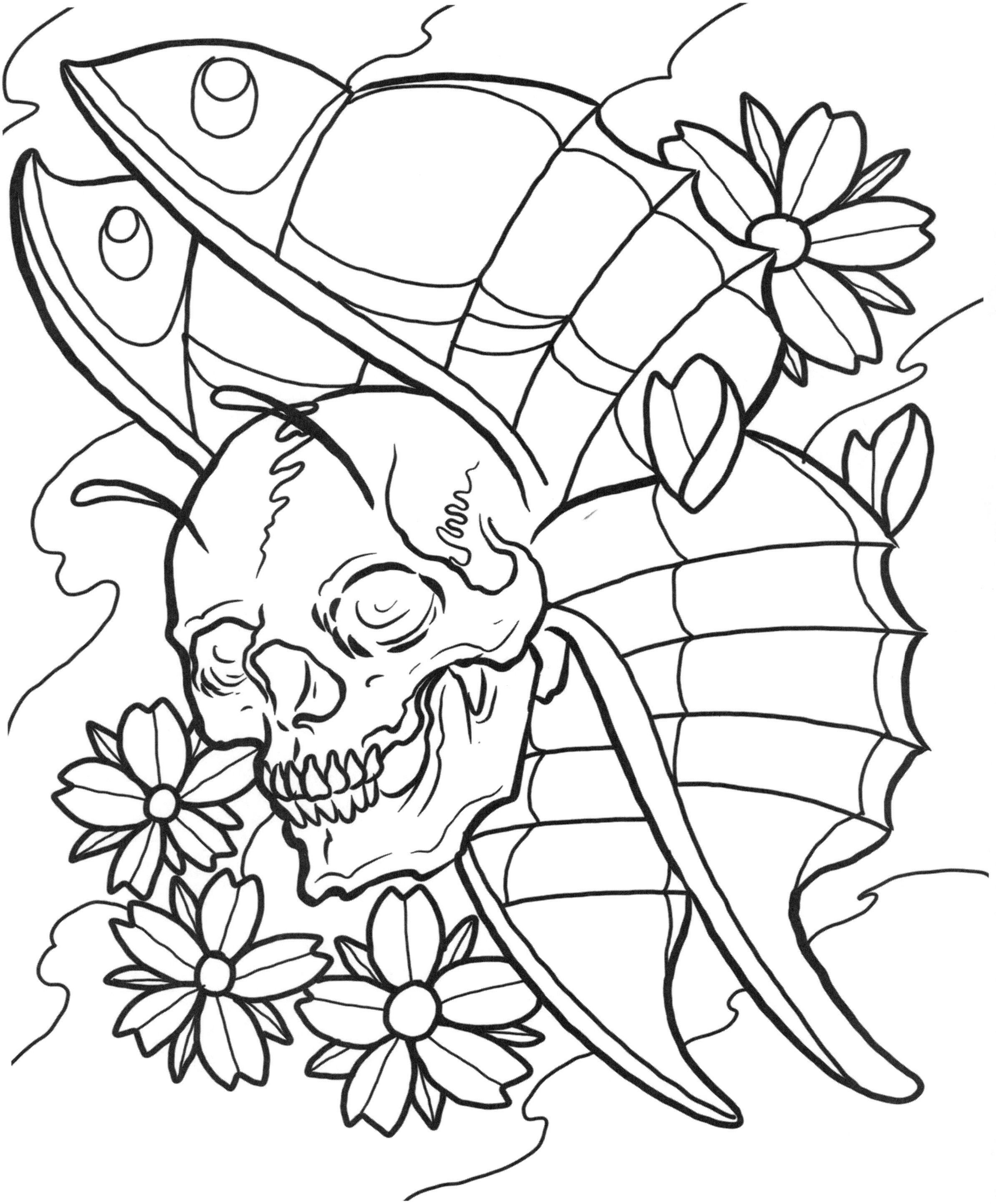

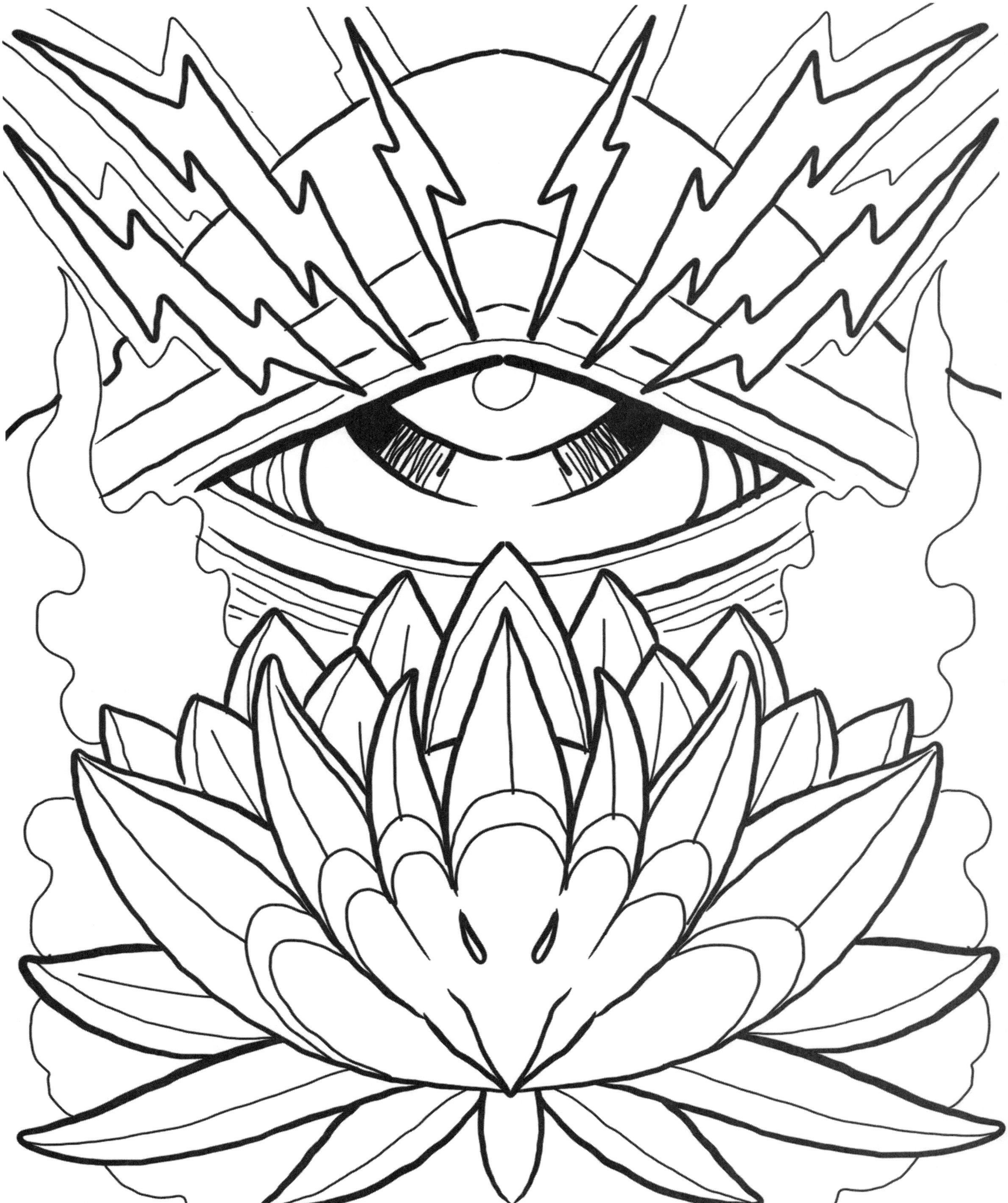

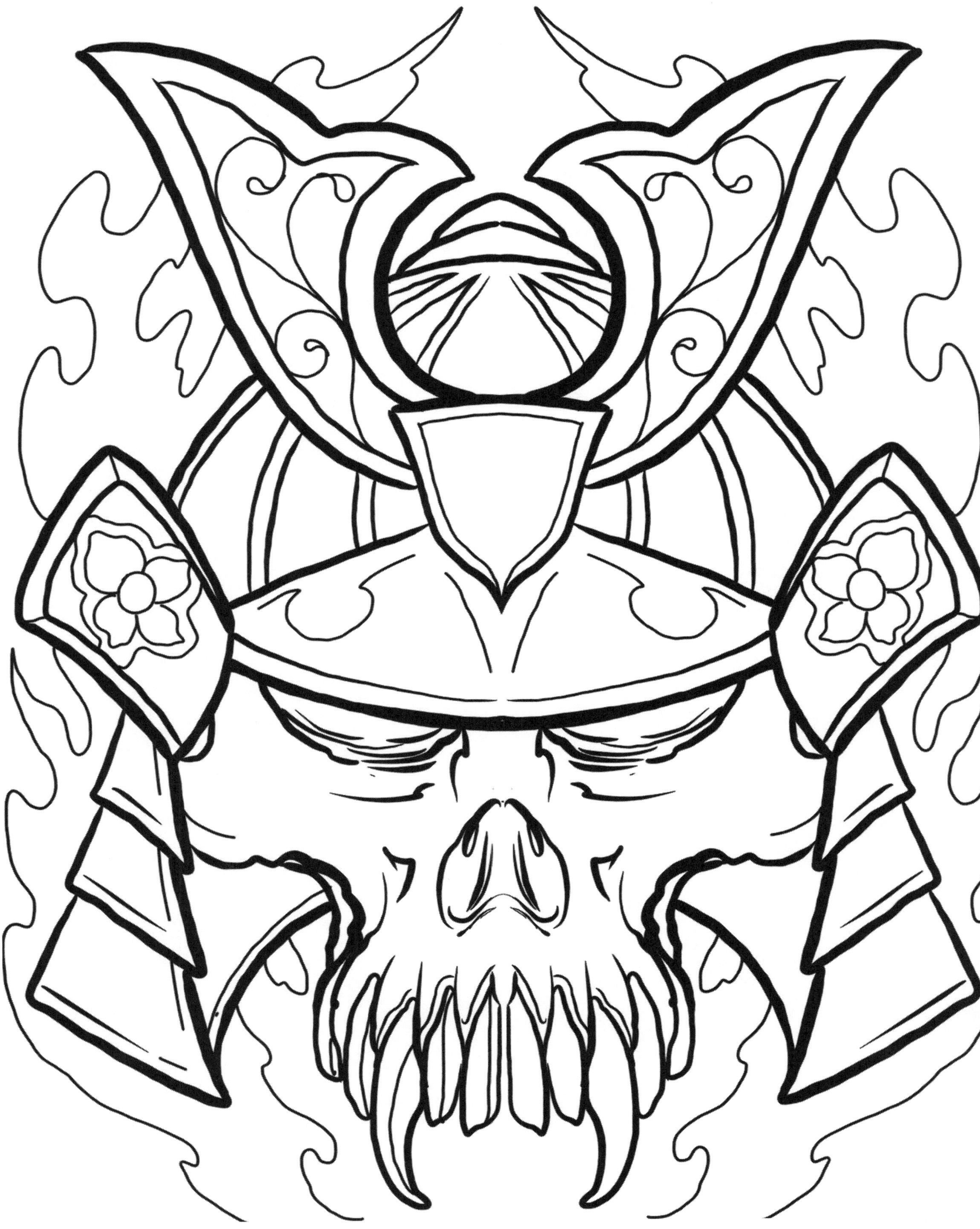

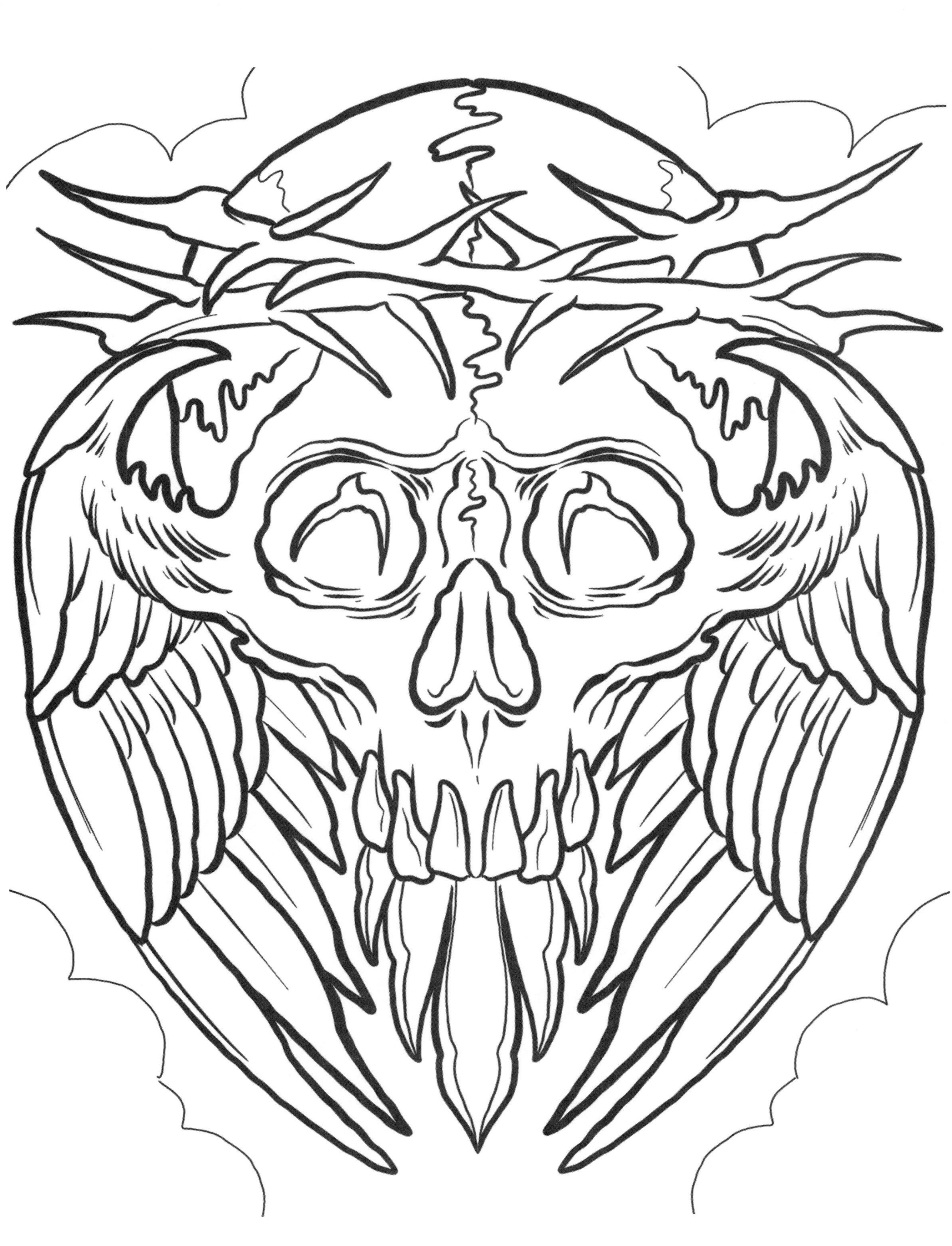

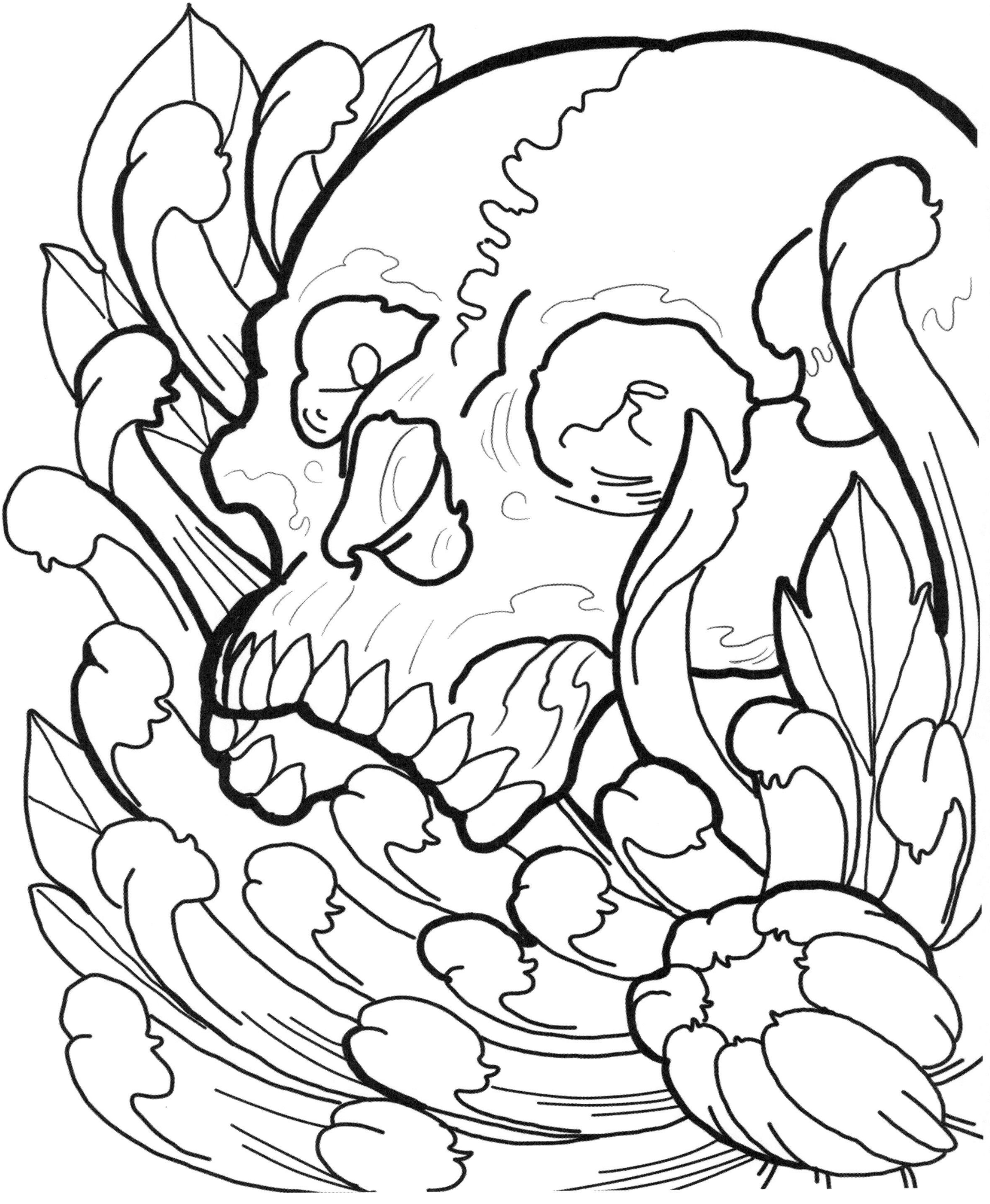

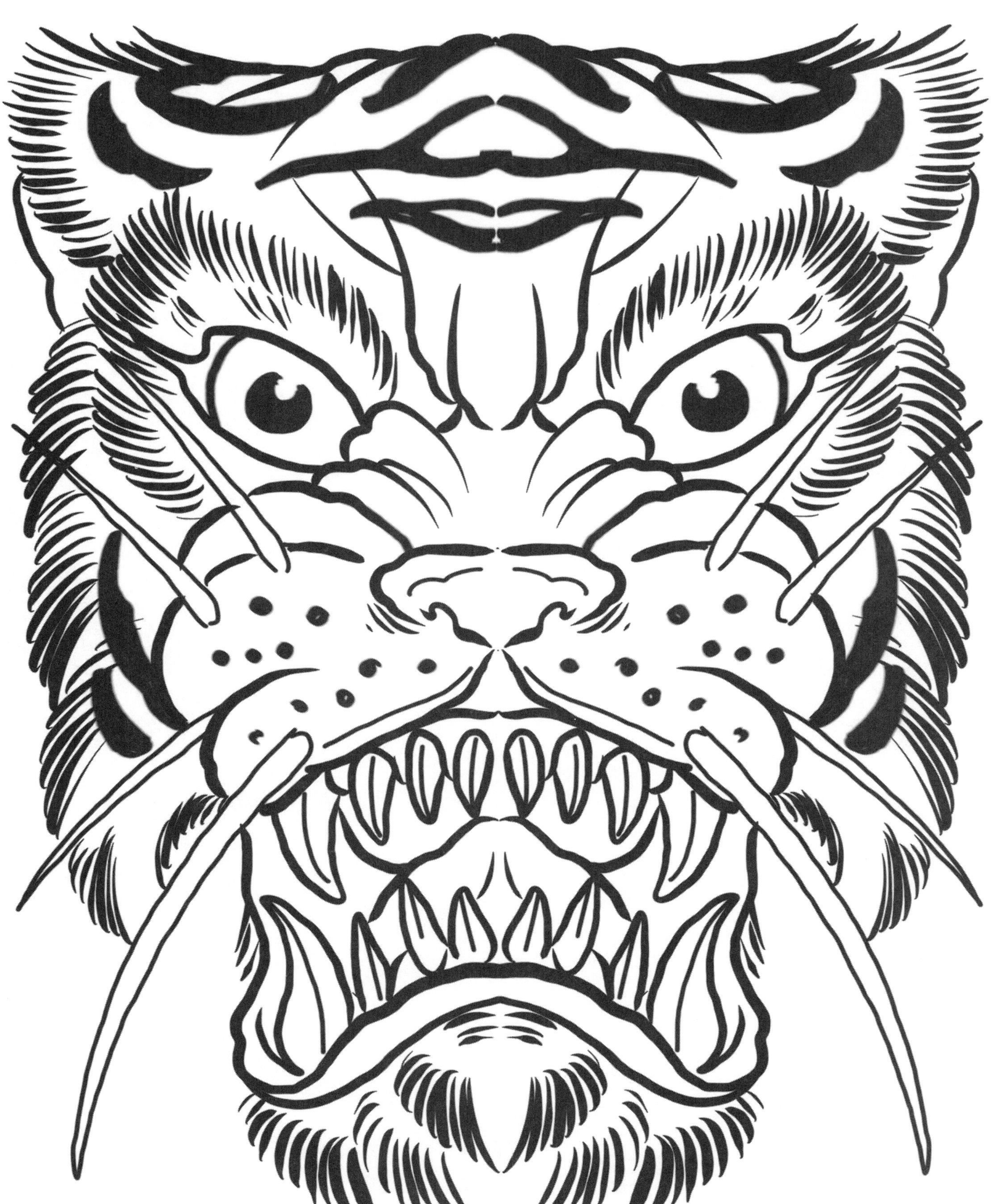

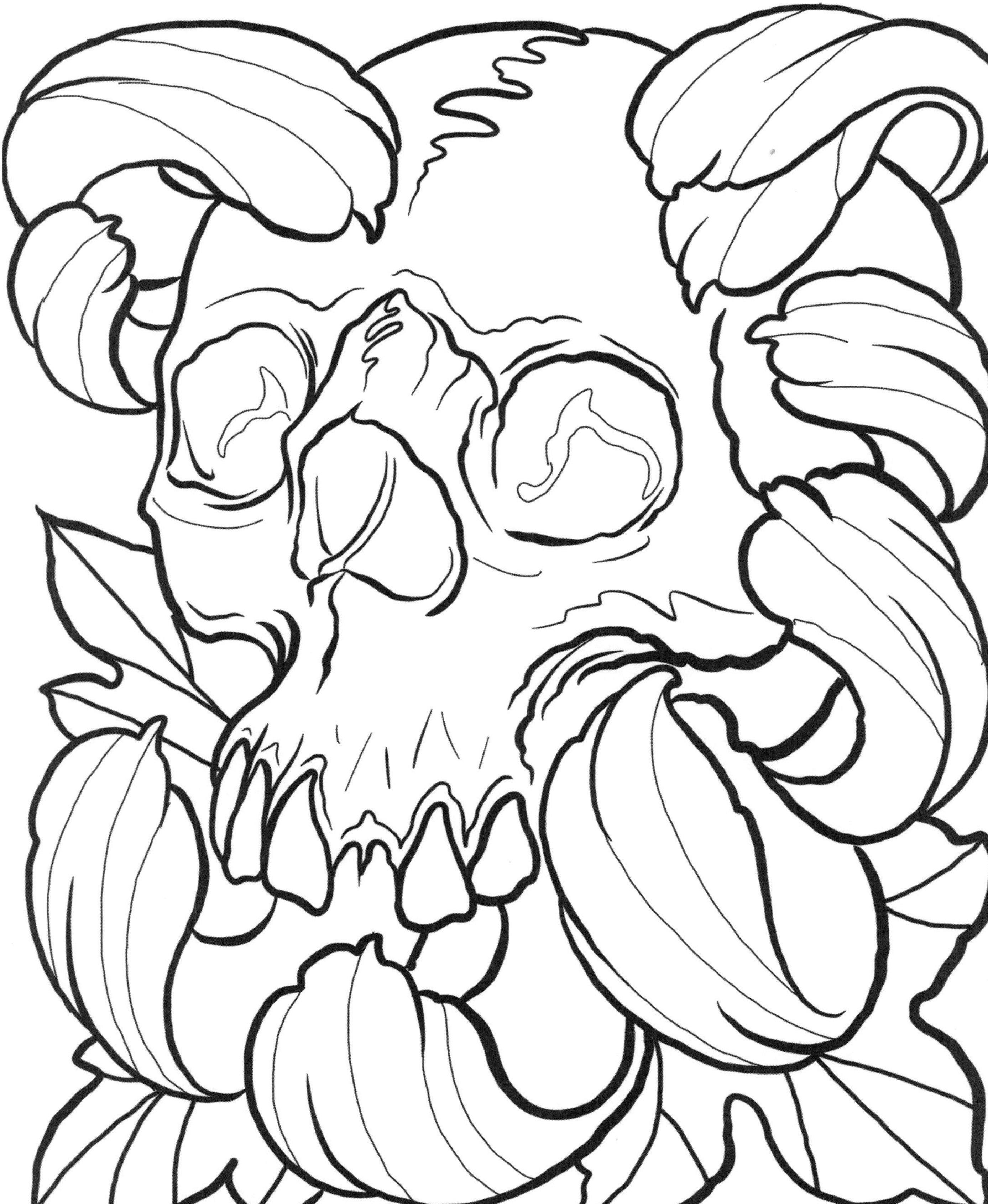

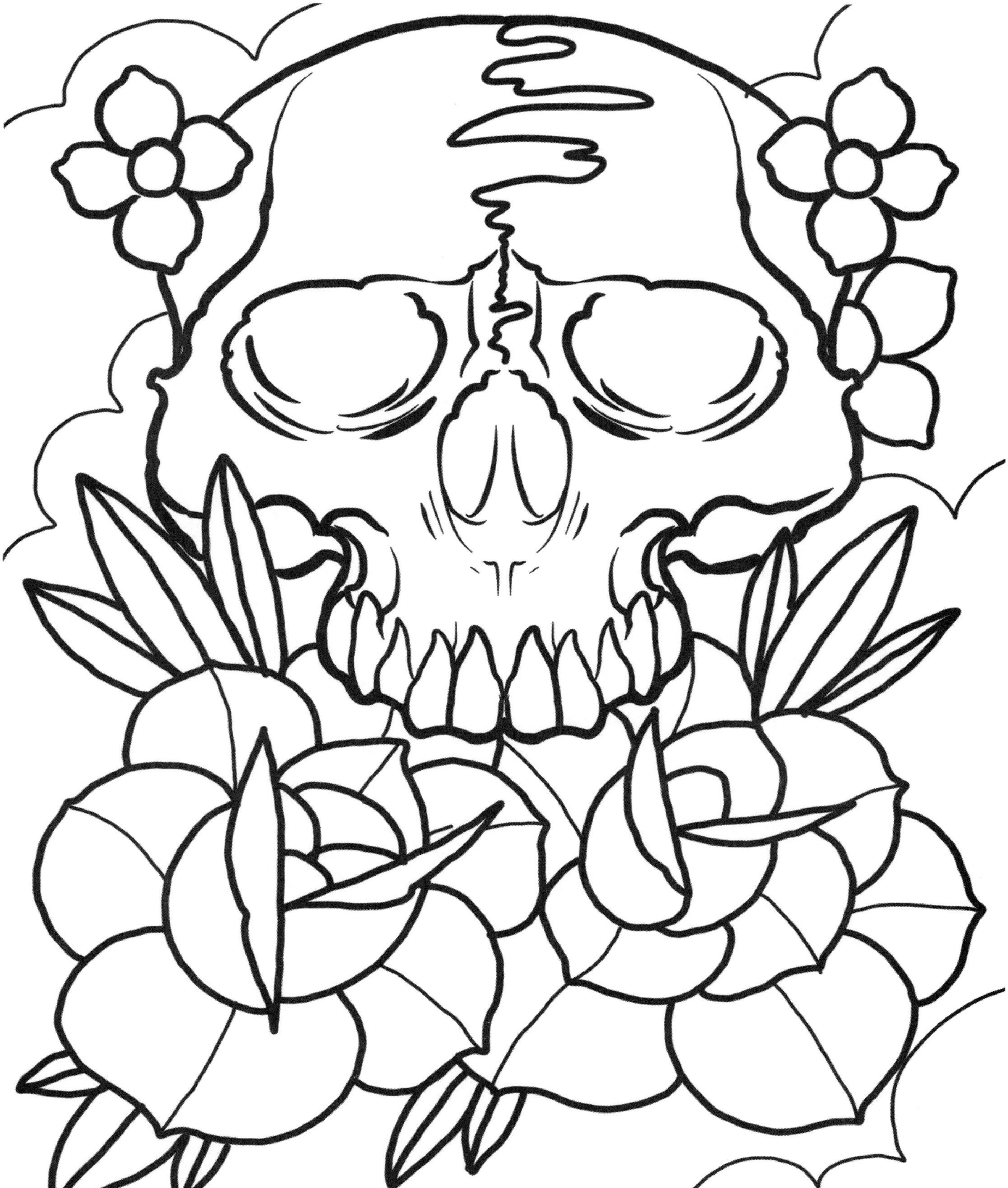

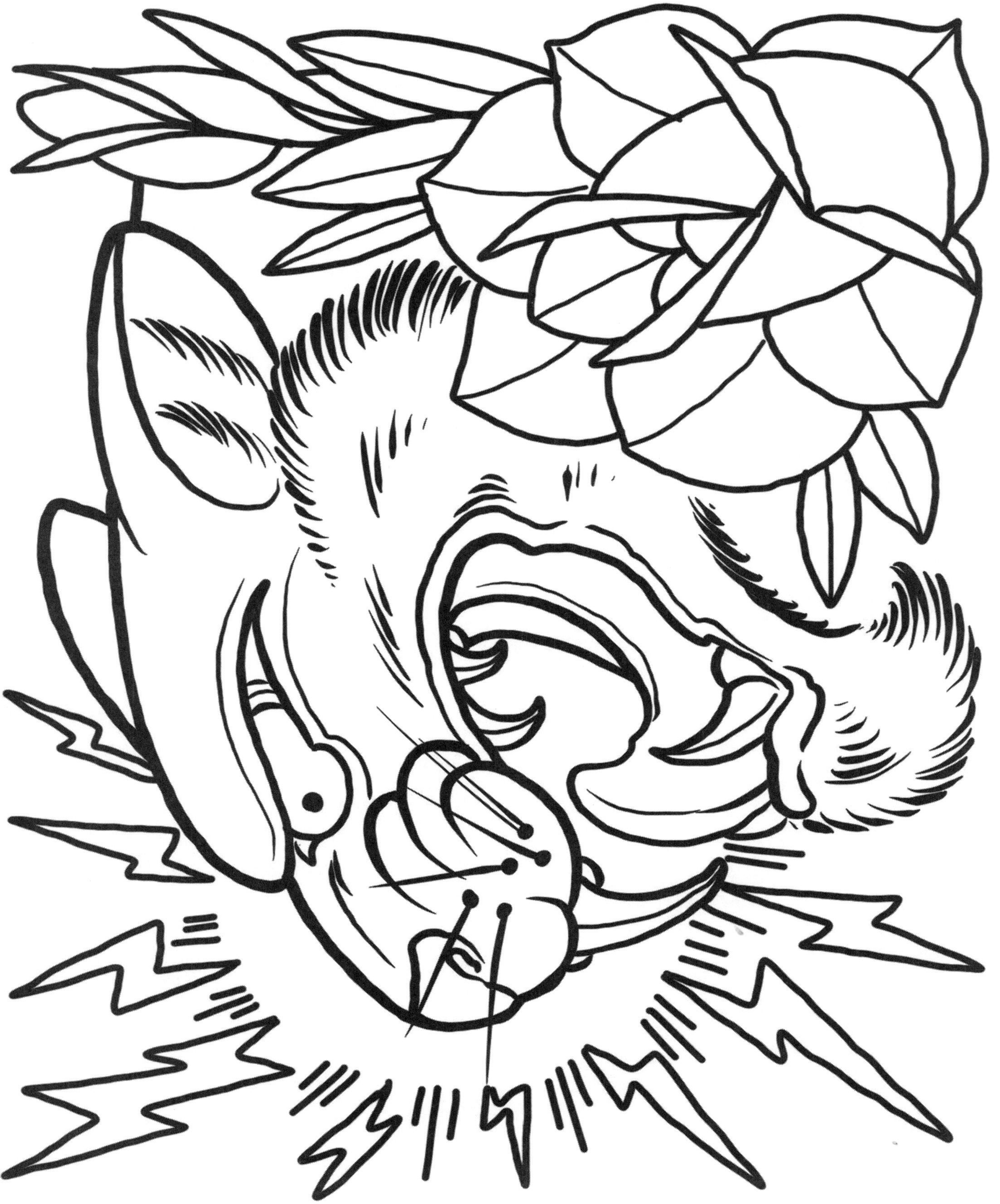

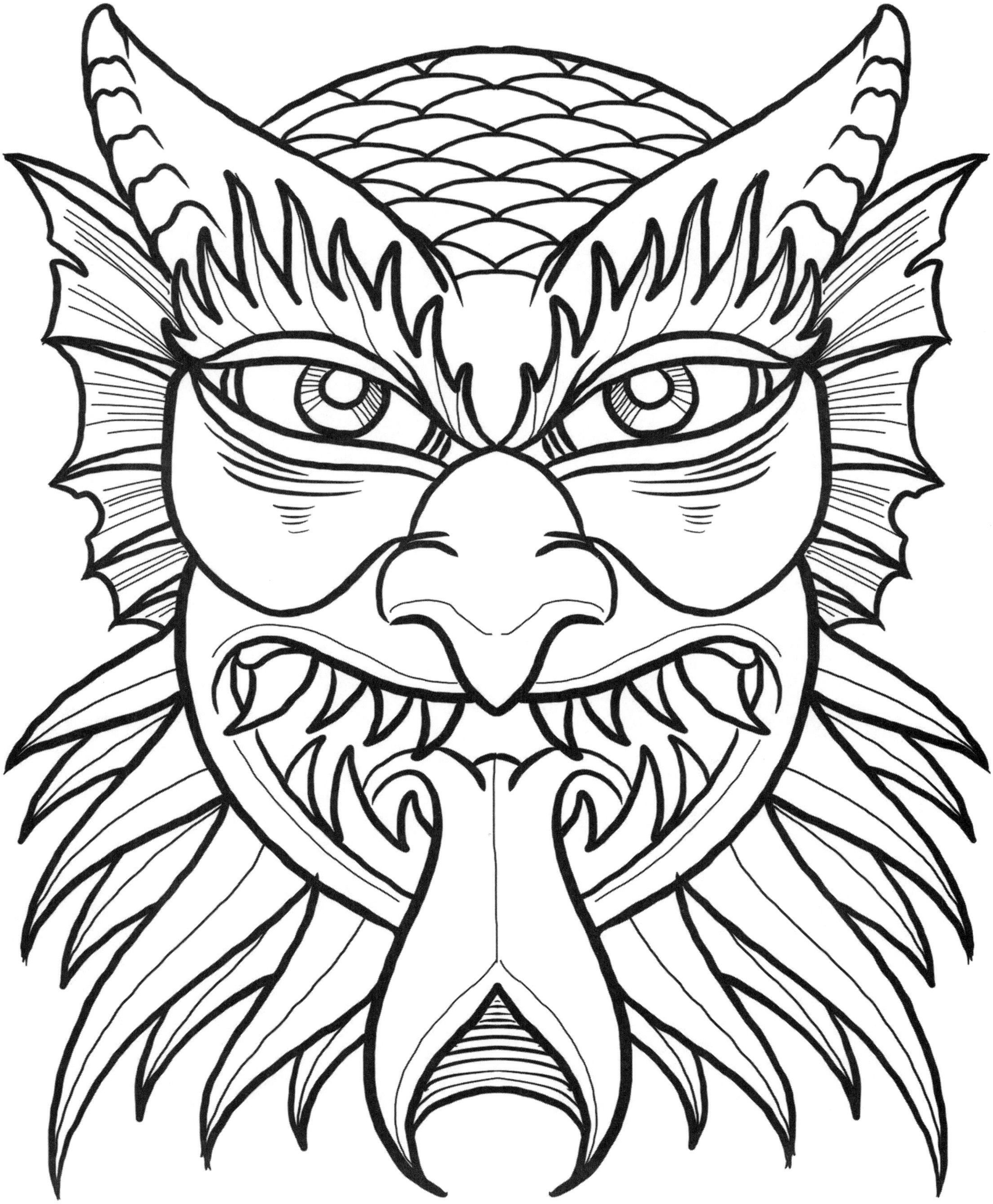

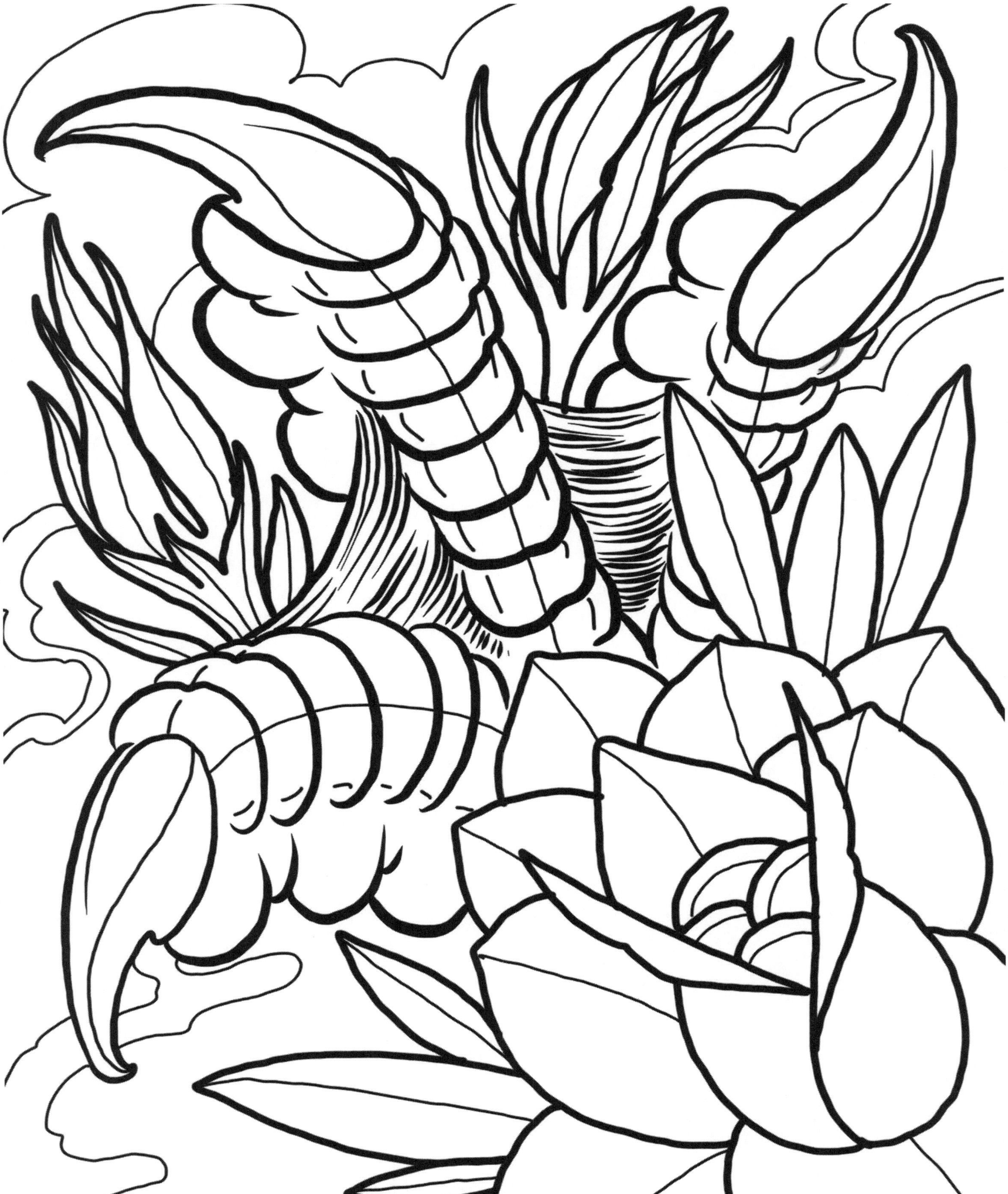

← 83

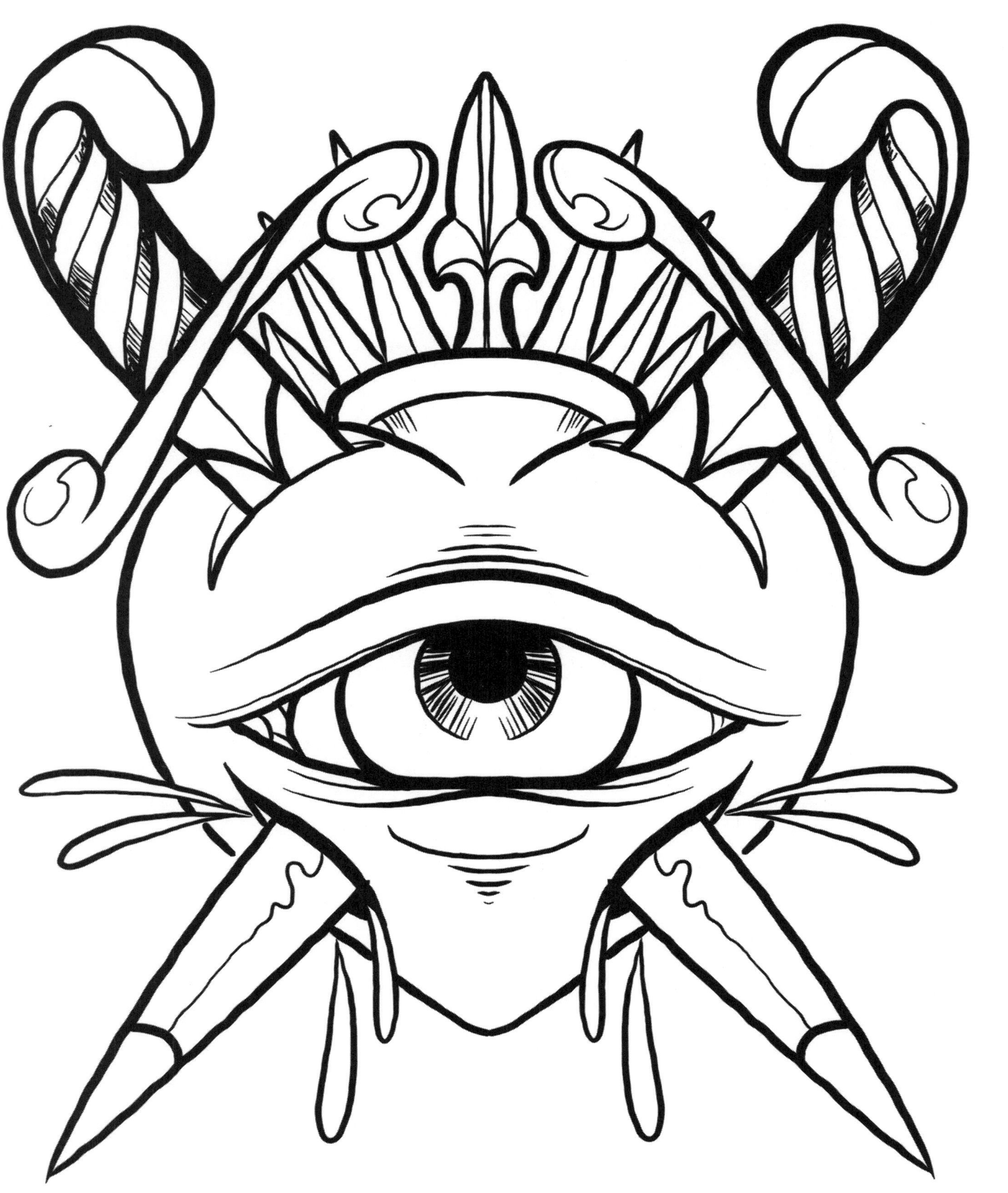

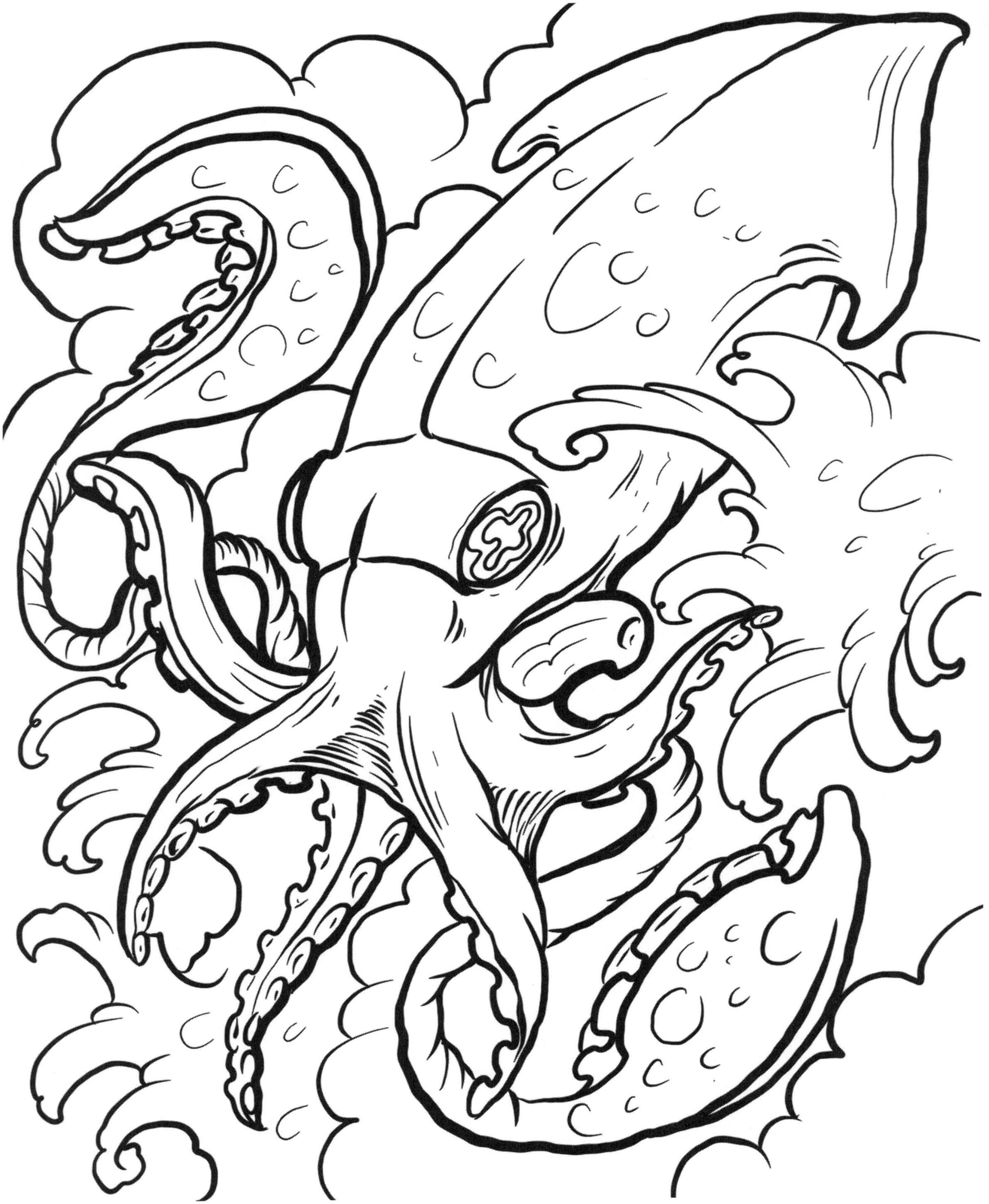

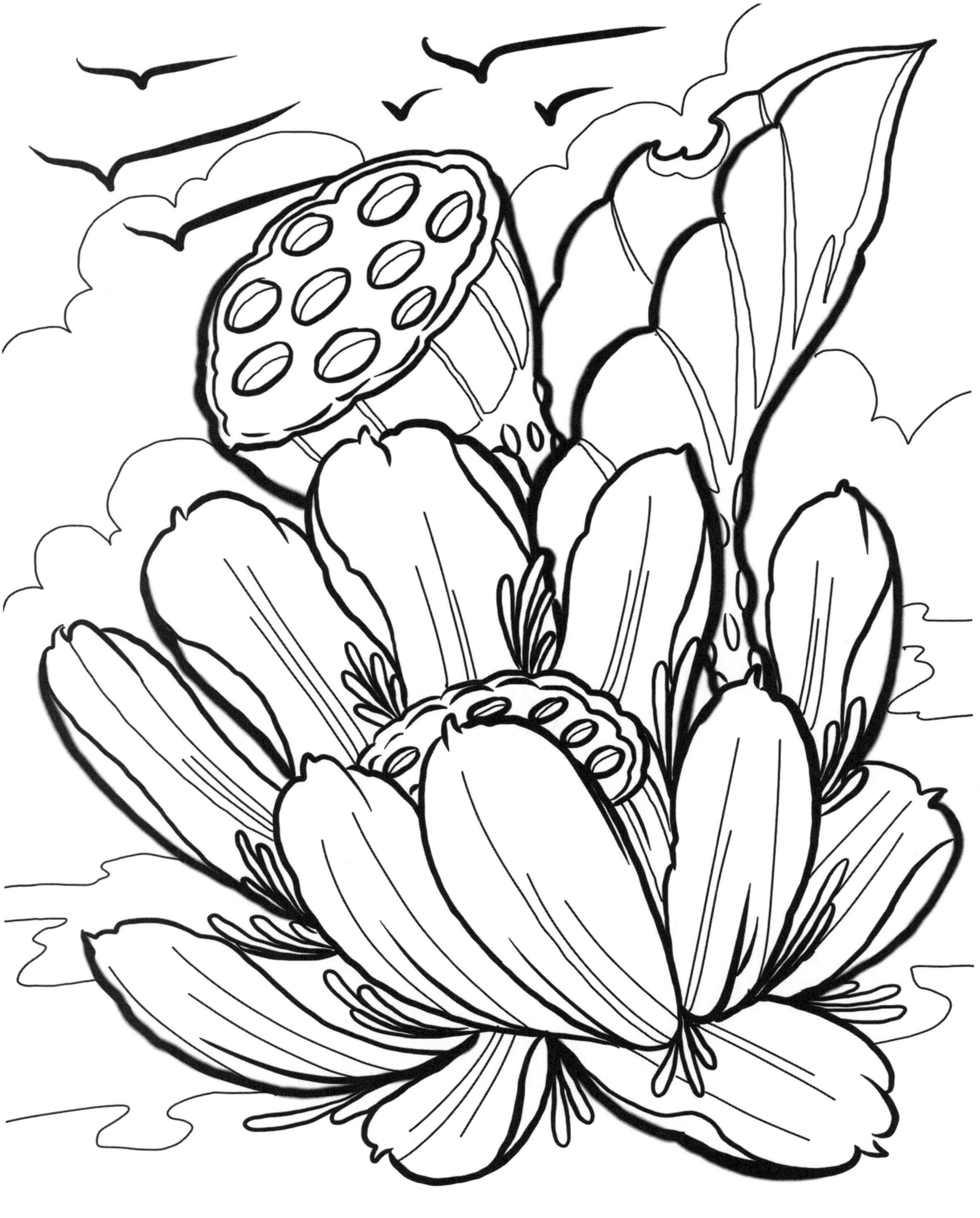

← 86

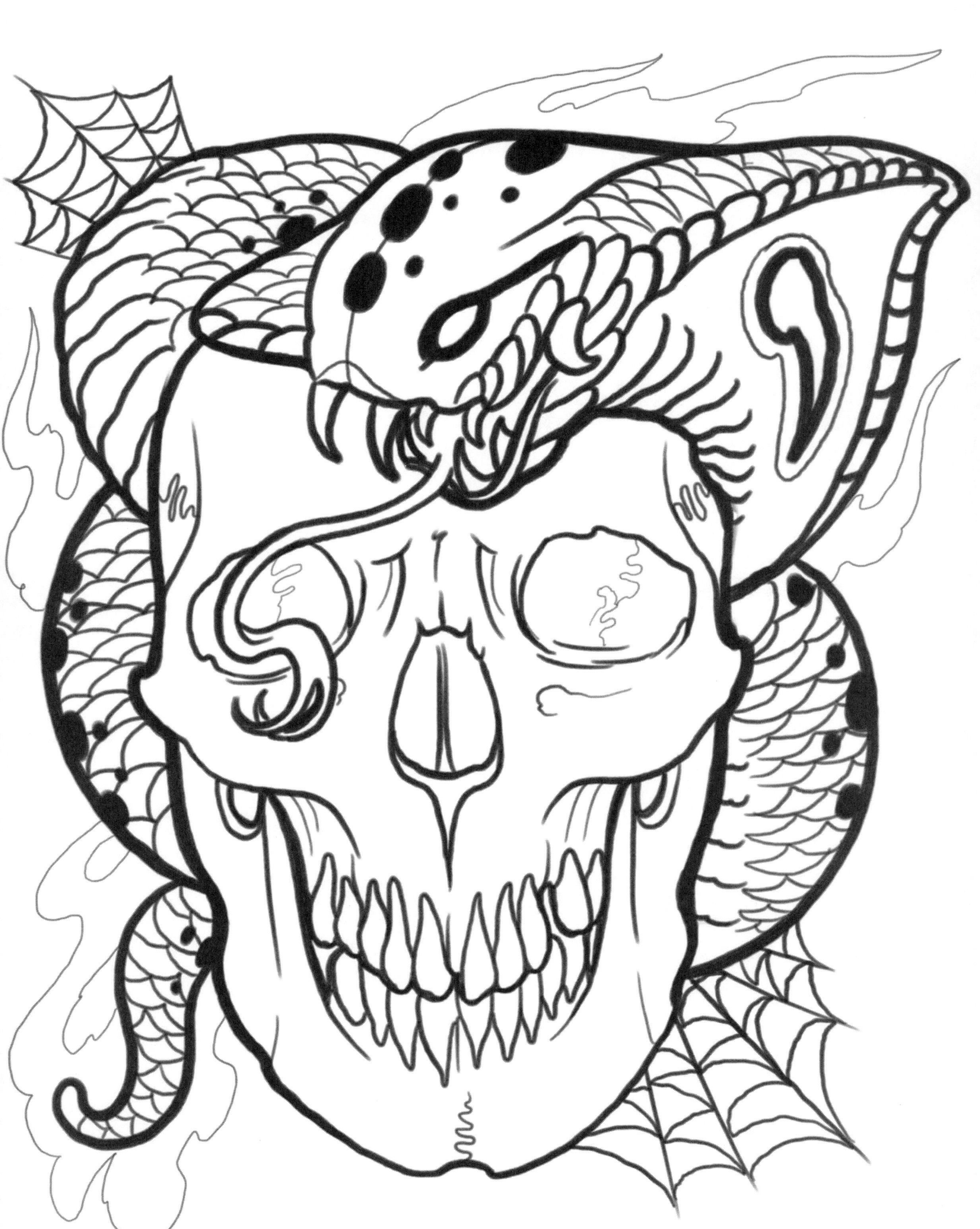

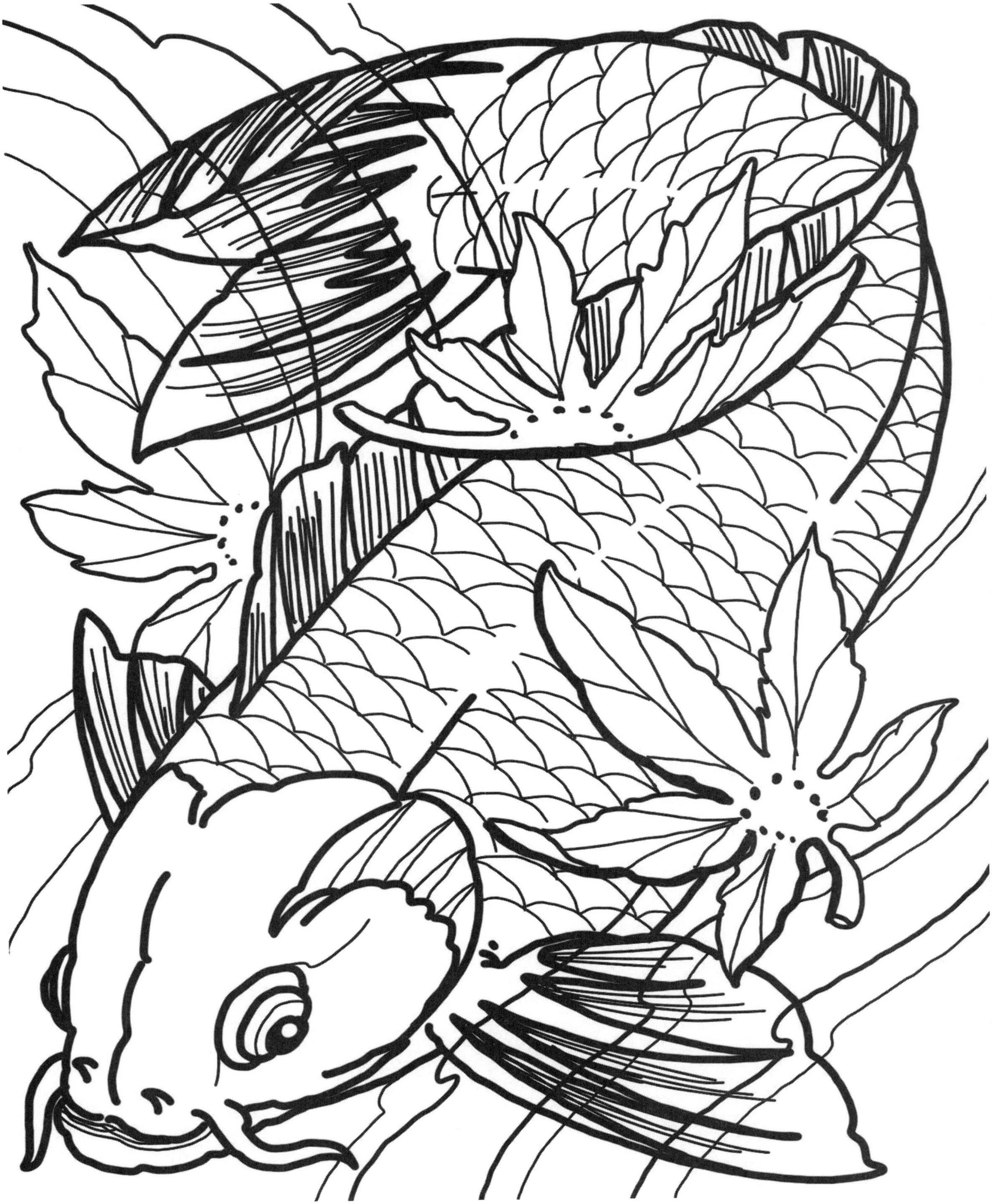

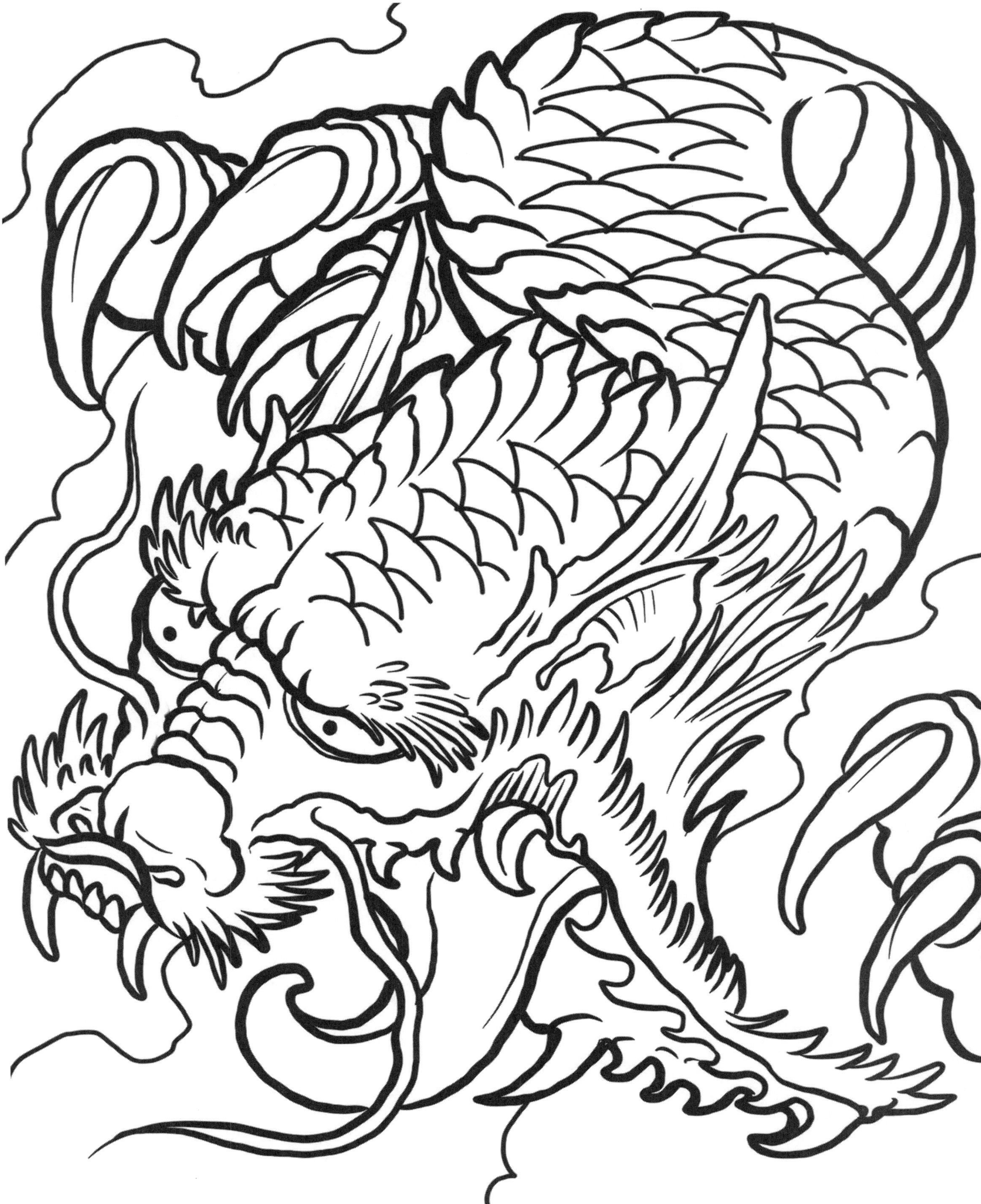

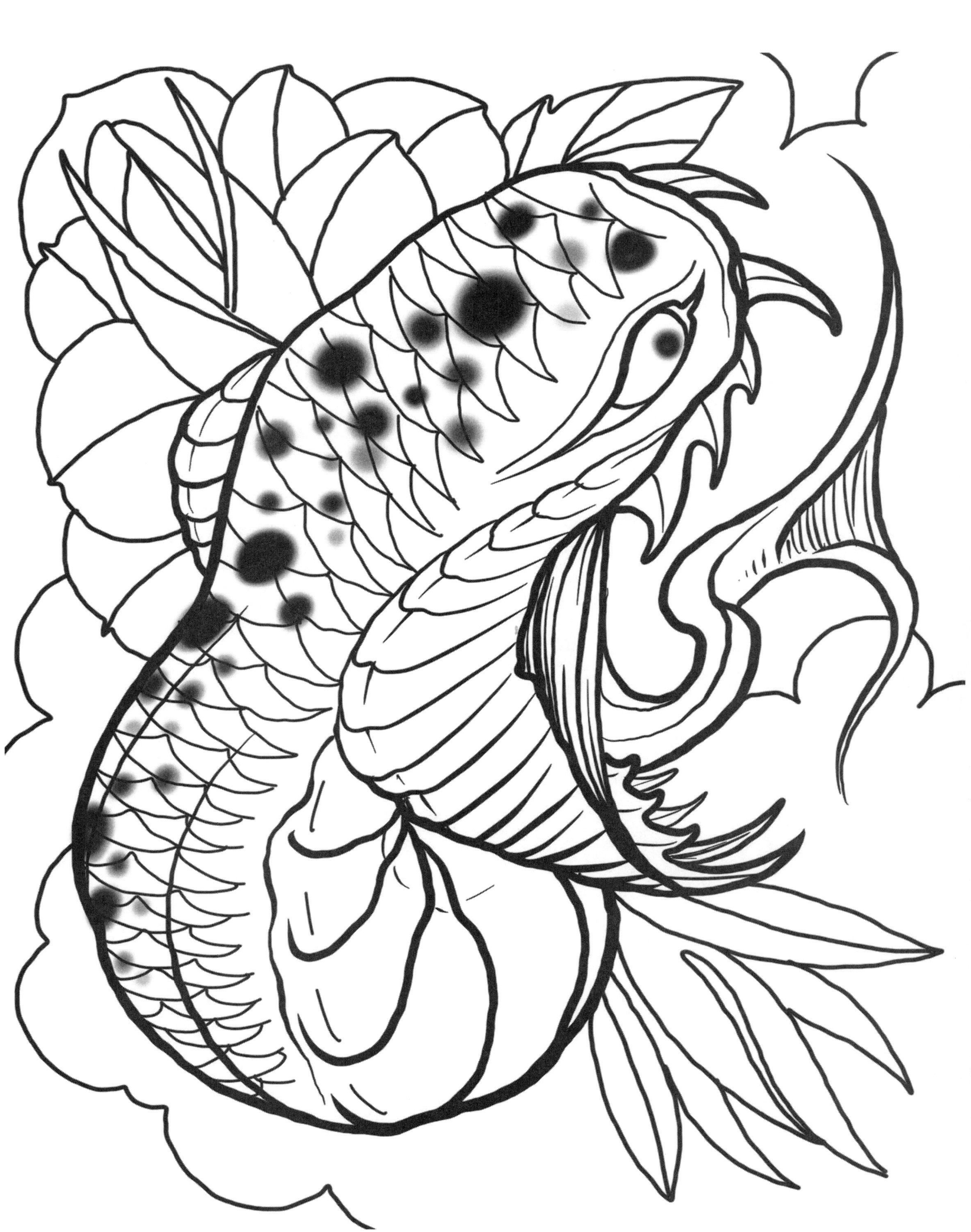

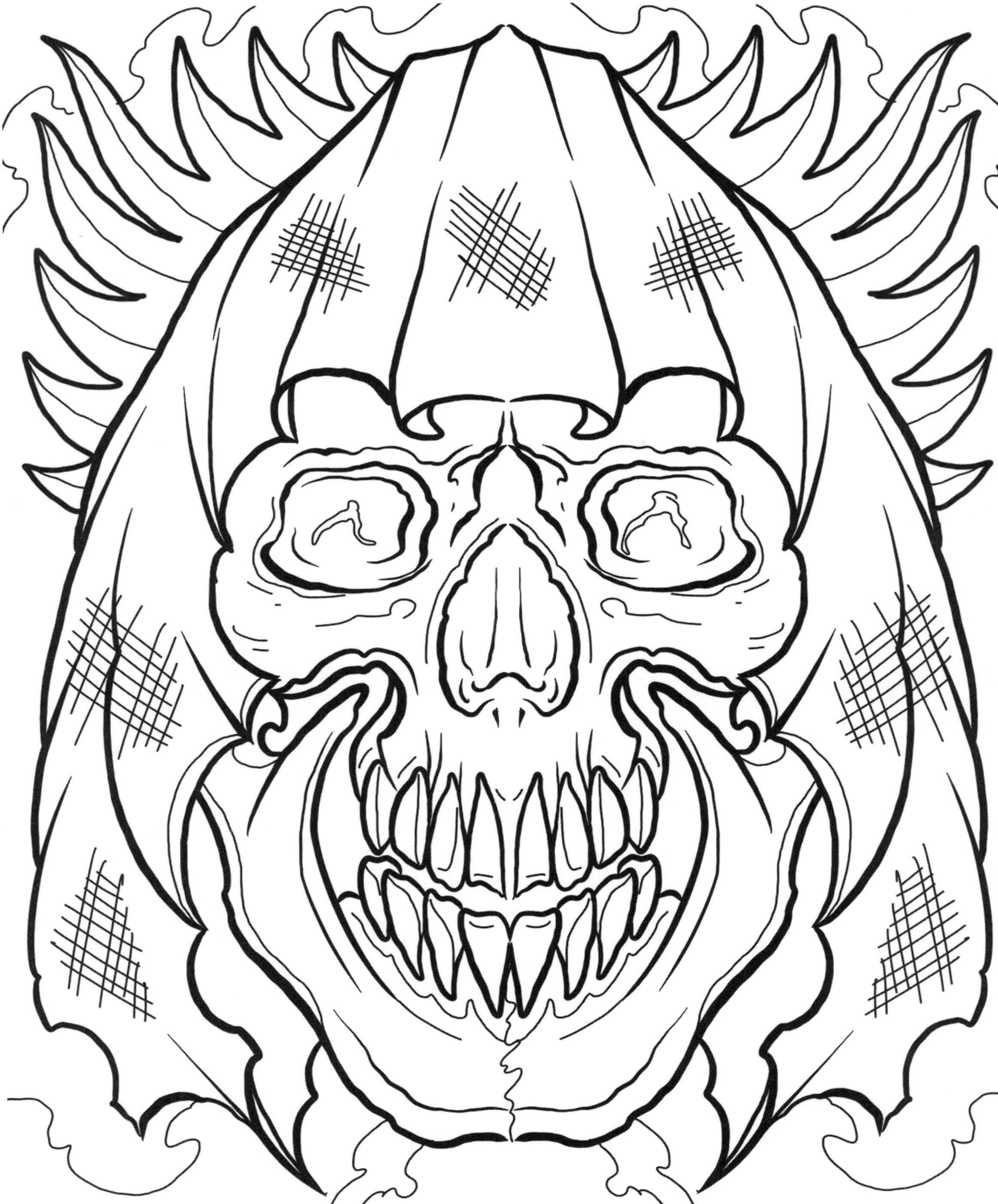

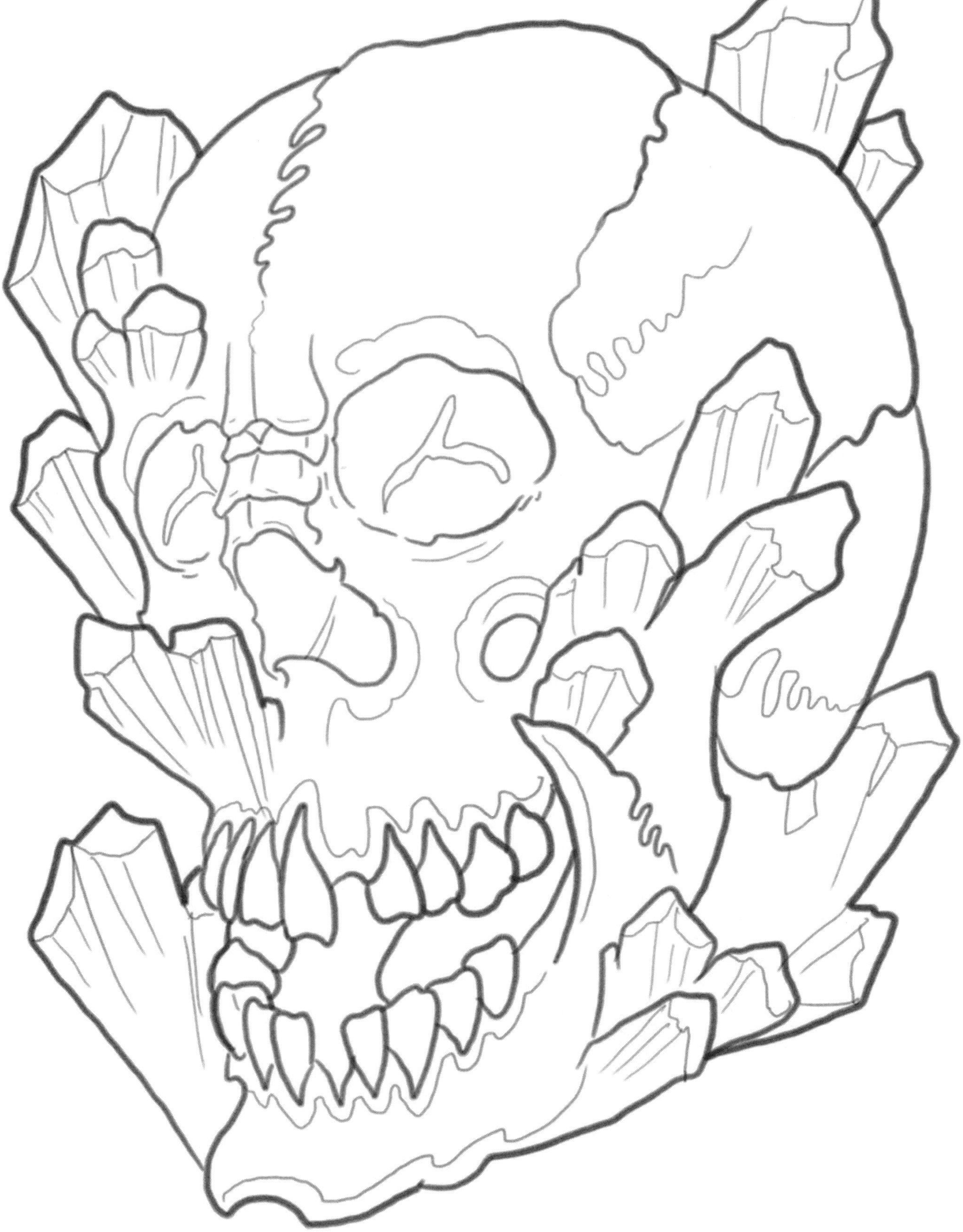

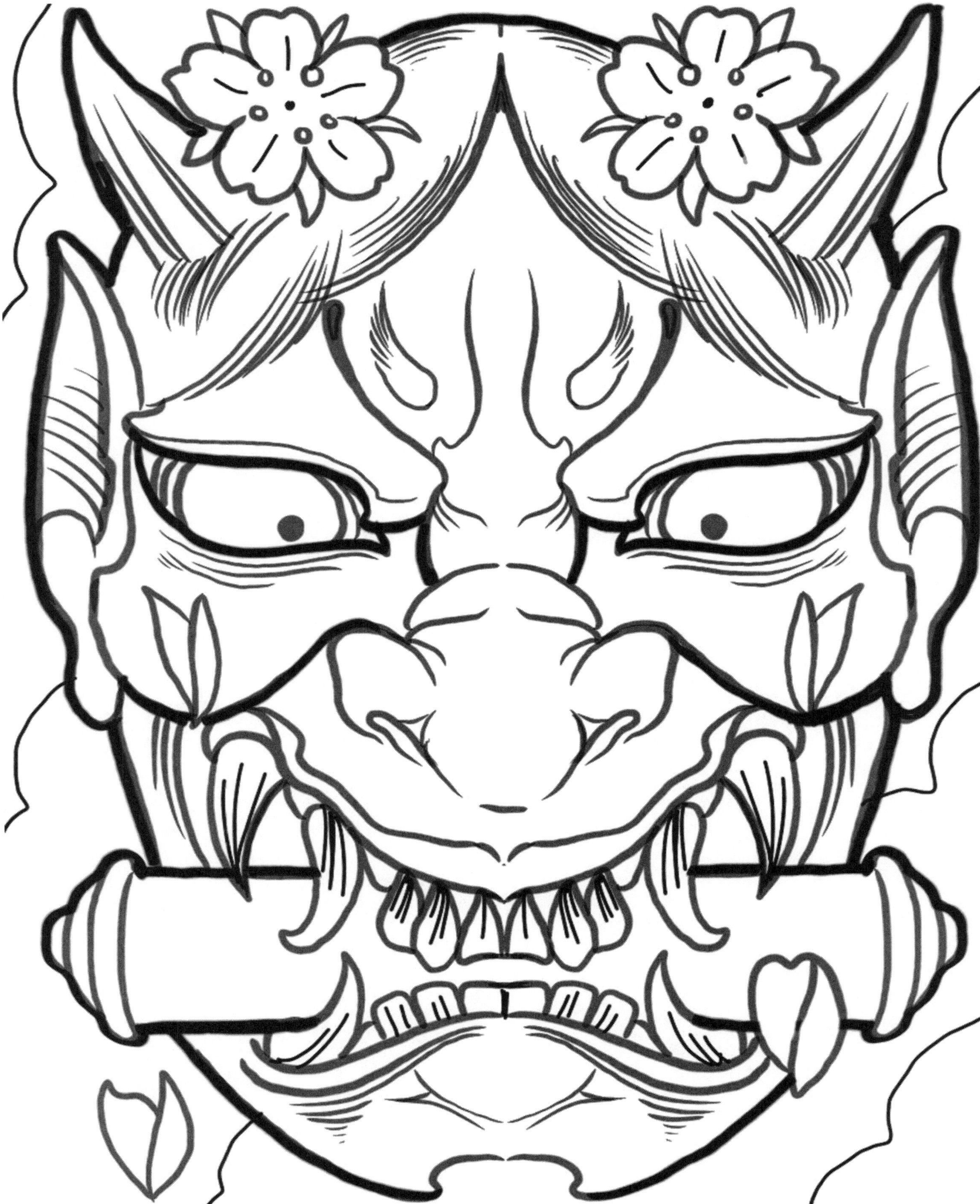

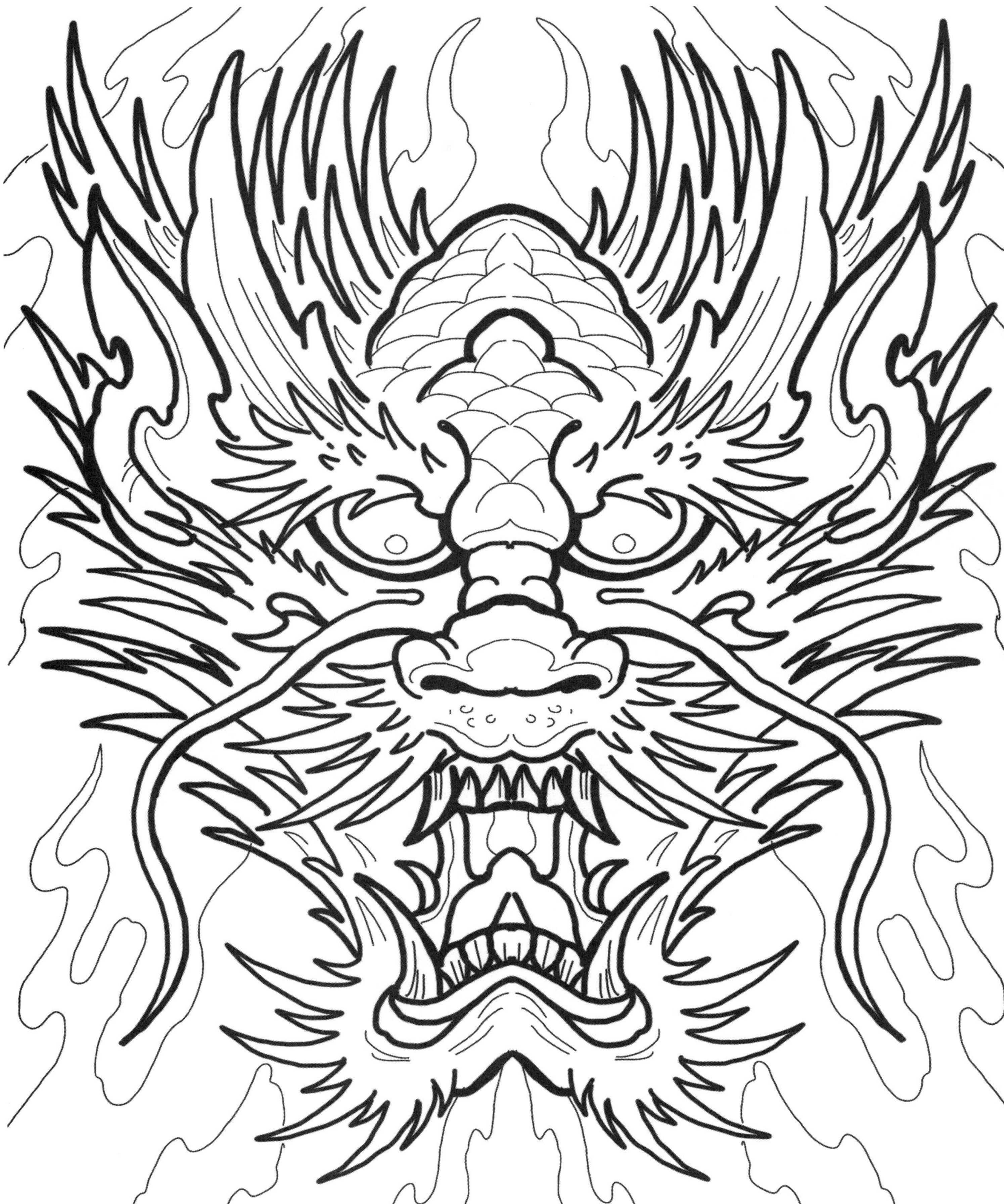

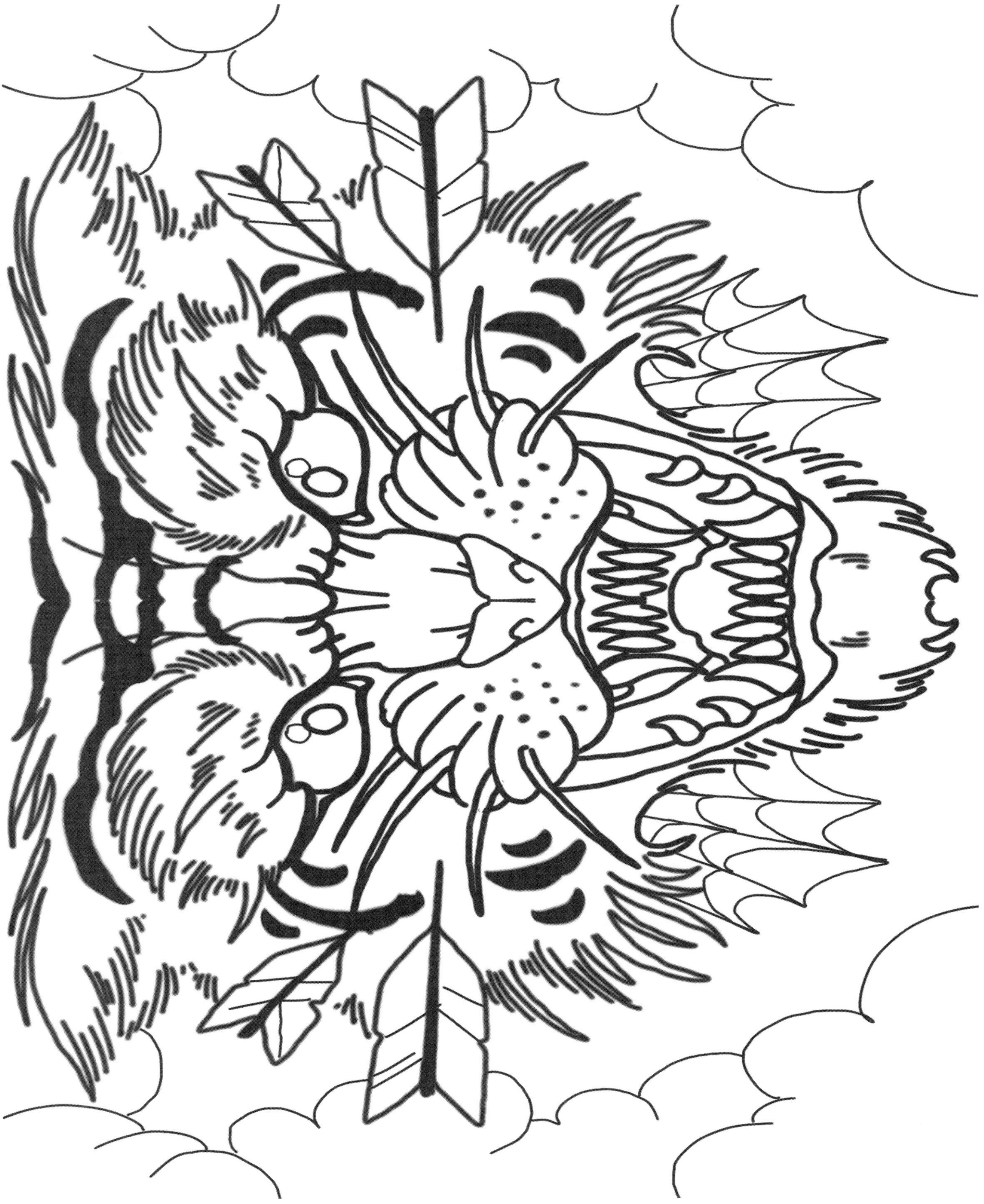

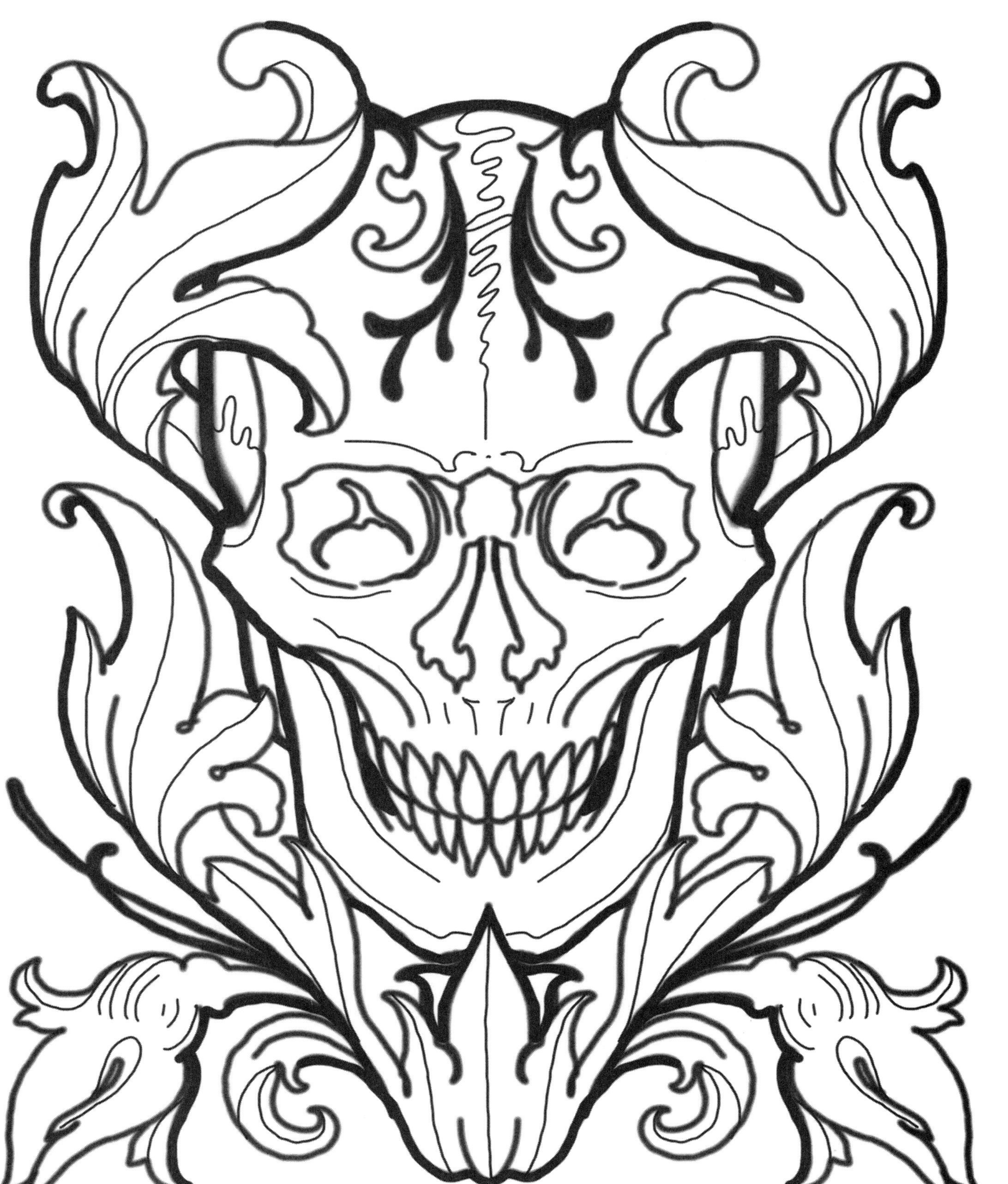

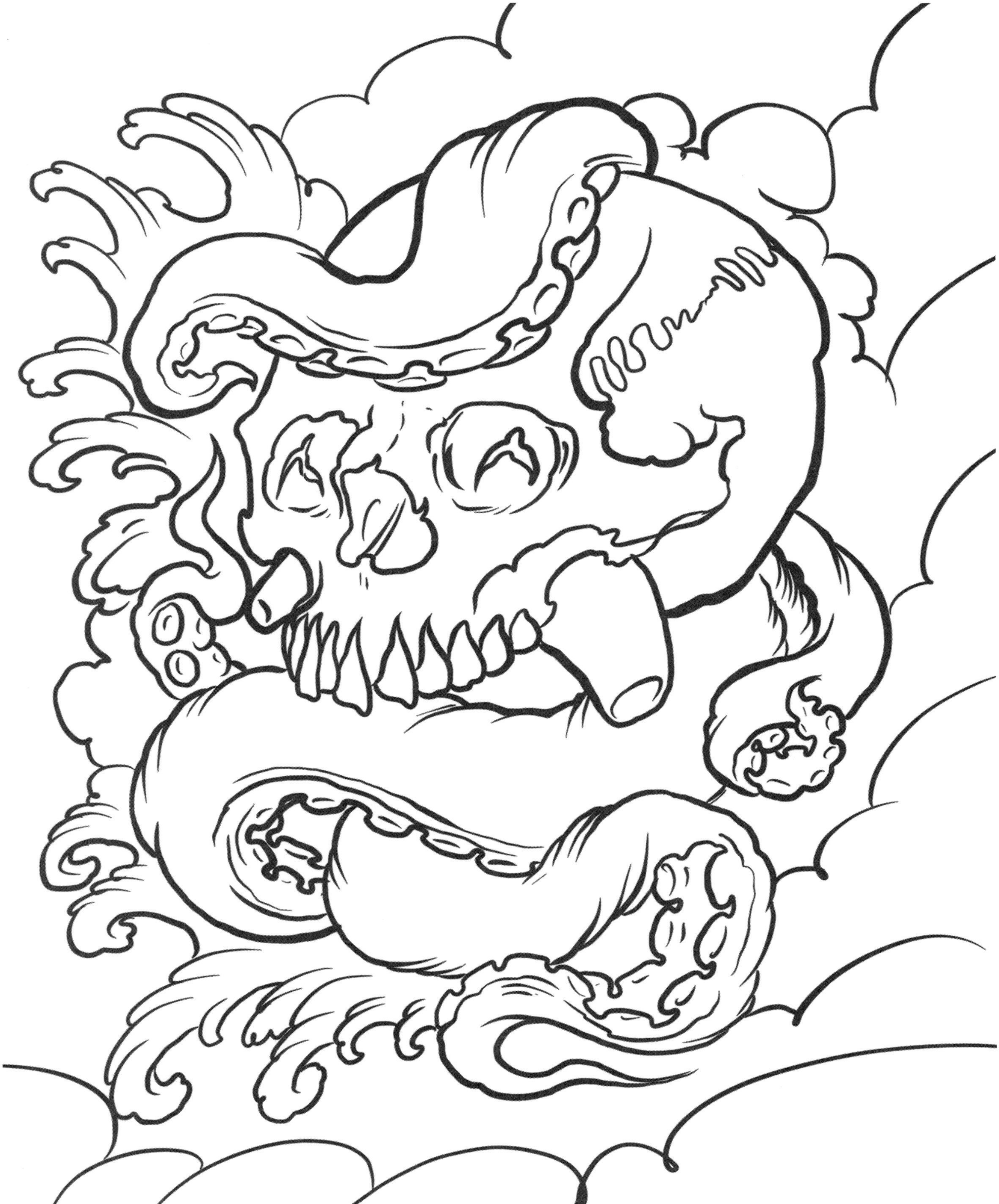

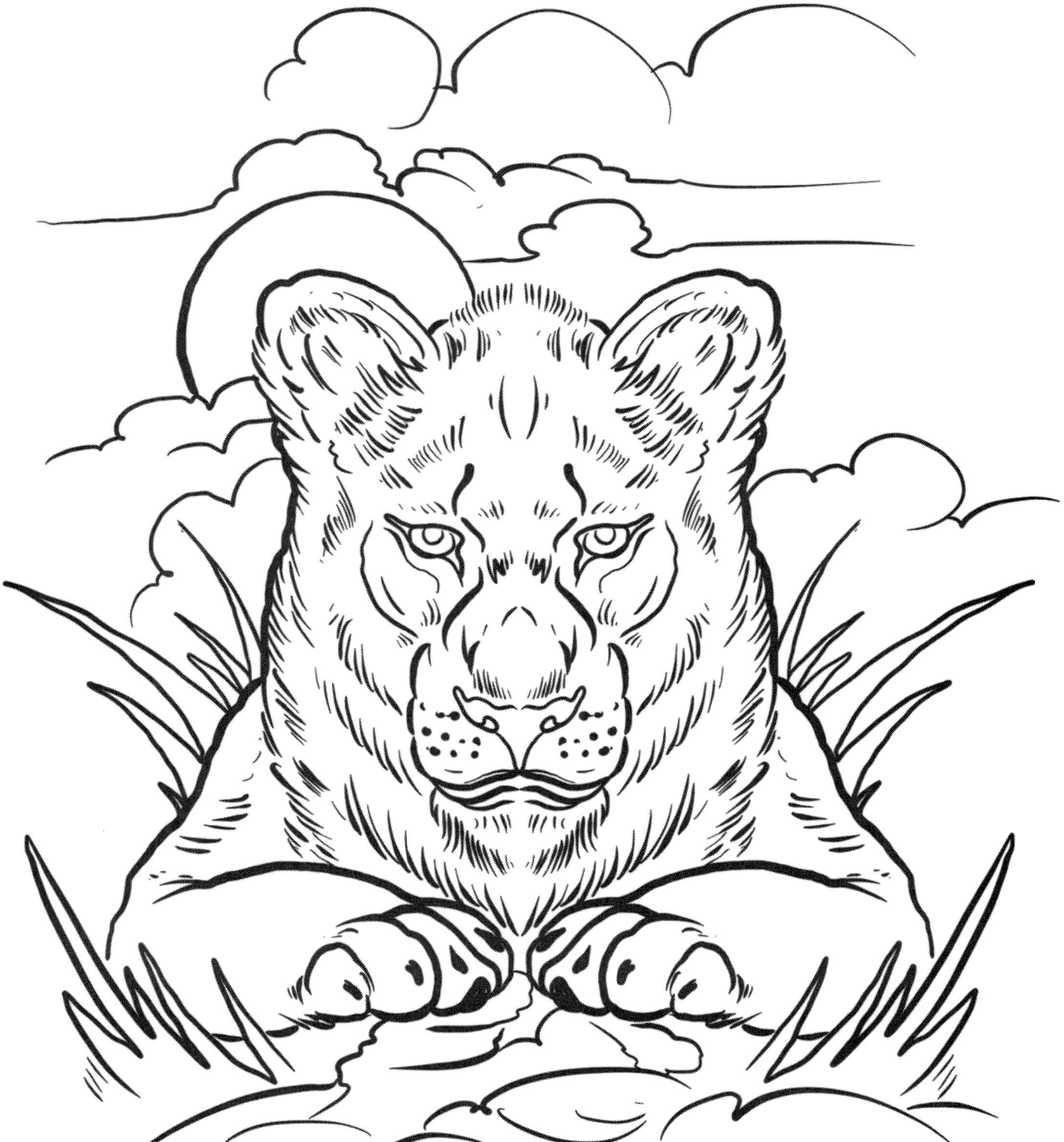

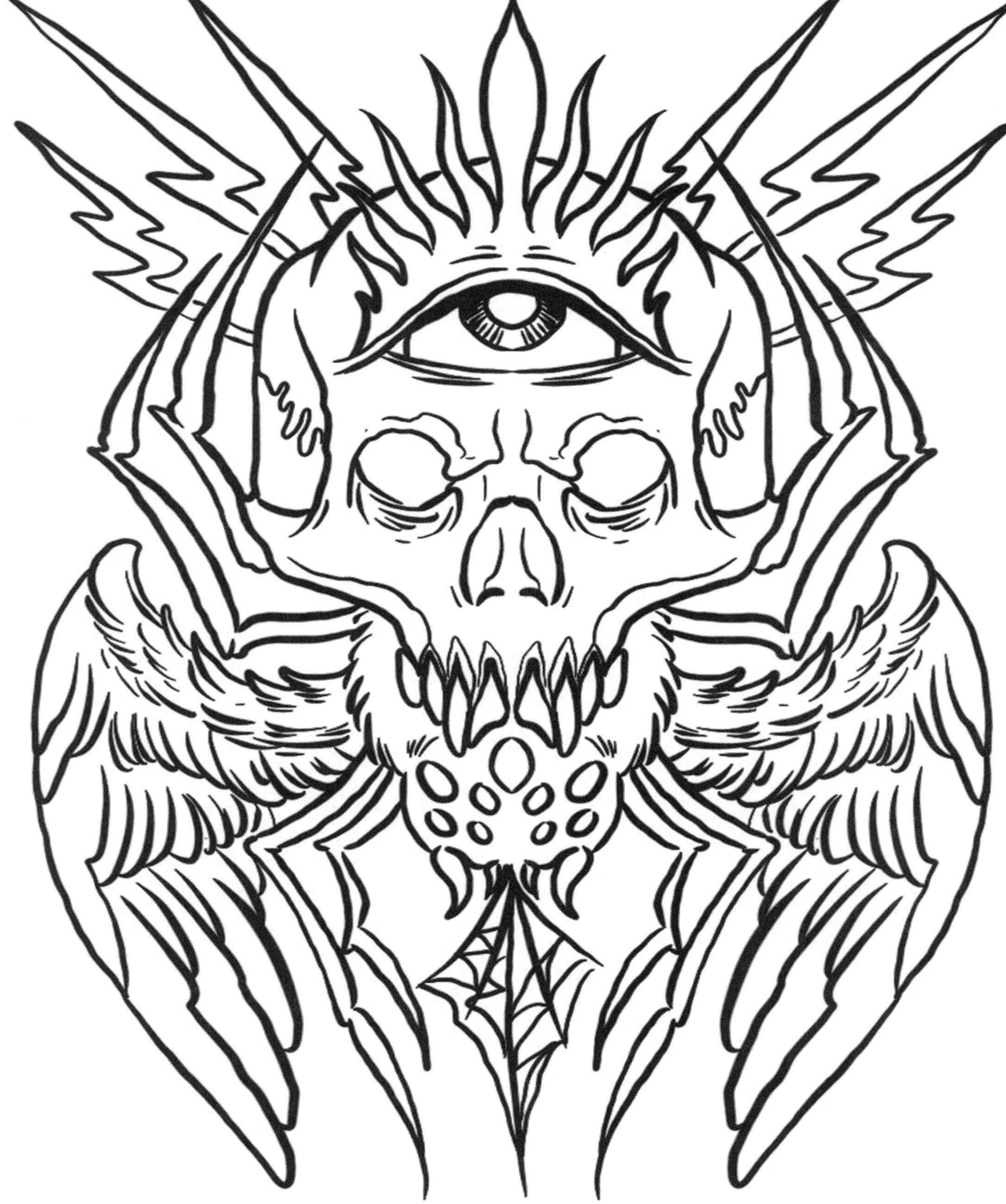

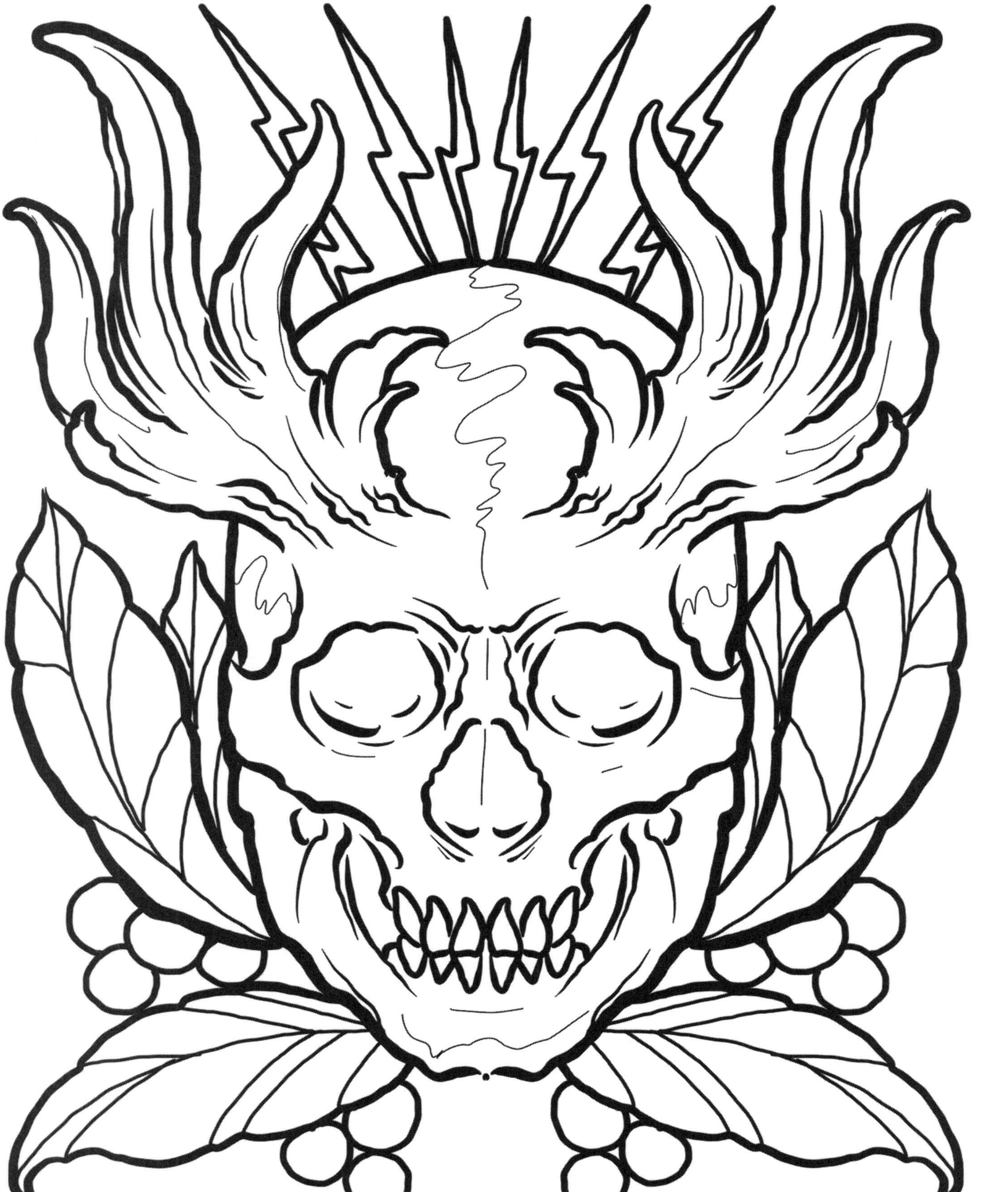

← 100

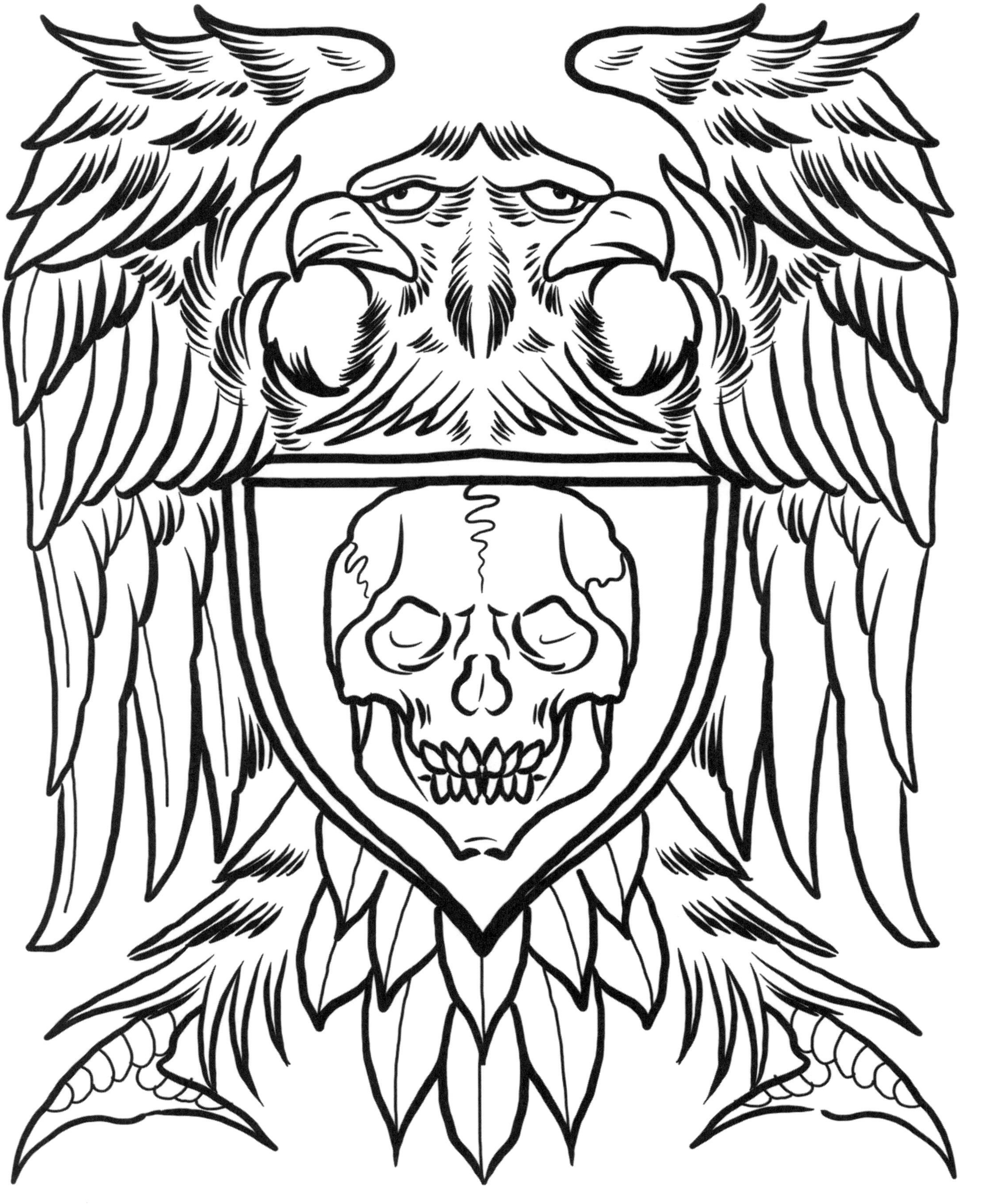

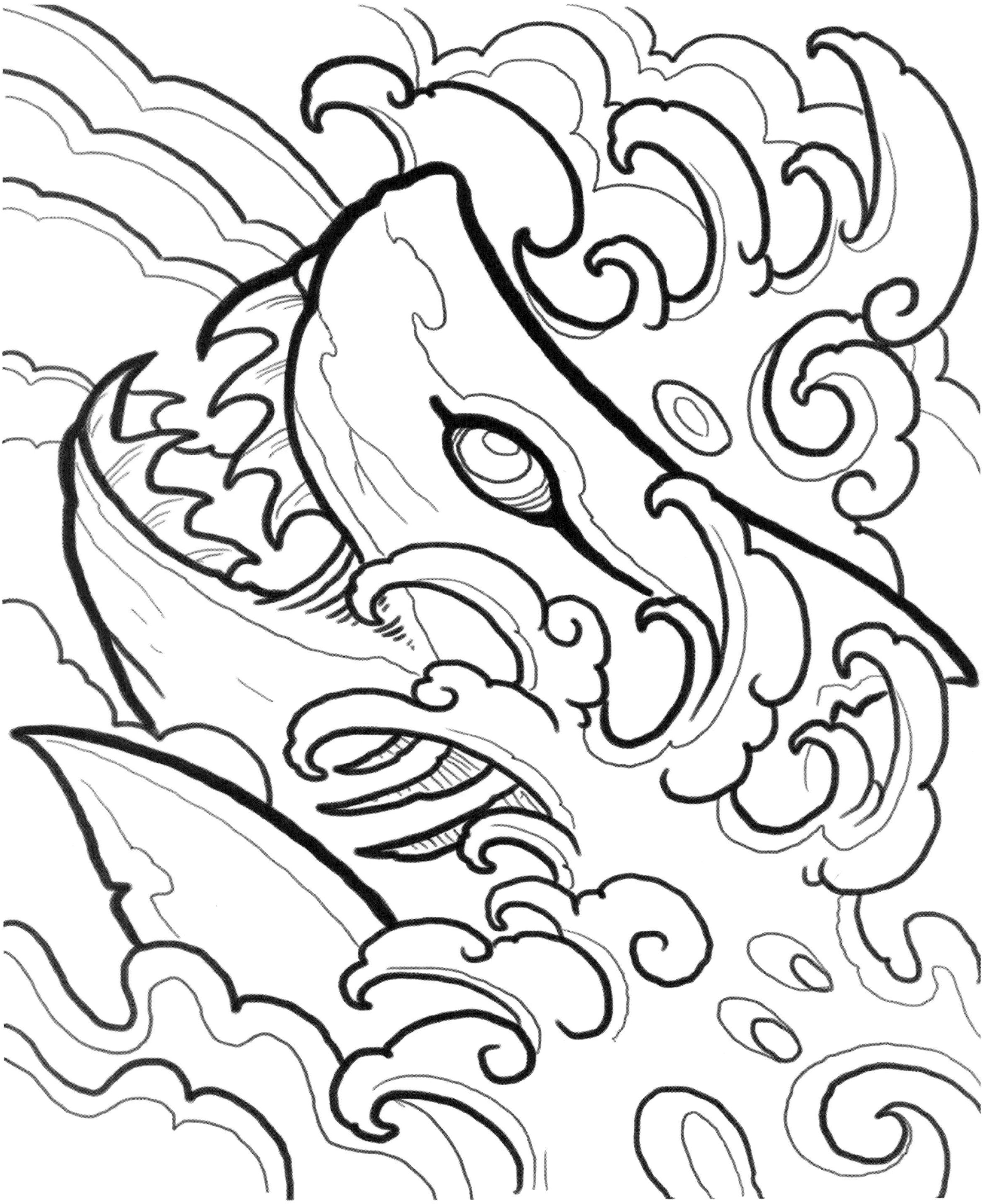

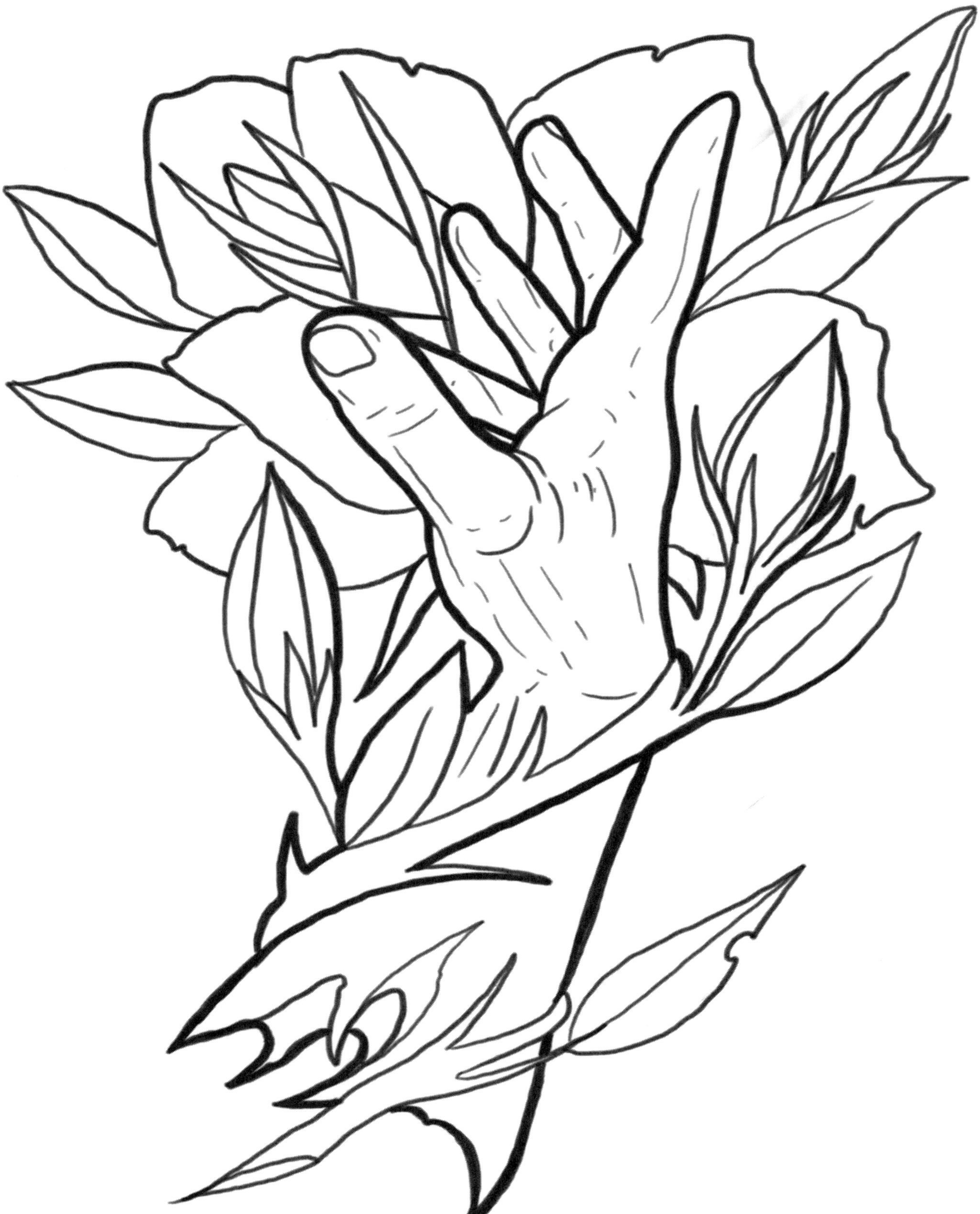

← 103

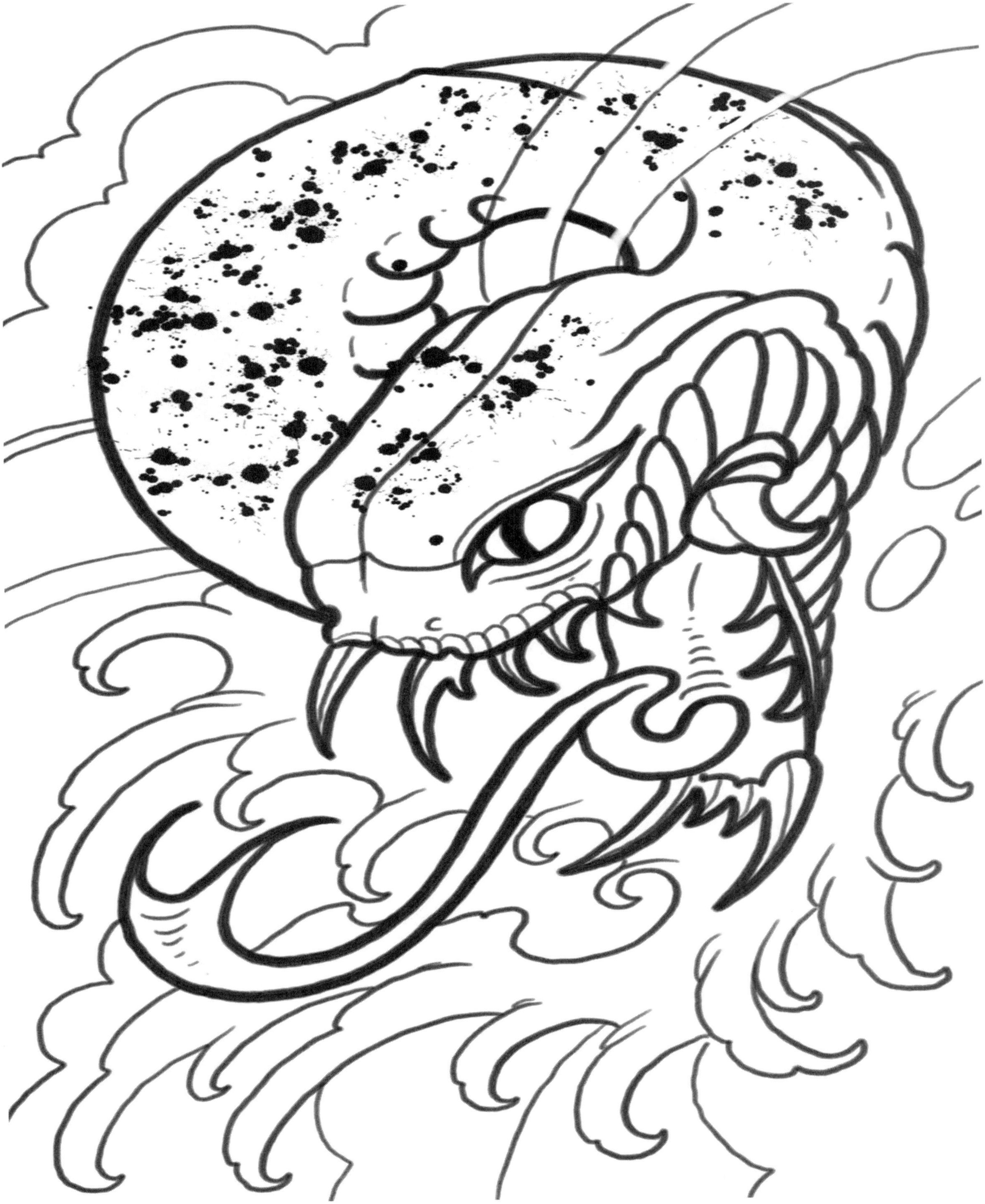

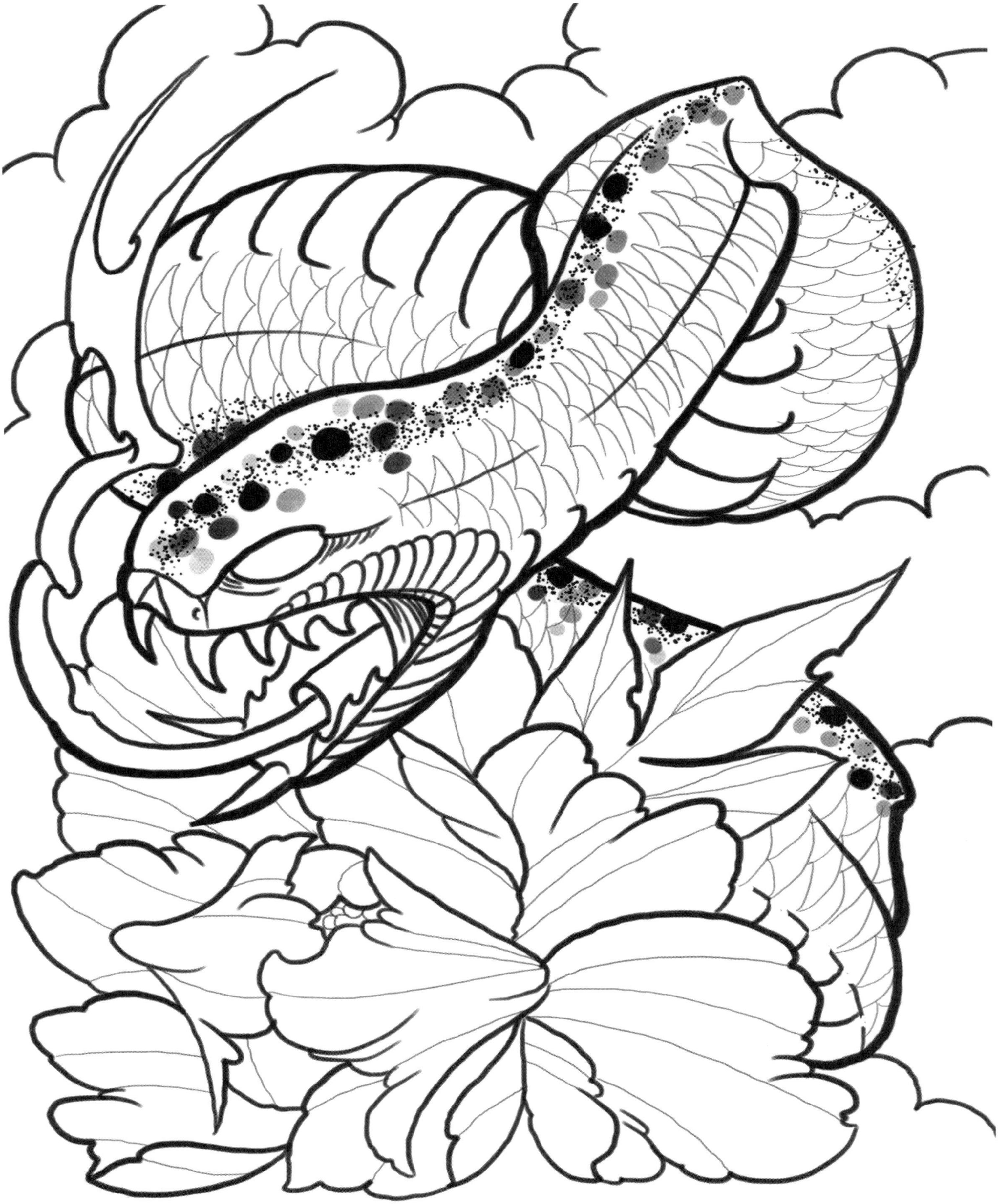

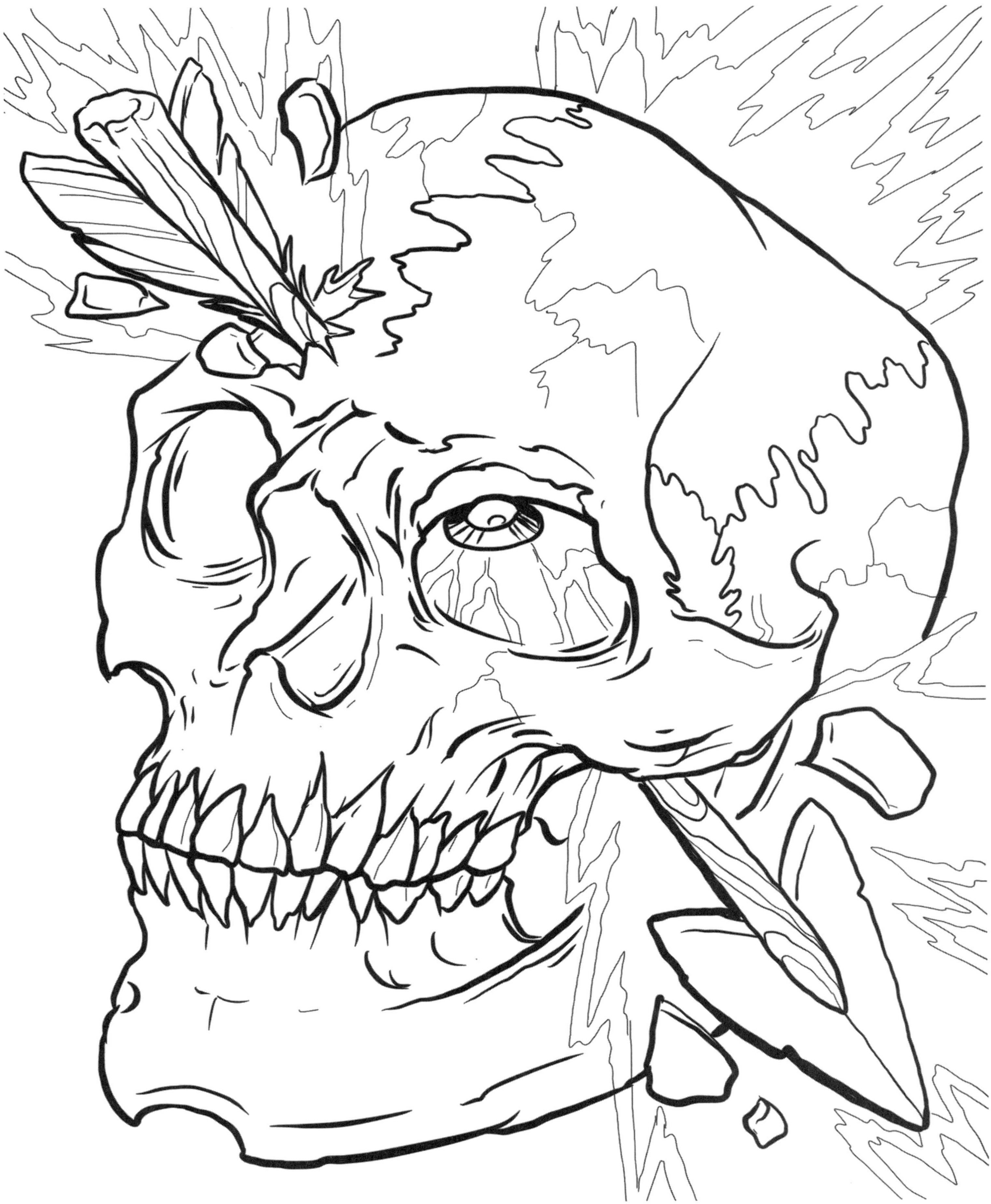

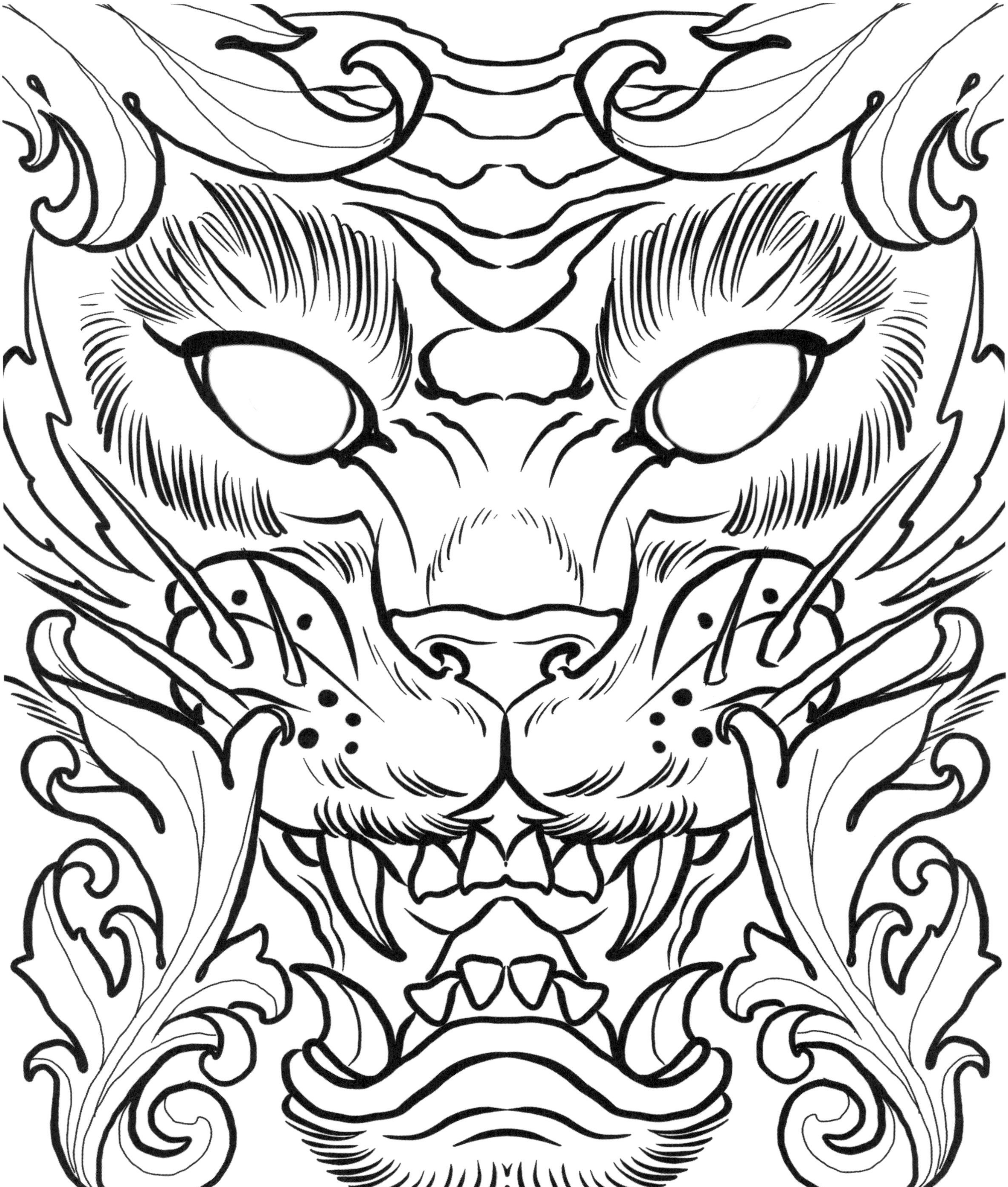

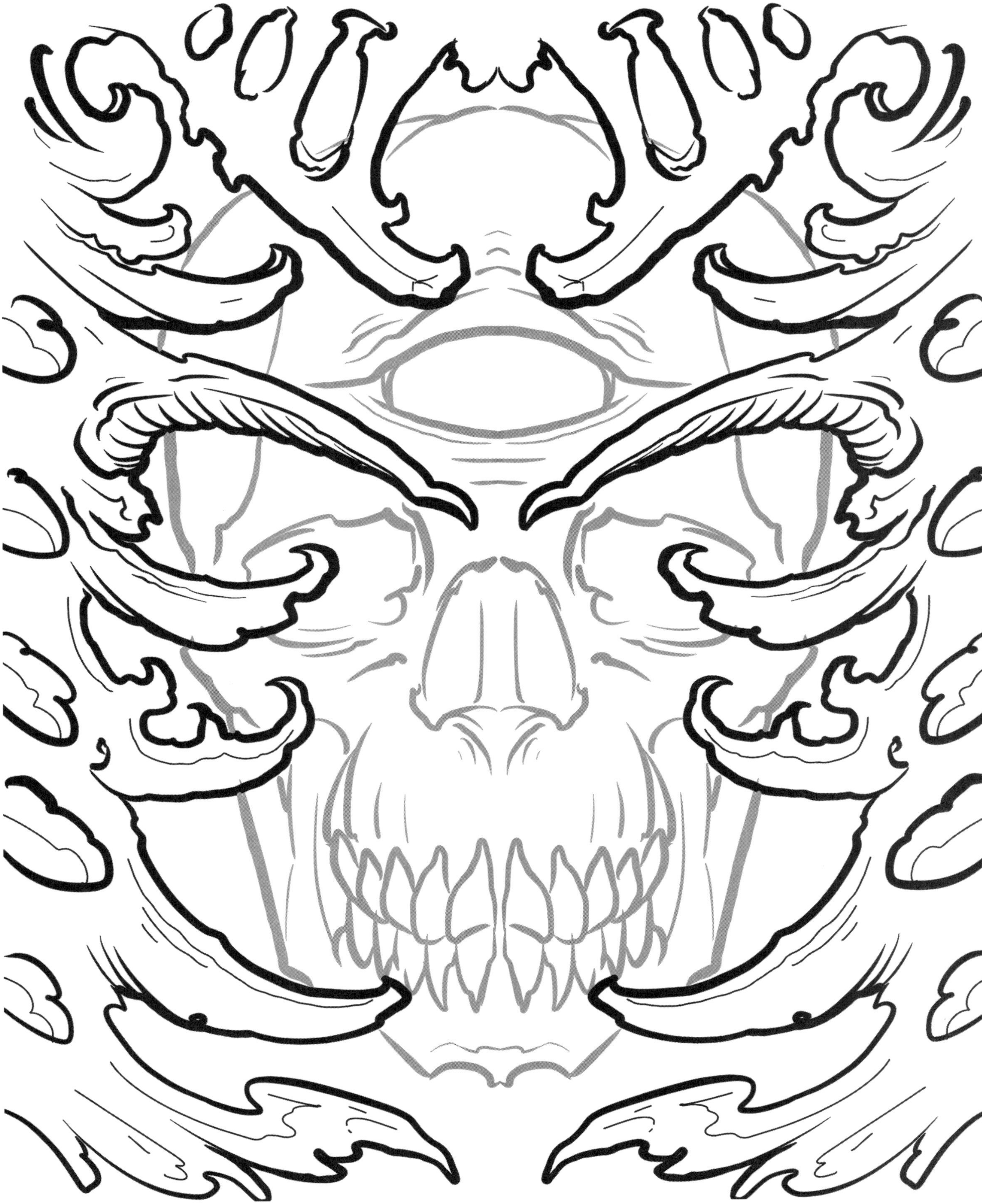

← 108

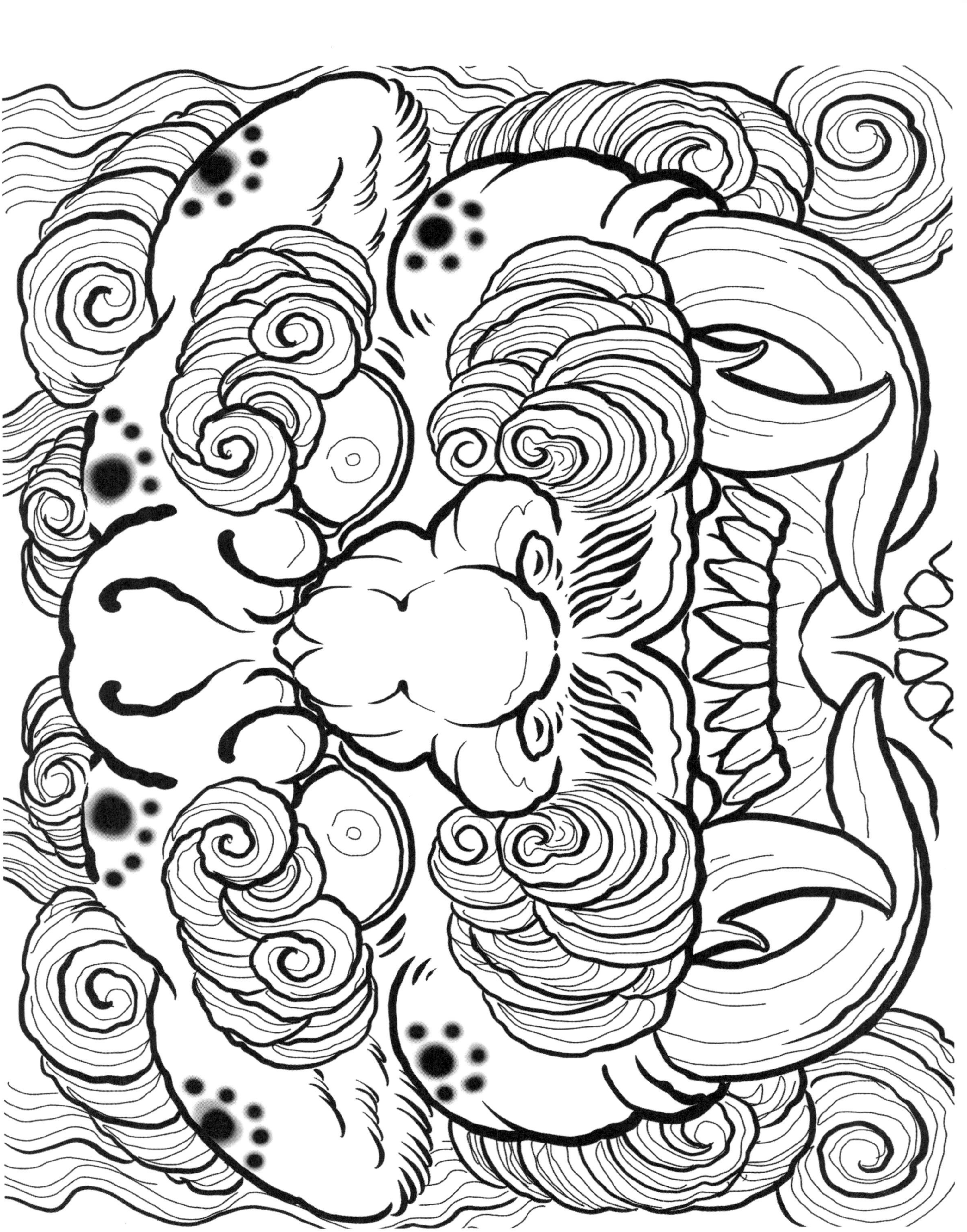

Palette Bars

Use these bars to test your coloring medium and palette. Don't be afraid to try unique color combinations!

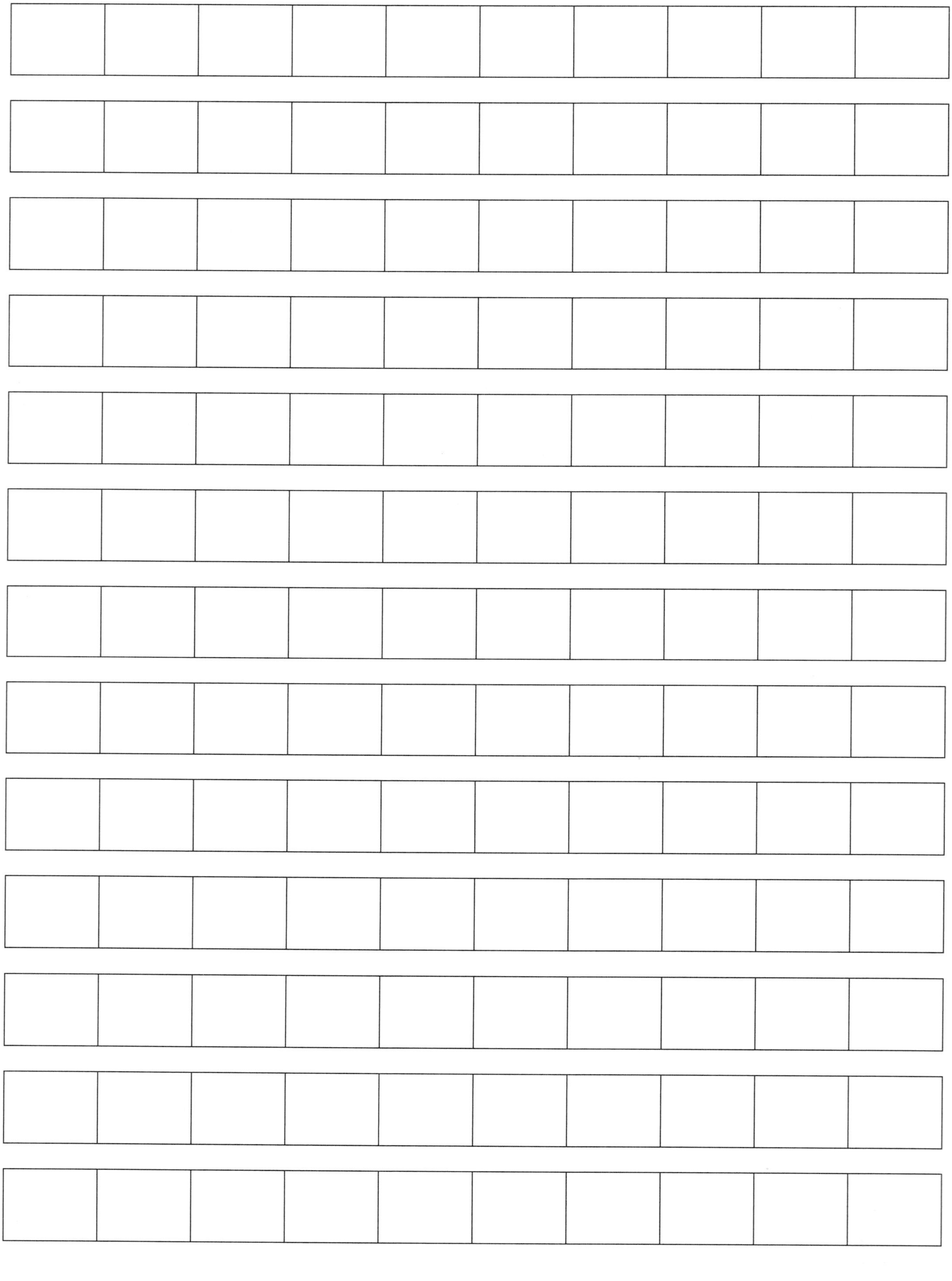

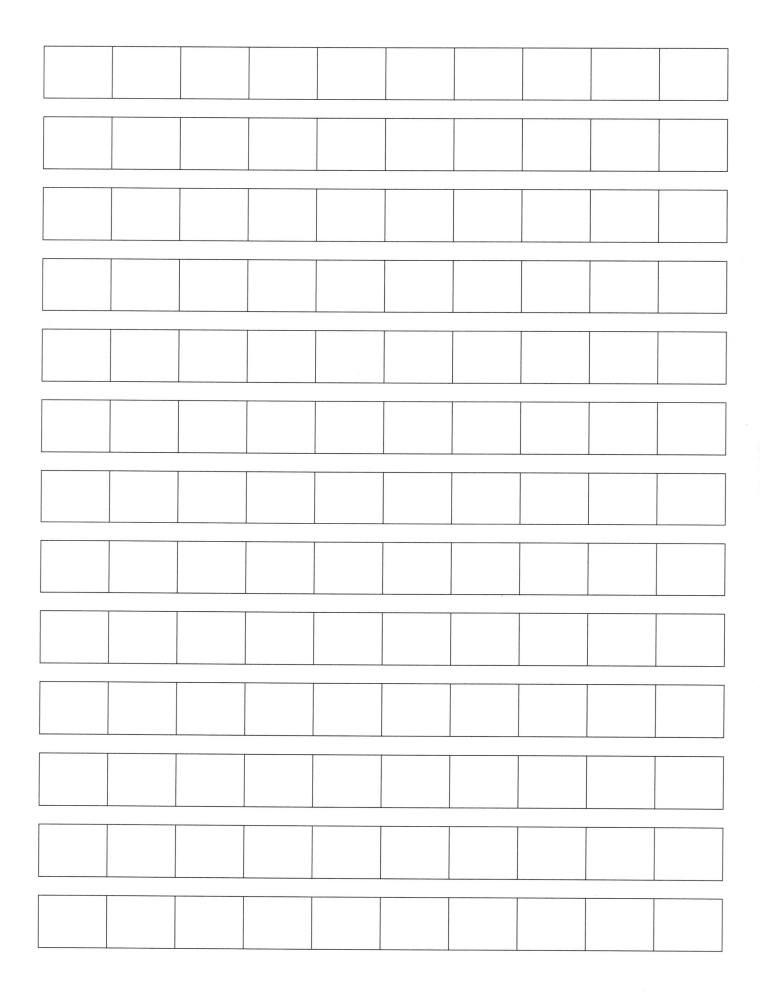